A WOMAN
of
FORTITUDE

Rosemary Laird

ROSEMARY LAIRD

Copyright © 2025 by Rosemary Laird

Life Inspired Publishing

eBook 978-1-80541-679-1

Paperback 978-1-80541-680-7

Hardback 978-1-80541-681-4

All rights reserved. No part of this book may be reproduced or used in any manner without written permission of the copyright owner except for the use of quotations in a book review. For more information, contact: rosemarylaird2@gmail.com

FIRST EDITION

rosemarylairdauthor.co.uk

ACKNOWLEDGMENTS

Many thanks to my parents who reared me with love and wisdom giving me a secure childhood to build the rest of my life on; to my four sisters who have provided me with unwavering support, friendship and love; to my two adorable sons who've made me a proud mother; to my wonderfully loyal friends and to my husband who on a daily basis enables me to achieve my dreams and whose love is irreplaceable.

CHAPTER 1
Childhood

Everyone's life, like a book, is made up of chapters and the longer the life the more chapters there are. "We all have a story to tell", as a turkey farmer I met in the swimming club sauna said to me recently. I've been lucky. My life has clocked up some colourful chapters and each new chapter has been distinct from the last. The first chapter in my life was, of course, my birth and childhood.

I was born in Windsor on Tuesday March 13th, 1945, towards the end of the second world war. My father was serving in the Royal Navy and at the time of my birth was stationed in Australia. I arrived a month late. It wasn't that my mother had miscalculated her dates. She knew exactly when I'd been conceived. It was while she was visiting my father for the weekend at Roedean School. She knew I'd been conceived that weekend as she didn't see my father for months afterwards.

During the war Roedean School pupils were evacuated to Cumbria and the school and grounds were used as a Naval Torpedo training base from 1940 until 1945.

When I was born, we were living in Bracknell and in the early hours of the 13th of March my mother took a taxi to Princess Christian Nursing home in Windsor. A nun put her to bed and left the room, and when she returned, I had arrived. All the nun said was "she's here". Rosemary Helen Lydiard Phillips had arrived when the daffodils were in bloom. They bloomed early that year. With only my mother present I had made my way into the world. It would appear my "can do" attitude to life was in evidence even at birth. I feel lucky that my mother told me about the slightly unusual circumstances of my birth. Knowing where I was conceived is an extra bonus.

I didn't meet my father until I was a year old. Every evening before I went to bed my mother showed me a black and white photograph of him which I kissed good night. But when he did finally return, I screamed and wouldn't let him near me. That must have been so disappointing for him. My father had to get to know his new baby and I had to accept a strange man in the house. He brought soft toy lambs and koala bears from Australia for my two sisters and for me. My lamb was made from sheep skin dyed blue and I called it 'Forget-me-not'. It was a perfect name as my father, when buying presents for his family, had not forgotten me, the new baby daughter he had never seen. My much-loved koala bear made from leather and real fur is now a little bald but still with me after 78 years.

When I was three years old another sister came along and then two years later yet another. So, then there were five. This meant I was brought up as a middle child of a family of five girls. Being one of a big family I considered to be a privilege; I hardly needed friends with so many sisters. We were creative in our activities and the house was full of life, and very often laughter.

There was a large and beautifully laid out public outdoor pool complex with two pools and a fountain opposite our house where we all learnt to swim. I loved the water and could swim by the time I was 5 years old. My affinity for water developed as a small child has stayed with me; I still love to swim.

We all learnt to ride a bicycle on a red fairy cycle which was passed down through the family. There were no stabilisers in those days, so the task was a little harder than it is today.

I had a zest for life and was continually active. My mother told me that when she put me in the pram in the garden, I used the hood to pull myself up, then jumped up and down to make the pram travel round the garden.

When I was nine, I was given roller skates which I was thrilled with. Then my father made me wooden stilts. I astonished the neighbours by casually wandering up and down the road on my stilts looking over their walls and into their gardens.

Our house was surrounded by farmland. There were fields of wheat scattered with scarlet poppies, and a copse with a beech tree which had thirteen trunks. We loved being outdoors exploring our surroundings. In those days it was safe for children to wander alone in the countryside, and we revelled in our freedom. A baker brought fresh loaves to the door, and unlike today we not only had a milkman, but our milk was delivered by a horse drawn cart.

My eldest sister, Ruth, invented the *Nibber Jibber Society*. The society midnight feasts took place in the bathroom. We all collected provisions for our feast during high tea and stored them in paper bags hidden under the table. My contribution one night was sandwiches spread thickly with chocolate spread. The problem was I'd used marmite instead of chocolate spread.

We all donated funds to the *Nibber Jibber Society*, (password *baked beans)*, from our pocket money and then arranged outings with the proceeds. One outing was on a bus which went from Bracknell to Finchampstead Ridges and then turned round and came back. We took a bag of halfpenny buns with us which we shared out, once we reached Finchampstead Ridges, and ate with relish on the stationary bus before returning home to Bracknell.

We had a big garden, and my parents were keen gardeners. They grew most of the vegetables we ate. Each of us was given a vegetable patch and a flower garden. Every summer we arranged a family fete in the garden and had a flower and produce competition. We picked bunches of flowers from our gardens and chose our prize vegetables which we entered into the competition. It was judged by our parents with suitable ceremony and prizes were given.

My flower garden was around the sandpit and when I developed an interest in pond life my father turned the sandpit into a pond. He bought me books so that I could identify the pond life and a microscope for me to study tiny creatures such as daphnia and hydra which I scooped out of the pond. This interest proved useful in the future.

We also performed plays. They were self-written and performed on the garden lawn. In winter the windowsill in the dining room became the stage. If we needed a larger stage, we used the dining room table. I had ballet lessons, and when we had visitors, I pranced around the garden in my tutu delivering my version of ballet. I loved an audience. I was a lively child, creative, stubborn but sensitive. My father used to call me "sunshine and showers". It was a valid description of me then, and still is, although I don't allow the black clouds to shed their raindrops so frequently now.

On my fifth birthday I started at Priestwood Infant School, which was a penny bus ride away. I'd only just returned from staying with an aunt and uncle for 3 months while my mother recovered from the birth of Marilyn, my youngest sister. I remember that day so clearly.

When I was 6 years old our chimney caught fire. Flames were coming out of the chimney pot and two fire engines arrived, but I didn't stay around to watch the fire being put out. I piled all my dolls into my dolls pram and wheeled them to the end of the road where there was a stream. I remember thinking the water would keep my dolls safe from the fire. Even in those days I was a thinker and a planner.

At 8 I moved up to the junior school and eventually took the 11+, which I failed. There was a lot of pressure put on children to pass the 11+ in those days so that they could go to a grammar school. The results were announced at school, and it was left to the 11-year-old children to deliver the good, or bad news, to their parents when they arrived home at the end of the day. I found it hard to believe I'd failed and as I walked along the pavement from the bus stop, I pondered how I was going to break the bad news to my parents that I was a failure. It had always been assumed that I would pass.

Although I hadn't earned a place at a grammar school there was still the hope that I could go to The Abbey School, an independent fee-paying school in Reading—that is, if I could pass the entrance exam. After failing the 11+ my confidence was waning. I wondered what exactly I was capable of.

Ruth and Sally, my two elder sisters, were already attending The Abbey School. Ruth had passed the 11+ and had been awarded a free place, whereas my parents were paying for Sally.

I took the entrance exam, and I passed but I still had to get through the interview.

The interview day arrived. Things weren't going very well at first. To make matters worse I was asked what books I read. I wasn't a keen reader of fiction so couldn't name any. I did read books on pond life though, so I told them about the life cycles of the creatures in my pond. I went into detail about the hydra, amoeba and daphnia and described what they looked like under my microscope. I must have sounded very enthusiastic as while I was talking, I noticed the panel of teachers in front of me visibly sit up and take notice. I mentally said a big thank you to my father for building me a pond and buying me books on pondlife, and a microscope.

I had gained a place at The Abbey School, but my parents still had to pay the school fees. Fortunately, they didn't have to pay them for long. At 13 I took the 13+, designed for late developers. To my delight I passed and was awarded a free place at The Abbey School. Success at last.

When I was 13, we moved to Reading. While living in Bracknell my sisters and I had caught a bus to school; the journey from Bracknell to Reading took an hour. My parents were hoping that my two younger sisters, Tessa, and Marilyn, would join us at The Abbey School so it made sense to move closer.

The house my parent bought in Reading was much bigger than our Bracknell house and more fitting to the size of our family. From our new home I could cycle to school in only 15 minutes which gave me greater freedom.

When I was 16 my father took me to visit my eldest sister, Ruth, at Girton College, Cambridge, where she was studying classics. My sister introduced me to her tutor who asked, "when will you be coming up?" Here was an assumption that sisters must have the same potential, but sadly it wasn't the case. I knew I would not be following in my eldest sister's footsteps. She was the academic achiever in the family. Not one of the rest of us was capable of achieving her great heights. I was very far from a star pupil at school, although I did win a national essay competition and was presented with a prize by the Duke of Edinburgh. That must have counted for something.

Frequently my lack of following in my eldest sister's footsteps was commented upon by teaching staff at The Abbey School. After a poor mark for my Latin homework the teacher asked, "are you sure you're Ruth's sister?" Judgement of my ability became a sore point. The assumption from the tutor at Girton that I was very intelligent was more encouraging than the condemnation I suffered at school. When you're a teenager you start to work out who you are, and any input is important to your self-esteem. Self-doubt can creep in with any thoughtless critical remark. The criticism that was heaped on me at school made me doubt my intelligence.

We had a family holiday every year. For many years we went to what we called "the hut" in Hill Head, near

Lee-on-the-Solent. It was one of a row of wooden bungalows built facing a shingle beach. The front door opened out onto the beach and at high tide the sea was only yards away. I loved it. I swam before breakfast and was in an out of the water all day. One day I clocked up seven swims. The water was cold, but afterwards we warmed up in front of the stove and drank hot chocolate. It was heaven.

When we were older my parents changed the family summer holiday for something more suited to our needs. Each year we went to the same cottage close to the cliffs near Tintagel in Cornwall. My great joy was to walk along the Cornish cliff path whatever the weather; rain and strong winds didn't stop me. On many occasions I was the only member of the family on the walk.

One year my parents hired two large caravans on the Isle of Wight for our annual holiday. They were perched on a cliff near Ventnor. The advertisement said you could "spit in the sea". Possibly true, except it would have had a long drop before it reached the water below. From the caravans we had to negotiate a very steep, rugged path to reach the beach. It was a long and strenuous climb back to the caravans.

We clambered down the path and found it led to a delightful sandy cove. On the beach we found two young men playing guitars. They'd walked down from their hotel, which was also perched on the cliff top. We chatted and they asked us if we were staying at the hotel. "No," said my elder sister, Sally, "we're staying in two caravans at the top of that path". I must admit I felt embarrassed about revealing to the young men that we were staying in caravans and not in the hotel. Again, I was feeling the sensitivities and self-doubt that a teenager can feel.

At that time I was 16 and thought the two young men were very good looking. I hoped we might see them again, but the next day it poured with rain, and we didn't go down to the cove. Instead, all the family, except my father, went for a walk. We were returning from our walk and just approaching the caravans when I saw my father coming towards us. With him was one of the young men we'd met at the cove. It was the tall one with blond hair, the one I thought was the most attractive. He'd tracked us down from my sister's description of where the caravans were and come to ask if I'd go to the hotel dance with him that night.

I had nothing to wear. I'd never been on a date before, let alone to a dance with a boy. My sister Sally had some lovely clothes. She was nearly 20 and her wardrobe was very different from mine. She lent me a full blue skirt, very fashionable in those days, with a wide, white, patterned border on the bottom. It had a matching top.

My handsome first date collected me in his father's car; he was 18 so already able to drive. The splendid hotel was impressive, a bit of a contrast to our two caravans. I was introduced to his parents who asked me what I would like to drink. I knew absolutely nothing about alcohol and they suggested a Cherry B. It came in a cocktail glass, and I remember being very impressed.

I had a lovely evening and a taste of the high life, then the young man drove me back to the caravans and we both climbed out of the car. He held me close; this was a new experience for me, and looking down at me he said, "can I kiss you?" I was embarrassed and didn't know what to say. I'd only ever been kissed in party games such as *Postman's knock*. I also thought my parents might have heard the car and be looking out for me, so I said, "you'd better not". He kissed me anyway. It was wonderful. I didn't see my first date ever again, but I'd had a taste of being held and kissed by a boy, and I liked it.

It was a year later when while cycling to school, I started to notice a boy in school uniform walking along the pavement towards me. He was on his way to Reading School, a boys grammar school, wearing his school blazer, with his school cap perched on top of his head. One day my boater flew off just as I was cycling past him. He rushed to pick it up and to my surprise and delight asked me to the Reading School sixth form dance.

I was 17 but my wardrobe hadn't grown much since the dance on the Isle of Wight. This time my sister Sally lent me her white and silver brocade dance dress with a large bow on the belt. I thought I looked the business, but when my date arrived to collect me, he said, "you looked better in your school uniform". He later denied it. Apparently, what he remembered saying was, "You looked just as good in your school uniform". Either way his reaction to my splendid white and silver brocade dress, or rather my sister's, hadn't boosted my confidence in any way.

We arrived at the dance and the MC called upon the Vice Head Boy and partner to come onto the dance floor to start the dancing. My Reading school boy took my hand and lead me onto the dance floor. The quiet, unassuming boy I'd met in the middle of a road was Vice Head Boy of a large boy's school. This was the first of many surprises he held for me.

I loved nice surprises, and still do, but in my teens, I expected them. My father had obviously noticed this as he called me into his study. "I'm worried about you, Rosemary," he said, "as you expect too much out of life and you're going to be disappointed". He was a perceptive man, and he was right. I expected too much from life then, and I still do. I remind myself of his words to this day every time my high expectations lead to disappointment.

I was quite a demanding teen and when I desired the impossible my father would say, "what you want is the magic wand department". From time to time, I still wish for a magic wand, but I know now that if I desire the impossible it's up to me to make the magic happen.

I started collecting boyfriends and it became a pastime. I met Bradfield College boys on a train, a Leighton Park school boy at our school dance, a Pangbourne Nautical College boy,

I can't remember where, and I added another Reading School boy to my list. I needed a filing system. I put all their letters in a cardboard shoebox and wrote each of their names on dividers for easy access to their letters. My family found this very amusing, but I just thought it was a good system to deal with a problem.

It was Christmas and time for The Abbey School sixth form dance. I hoped only one of my boyfriends in the shoebox would turn up. But one by one they came through the door and into the dance hall looking for me. I needed to think quickly. I came up with a plan. I decided to suggest to this accumulation of boyfriends that if they wanted to dance with me, they had first to dance with my classmates, and then they could take their turn with me. What was I like? Anyway, it worked.

Everything was going like clockwork until I started to worry about what would happen after the last waltz. What was I going to do if the last boyfriend to dance with me wanted to take me home? If he did it might be regarded as favouritism by the others. So, I made a decision. I decided that if I went home with my neighbour, I would avoid showing favouritism to any particular one of them. My Reading School boyfriend claimed the last waltz, and I went home with Isobel.

Disappointment did come my way a little later. The Pangbourne Nautical College boyfriend invited me to a ball at his home in Pembrokeshire. My sister's silver brocade dance dress had been dry cleaned and when I went to bed was hanging on a coat hanger ready to pack the next morning. I planned to take a train to Haverfordwest where the young man would meet me and drive me to his parents' stately home. It seemed too good to be true.

When I woke the next morning, I was covered in a rash. My parents were away so my sister Sally called the doctor. He diagnosed German measles saying, "good that you've caught it now, not when you're pregnant". I was heartbroken. I didn't think it was good that I'd caught it now and what could happen if I was pregnant didn't interest me in the slightest. I just wanted to go to the dance, so the doctor was no comfort at all. I was so terribly disappointed, and I didn't see my Pangbourne Nautical College boyfriend ever again.

My father obviously thought it was time to give me more advice, so he called me into his study. "You've got a lot of boyfriends Rosemary," he said. "What you must realise is it will never be possible to find all the qualities you desire in one person." I wasn't serious about any of them, I was just having fun, but he had a point. I've now learnt it's important to appreciate people's good points and accept the rest, not to expect perfection.

It was time to decide what I'd do when I left school. In those days girls in the second year of the 6th form were given four choices for their further education. The brightest could apply for university, the not so bright could train to be teachers, or nurses, and the remainder could go to secretarial college. At the beginning of my first year in the 6th form the school chose teaching for me, saying I was a born teacher, although I can't think why. They arranged for me to teach at The Abbey Junior School two afternoons a week to gain experience in teaching. As a result, I was only timetabled for two 'A' levels: botany and geography. I really wanted to study biology and art as well but was told the timetable wasn't organized for Rosemary Phillips.

My father wasn't happy with the arrangement as he thought I should go to university, so he suggested he discuss it with the headmistress. I insisted that the school knew my potential better than he did, and I should do what they suggested. I was probably wrong. My father knew me, and as I've said before, was a perceptive man. I was conscious throughout my childhood that he believed in my ability more than I did but I was stubborn. I eventually went to Roehampton Froebel Institute for an interview and was accepted to train as a teacher.

The last day of school was fun. We all jumped into the swimming pool fully clothed. It's strange to think what schoolgirls did to celebrate in those days. Youth is a wonderful thing.

Soon after I left school my mother put me on a train to Cornwall. She'd arranged for me to work in a friend's chemist shop in Fowey for 8 weeks before I started college. I felt very packed off and I don't know to this day why I was. I wasn't really cut out to stand behind a shop counter all day. My motto, "It's not what life throws at you but what you do about it that matters" came in handy. So, when my mother's friend suggested I joined the sailing club for young people I joined it, even though I knew nothing about sailing and had never stepped into a sailing boat. It wasn't long before I'd acquired a boyfriend who taught me to sail his wooden clinker-hulled dinghy. Eventually he let me take the helm and race and from then on, I was a very keen sailor.

My 3 years at Roehampton Froebel were a lot of fun socially. The first year I shared digs with 5 other girls, and 4 of us stuck together throughout our time at Roehampton. Sue, my roommate for the first year, already had a boyfriend who she later married. Jude, Elaine, and Anna shared another room in our digs. Elaine already had a boyfriend too who she later married.

But Jude and Anna, like me, were "fancy free". Jane had a single room and found other friends at college although we've remained in contact with her to this day.

We went to university *hops* together in central London every Saturday night. We stood or sat at the edge of the dance floor and male students who liked the look of us would cross the dance floor to ask us to dance. We were there to have fun but more importantly one of us needed to find a potential boyfriend who had a car and could give us a lift back to our digs. When asked to dance anyone who had a car was a keeper. I managed to accumulate a lot of boyfriends by going to *hops*;

engineering students, medical students, estate management students, the boyfriends mounted up. It was difficult to find time to see them all.

I was less happy with my studies. I began to feel bored. The course didn't satisfy me. When I went home at the end of the year I told my father how I felt about it. Predictably he suggested I applied for a place at university. His suggestion met the usual rejection from me. I replied, "I've started so I'll finish". Perhaps I was too stubborn for my own good.

I finally settled down and enjoyed the teaching course, particularly child phycology. In those 3 years I grew from a rather naive child to an adult. Twenty-one was when you were recognized as an adult in those days, and I celebrated my 21st birthday just before I qualified. An ex-boyfriend brought a box of large cigars to the party, and I thought it was time to try one. One puff and a lot of choking convinced me that I never wanted to take up smoking.

During my last year at Roehampton my very first boyfriend at Reading School contacted me. That's the one who picked up my boater when it blew off in the middle of the road as I cycled past him on the way to school. When he left school, he went to Wadham College, Oxford to study physics. He started visiting me in my third year at Roehampton and in winter he bravely rode his scooter from Oxford to Roehampton in freezing temperatures. I remember one Saturday morning he arrived practically frozen in a sitting position. He had to slowly prise himself off his scooter. I admired him for that. Such determination and disregard for personal comfort. That trait I later discovered ran through him like "Brighton" in a stick of rock.

My childhood was over, and I was an adult. I felt grateful for the happy and stable life I'd had growing up. I firmly believe that a happy, secure childhood gives you a firm base on which to build the rest of your life. As I went through life, I met some tough challenges but the rock my life was built on kept me stable. Only once did I nearly topple off my foundation rock.

CHAPTER 2
Teacher and Wife

At the end of three years at Roehampton Froebel I was a bit surprised to find I'd qualified as a teacher. I've no idea why I could possibly have been surprised, but it was the way I felt. I think I was disappointed. I thought the world was my oyster and held something more exciting than teaching for me. An ex-boyfriend once said he thought I'd "rise out of teaching and have a more exciting career". Did no one, other than The Abbey School, think that teaching was the ideal career for me? My father obviously didn't, and he had a habit of being right. He was certainly right about me expecting too much out of life and being disappointed.

My school boater retrieving Reading School boyfriend was accepted to study for a Ph.D. in geophysics at Imperial College, London. As our relationship was getting closer, I decided to stay in London and get a job. I'd qualified as a teacher, so it made sense to teach. I took up a teaching post at Pinkwell Junior School in Hayes and having found a reasonable flat in Ealing, I settled down to get on with life and see how it panned out.

Despite my reluctance to become a teacher I found once I started work, I enjoyed teaching. I loved the children's enthusiasm and their refreshing approach to life. I felt a sympathy for the ones who were struggling and gave them extra attention. An 8-year-old girl was seeing a child phycologist when she moved into my class, and I did my best to help her. At the end of the year her parents came to the school to thank me. They told me their daughter no longer needed to see the phycologist as the result of spending a year with me. It brought me joy to think that I'd been able to help.

After a year teaching, I was offered a one-year course which would convert my Teacher Training Certificate into a B.Ed. degree. I was eligible for the course as I'd done well in my finals. I gained a place to study but couldn't get a grant as I'd only taught for one year, not the required 2 years. The chance of getting a degree and finally fulfilling my father's dreams for me slipped out of my grasp once again.

There were several highlights during the next three-years. I had innovative ideas which were noticed by the education authority inspectors. I was asked to join a committee to arrange a teachers' conference at Keeble College, Oxford. That was a lovely surprise. Recognition of my talents gave me a big boost.

In my third year of teaching, I signed up for a course in producing and presenting children's TV programmes. Greater London was developing a close circuit TV educational programmes system. At the end of the course a team was selected from the participants for technical jobs in TV programme production. They read out the names of those chosen but to my chagrin mine wasn't amongst them. Disappointment engulfed me once again. Then the organiser announced that he would like me to be the presenter. I was amazed and thrilled beyond words. I remember going to bed that night finding it hard to believe I hadn't been dreaming.

The job of presenting children's educational programmes was mine. The TV studio was equipped, and I was due to start the career of my dreams. But education budget cuts intervened, and the project was cancelled. My dreams evaporated along with my TV career. It's one of the disappointments in my life that I've never quite been able to come to terms with.

Despite my TV disappointment I had three satisfying years teaching and I found it stimulating and fulfilling. For the 8 and 9-year-olds in my class, life was like a box overflowing with new and exciting experiences. I loved that. When my class wasn't studying the three R's, we had fun. We took seeds from ripe tomatoes and germinated them. The children learnt how to care for the plants and finally we made tomato sandwiches out of the tomatoes we grew. They were fascinated by this project and the many other projects and experiments we carried out.

In a swimming pool in London, while taking a scuba diving course, my Reading School boyfriend, Rodney William Calvert, asked me to marry him. He had a penchant for the bizarre even in those days. He tried to prevent me from getting out of the pool until I said "yes". But I escaped, and it wasn't until I'd taken all my scuba diving gear off that I agreed to marry him. We celebrated in a pub afterwards and were given the glasses we'd used for our celebratory drink to take home. Life was good.

My fiancée's Ph.D. in geophysics was to substantiate the theory of continental drift. He spent months in Iceland building concrete posts and taking measurements. Naturally I missed him. So, I felt very fortunate when Imperial College offered to pay my fare to Iceland and my accommodation expenses if I worked as his assistant during my summer holiday from teaching. I was required to record figures and information for him while he took readings. It was the beginning of an amazing adventure.

The weather in Iceland can be bad, even in the summer. One night we pitched our tent over a small fumarole to keep warm. Steam seeped out from a vent and circulated round the tent. Next morning we left the tent and went off to take measurements. We'd camped in a remote part of Iceland and at the end of the day we had to negotiate uneven terrain to reach our tent. As the Land Rover slowly ground its way forward in low range, we noticed a familiar looking object lying on a rock.

It was our lilo. A few minutes later we found the remains of our tent. When we finally arrived at the site all that was left were heavy items that couldn't become airborne. The tent may simply have blown away in a gust of wind, or the fumarole could have had something to do with it. We'll never know!

With little camping gear left we checked into a hotel and had our first taste of Icelandic cuisine. It seemed to be greasier than food we were used to. I think some of it must have been whale meat. There were copious amounts of cooked cucumber with a pink sauce served with every main course. In Iceland large quantities of cucumbers are grown in their thermally heated greenhouses and frequently used as a cooked vegetable. We were introduced to Skyr which I didn't see in British supermarkets until the 2020's. The Icelandic Skyr was thick, creamy and served with creamy milk and sugar. It seemed to appear at every meal. I've heard that longevity of the Icelandic people has been attributed to the large amount of Skyr they consume every day.

Taking a bath was an interesting experience. I turned the tap on, and bright orange water gushed out. It remained bright orange, and I was confronted with the decision of whether it would make me cleaner or dye me orange. Hot water in Iceland is thermally heated and comes straight from the ground full of large deposits of iron oxide. Anyway, I got in the bath, and it didn't dye me orange. Looking on the positive, side the minerals may even have had health giving properties.

Our time in Iceland was packed full of new and exciting experiences, many of which had something to do with my fiancée's penchant for the bizarre. We found a cave full of thermal heated water at a temperature above blood heat. It offered us a great chance for a real warm up. We ate lunch in the wonderfully warm water floating around as we sliced into a loaf of bread balanced on a rock. I don't remember what we put on the bread, but I do remember it was great fun, and different from anything I'd done before.

Another time we came across a large hole full of bubbling mud and tried to cook in it. We lowered a saucepan of cold water containing pre-cooked sausages into the mud hoping to heat them up. The mud bubbled and then spurted. The spurt curled over and landed in our cooking pot. It wasn't a great success, but worth a try.

There were wonderful tourist sights to visit such as the geysers at Hverir geothermal area and the thundering waterfalls of Gullfoss and Dettifoss. Everything was so new and awe-inspiring. For me Iceland was a landscape I could only wonder at.

We took a couple of weeks off from taking measurements and building concrete posts to explore. There was a narrow dirt road which ran through the centre of Iceland from south to north, between the Langjokull and Hofsjökull ice sheets. We decided to give it a try. We set off from Reykjavik in our Land Rover and drove north with Akureyri as our goal. It was an experience I could never have imagined. We drove through a landscape of black barren lava which stretched to the horizon, we forded several large rivers, one of which was in flood, and camped in remote huts. The huts were for travellers' use and were relatively accessible from the track.

One night we stayed in a hut at the edge of Langjokull ice sheet. It was kitted out with bunks and a stove. After cooking up a very basic meal we climbed into our bunks and snuggled down in our sleeping bags. In the early hours we were woken by noises, and I felt someone climbing into my bunk and lying down beside me. A German lad, who had arrived at the cabin in the middle of the night, in the pitch dark, thought my bunk was empty and was trying to settle down for the night next to me. It was quite a surprise to us both.

There was a ladder in the hut which led to a small attic room with a window. I climbed up the ladder to enjoy the view. I could see Langjokull ice sheet and a vast expanse of barren terrain. There was no vegetation for miles except for one clump of grass growing below the hut window. As I watched a goat appeared, as if from nowhere, ate the clump of grass and moved on.

We continued along the track and reached Akureyri in the north of Iceland. There are 5 volcanos in Akureyri and my fiancé chose one with a cinder cone to climb. I couldn't make any headway up the ever-shifting slope of cinders, so he tied a rope round my waist and hauled me up. There was a stunning view at the top and a large crater lake. Looking down we had a fantastic view of Lake Mývatn. It had been worth the struggle to reach the top.

When my time in Iceland came to an end I flew back to England and travelled to my parents' home. During the holidays, when I was teaching, I lived in my childhood home as it was far more comfortable than my rather basic flat in Ealing.

I arrived home, and was greeted by my mother, but my father wasn't there, which surprised me. "Where's Daddy?" I asked. "He's gone," replied my mother. "Gone where?" I asked. I wasn't expecting the news I was given. My father had left my mother and gone off with a young woman. I was heartbroken for my mother. She'd raised 5 children and sacrificed so many things to nurture and care for us. She was an intelligent woman and had tried to fit other pursuits around her nurturing task, and I knew there had always been sacrifices. I had a close relationship with my father, so I was heartbroken for myself as well. I needed to help my mother, so I gave up my flat in Ealing and moved back home. I hope I was a comfort to her as she faced the enormous task of sorting out and packing up our 7-bedroom family home.

I was now only seeing my fiancé at weekends, and we thought it was time to fix a wedding date. We'd known each other since I was 17 and my fiancé was 18 and we longed to be together. We chose a date and let our parents know.

The reply I received from my fiancé's mother surprised me. Instead of congratulating us and saying how pleased she was that we'd fixed a wedding date she wrote, "Your marriage does not have my blessing, and I won't be coming to the wedding". After more negativity she continued with, "If you marry while my son is a penniless student, love will fly out of the window as poverty creeps through the door". All rather dramatic and upsetting. Was she worried about our happiness or was the real reason that she didn't like me, or perhaps that she didn't feel I was good enough for her son? She clearly intended to make our marriage as difficult as possible. On reflection, her reaction to our proposed wedding date was only the first time she expressed her disapproval of me. She later earned the nickname of my mother-in-law from hell. As years went by she proved herself to be one of those disappointments in life my father had warned me about.

Finally on July 26th, 1969, we married in Reading and my future mother-in-law did come to the wedding. But my father, who I loved so, much didn't give me away. By then he was estranged from the family. I walked down the aisle on the arm of my bachelor uncle, and he gave me away. Naturally I was saddened I couldn't be on my father's arm, but I know how proud my uncle felt to take his place, and I believe it made him feel he held an extra special position in the family. Out of heartbreak good can spring.

The reception was perfect in every way. It was held in Caversham Bridge Hotel. Lush green lawns stretched down to the Thames which sparkled in the sunshine. I caught sight of myself as I passed a mirror in the hotel. I radiated happiness and I was surprised to see I looked beautiful. I spent my wedding day floating on a cloud of euphoria.

We found a pretty cottage and I supported my husband with my meagre teacher's wages until he finished his Ph.D. It led to some creative cooking on my part. I boiled bones, with a little meat still attached to them, given to me by the butcher. With added vegetables it became my signature dish.

My husband applied to work for Royal Dutch Shell and was accepted. As soon as he'd finished his Ph.D., we took the ferry to Holland. We travelled first class and from then onwards our meagre existence was exchanged for one of privilege. Our life together as expatriates had begun.

Shell checked us into a hotel, where we basked in luxury while we looked for somewhere to live. We stayed in the Europa Hotel in Schreveningen for a month and ate like kings, or rather a king and a queen. Chateaubriand was our favourite main course and lobster bisque soup our favourite starter. We had to pay for the alcohol we consumed, but if we ordered lobster bisque the waiter would pour whiskey over it until we said stop. These meals were a luxury neither of us had experienced before.

We asked what cheeses they had and were rather amused at the selection. The Dutch waiter listed their cheeses "We have young cheese, we have old cheese, and we have middle-aged cheese". That was the extent of the choice of cheeses. I later learnt about old, 'oude', and young, 'jonge', Dutch cheese, but I've never seen one labelled "middle aged" cheese before or since. After a few weeks we began to get tired of luxurious food and overeating and longed for something simple like sausages and baked beans.

All the new intake on the Shell introduction course staying in the hotel went flat hunting. The flat we found was in Voorburg, and on the ground floor with one bedroom. It had a garden, which was perfect.

We moved in and I can remember taking my new wifely duties very seriously. I cleaned and polished the flat every Wednesday. There was no washing machine, so I put the washing in the bath once a week, jumped in with it and gave it a good pummelling with my feet. Before my husband came home each evening, I touched up my make so that I would look as attractive as possible for him. I really wanted to be the perfect wife.

There was a Dutch lady living alone in the flat above us who gave us our first introduction into Dutch culture. Checking up on other people and making sure they follow the rules, we discovered, was part of the Dutch way of life. One day we were contacted by our landlord who said he'd received a complaint and needed to visit us. The moment we opened the door he realised what had caused the complaint. Inside the door, above the coat rack, was a shelf full of fancy bottles. He told us the neighbour had reported to him that we were alcoholics, and the flat was full of empty bottles. She'd obviously looked in through our front door on her way up the stairs and seen the bottles. This wayward behaviour, she obviously thought, should be reported to the landlord. However, the landlord quite understood that we liked keeping attractive bottles and using them as decoration.

The Dutch trait of not minding their own business rather irritated me. Walks in the sand dunes were marked out with wooden posts and each post was topped with a particular-coloured paint to let you know which walk you were on. If you put even a foot the other side of one of the posts, you were likely to be tapped on the shoulder and told to get back on the path. It seemed that every citizen wanted to make sure no member of the public broke the rules. A car drove over a railway crossing after the red lights started to flash and another driver noted down their number plate and reported them to the police. The Dutch *Neighbourhood Watch* was like our neighbourhood watch, except theirs was on steroids!

We remained friends with the Shell newbies we met in the hotel after we'd all moved into our flats, and we started to enjoy Holland together. We went swimming in a group and wives met for coffee in each other's flats. Treats served with coffee began to escalate as competition kicked in. We started with biscuits and coffee, then cakes and coffee, then bigger and more elaborate cakes, and finally a strawberry flan with cream.

I was responsible for the strawberry flan. I'd had a problem making it as I didn't know the Dutch word for "gelatine". I bought a packet of transparent strips which looked like gelatine and poured hot water over them. They softened but didn't melt. So, I mashed up the soggy transparent mass I'd created and poured the mixture over the strawberries. The other wives said how much they enjoyed the flan and indeed it tasted okay. Sometime later I discovered that what I thought was gelatine had in fact been Indonesian dried bean shoots.

With my full-time teaching career over I needed something worthwhile to do, so I called in at the Berlitz language school in the Hague to see if they'd give me a job. My teaching qualifications proved useful, and I was taken on to teach English as a foreign language. I was given a set of three Berlitz method English language books which provided me with a structure to work with. One quick flip through the books and I was ready to start teaching again.

The most difficult pupils were a class of 12 teenagers sent by their parents to improve their English. The teenagers didn't want to learn English, they just wanted to lark around and have fun. They were not cooperative students, and the lessons were frustrating and difficult. My favourite pupils were businessmen. They signed on for crash courses which were all day and every day for a week. My job included taking them out to lunch and having a normal conversation with them as we ate. This gave me a free lunch and I was also paid for my time. As a bonus I learnt about many different professions. It was a brilliant job.

After the initial 6-month Shell training course my husband joined a team analysing exploration data. He worked in a building full of computers which were massive in those days. I could see them though the windows of the data processing centre standing in a row like giant wardrobes. There were two vast metal wheels holding a tape attached to the front of each machine. Watching them rotate backwards and forwards rhythmically as I waited to pick up my husband at the end of the day was quite mesmerising. How times have changed!

While living in Holland it easy to find friends as there was a large British expatriate community. We were all foreigners and spoke the same language, so we had plenty in common straight away. In the 1970s very few of the Dutch spoke English so friends with a shared language were important.

One evening while watching a film in an ancient and somewhat dilapidated Victorian theatre, built when Scheveningen was a Victorian seaside resort, the roof started to leak. I could see large drops of water falling from the ceiling and landing on an English couple sitting in the seats in front of us. I tapped one of them on the shoulder and suggested they moved back with us as we weren't getting wet. We got chatting and at the end of the film the couple invited us back to their flat for coffee. It was the start of a wonderful friendship which has lasted to this day. Liz and Keith became precious friends. We liked doing the same things, so we met up frequently. We spent weekends camping with them and went on skiing holidays together. How serendipitous the finding of friends can be.

Our new married life had got off to a flying start and we were revelling in being young, active and free. My husband was a very outward-bound sort of person. He paid little attention to his comfort. As you may remember I'd discovered this sometime before when he arrived on his scooter, one winter's morning, to visit me in Roehampton. When I went out to greet him, I found him sitting on his scooter frozen in a sitting position too cold to move. Knowing his disregard for personal comfort it was of no surprise when he suggested we camped with our newfound friends for one weekend every month of the year, throughout the year. Liz and Keith were on board with the idea but when we arrived at campsites in November, December, January, and February equipped with camping gear we met incredulous campsite owners. Despite our quizzical welcomes we stuck to our target and at the end of the year we'd achieved our goal.

We loved the freedom of camping and often took a boat to Vlieland, one of a chain of Frisian Islands situated off the north coast of Holland. We camped in the sand dunes, hired bicycles and explored the islands, eating pancakes in traditional Dutch pancake houses. Everything we did with Liz and Keith was fun. We were a foursome that really gelled, perhaps because we all had a slightly whacky taste in activities.

The ski slopes of Switzerland weren't difficult to reach from Holland so one winter a group of us rented a chalet and drove to there. We took it in turns to cook, but instead of cooking in couples we mixed the couples up. Each evening everyone, except the cooks, went out for a drink and came back to a meal, of sorts. Sometimes the meals were a bit odd, but the arrangement worked well.

Life in Holland had been full of fun. We were young, childless and free, with boundless energy and enthusiasm. It was a unique chapter in my life. But the time to move on had arrived. After 2 years in Holland, we left for Dallas to start a new chapter in our lives.

CHAPTER 3
Life in Dallas

The only thing I knew about Dallas was that President John F. Kennedy had been assassinated there in 1963. I was in my first year at college when the news shocked the world. It was one of those events when you remember exactly where you were when you heard the news. I was with my roommate in my digs in Putney.

I wasn't very happy about a posting to what I believe to be dangerous Dallas, but I didn't have a choice. Texas Instruments was building an Advanced Scientific Computer for Royal Dutch Shell, and my husband was needed in Dallas for 6 months to ensure the computer was built to Shell's specifications. I was allowed to accompany him, but as it was such a short posting we could only take minimal personal effects. We were told we could fill one large trunk which Shell would air freight to Dallas.

The flight to Dallas offered us an opportunity to arrange some side trips en route so we started planning a holiday in the West Indies. First, we'd go to St Lucia, then Antigua and finally to Barbados. We found we could get a direct flight to Dallas from Barbados. We hired a car when we arrived in St Lucia and drove to our B&B in Soufriere. It was run by a warm and welcoming couple who owned a fruit plantation. Our hosts took us to our room where there was a four-poster bed shrouded in yards of mosquito netting. They told us to be sure to use the netting every night and to keep the windows open as there was no air conditioning. We realised having the windows open all the time would give the mosquitos 24 hours a day access to us. Clearly, we were about to experience the negatives, as well as the positives, of holidaying in the tropics.

The B&B was close to a cove and the impressive volcanic plugs forming the Petit and Gros Pitons stood dramatically at one end. There was a lovely sandy beach and warm, clear water lapping the shore invitingly. I couldn't wait to wade into the crystal-clear water.

The next day after a swim our charming hosts took us on a tour of their tropical fruit plantation. They handed us slices of one fruit after the other until we could eat no more. We had our first taste of soursop, pomelo and sweet papaya. Then we were taken back to the B&B and presented with an enormous lunch. Long slices of fried plantain were arranged around delicious looking pieces of fresh fish and other vegetables. We didn't want to offend our hosts, so we tried to eat at least some of it. They were such a delightful couple and so very hospitable. When we left, they asked us to return when we had children.

We flew to Antigua next and hired a car. The atmosphere in Antigua was very different from St Lucia. A group of people standing beside the road spat at our car as we drove past. Antigua was beautiful with magnificent sandy beaches, but we were happy to leave for Barbados.

The cost of hiring cars was mounting up so when we landed in Barbados, we took a local bus from the airport to a hotel we'd noted down from a travel guide. We climbed onto a crowded bus full of people sitting with giant carrier bags and boxes full of produce. Some were clutching live chickens. We gave the driver the name of our hotel and asked him to tell us when we arrived. At our stop we jumped off, and as the bus pulled away, we noticed there was no hotel, just an empty piece of ground. The hotel had burnt down two years earlier, but the bus stop still bore its name. It taught us a lesson. Next time we'd make sure we bought an up-to-date travel guide before travelling.

Eventually we found an apartment with a view of the sea and my husband hired a moped. It was perfect for Barbados which was more built up than St Lucia and Antigua. I sat on the back and clung onto my husband as we weaved through the streets of Bridgetown. But while mounting a steep hill the moped began to struggle. It obviously thought it could do better without its heavy load, so it suddenly surged forward and left me standing in the middle of the road. My husband was totally unaware he'd lost his passenger, and it was a while before he came back to find me.

When we arrived at Dallas Fort Worth International Airport, we hired another car, a yellow Pontiac. We checked into a hotel and when our trunk arrived shortly afterwards, we drove back to the airport to collect it. We'd stopped at traffic lights when I noticed steam coming from under the bonnet of the Pontiac. I imagined a hose had split, but the steam became darker until it was thick and black. We jumped out of the car. I ran to the car behind to ask the driver if he had a fire extinguisher, telling him our car was on fire. He didn't reply, just reversed out of the queue, and shot off at speed.

My husband pulled the trunk out of the car and a man appeared from nowhere and opened the bonnet. Immediately a wall of flames shot up and clouds of black smoke rose into the air. He tried to smother the flames with a cloth, but the fiery furnace that was once our engine, consumed the cloth within seconds. We phoned the fire service, then stood back and watched our hire car burn. As if by miracle a truck loaded with fire extinguishers drove by. It stopped, the driver jumped out, grabbed a fire extinguisher from the back of his pick-up and in a moment the fire was out. I felt as if I must have a guardian angel. Serendipity had dealt us a heavenly hand; such wonderful happenstance. By the time the fire engine arrived the drama was over and all that was left was a smouldering engine.

A crowd of curious passersby and shop keepers had gathered to watch. The manager of the nearby *Dunkin Donut* Cafe was amongst the crowd and took pity on us. He offered us coffee and as many doughnuts as we could eat for free. We sat eating doughnuts as we waited for the car hire company to bring us another car. We very much appreciated the manager's kindness. It's when things are really going badly that empathy from others is at its most valuable. We later discovered that the model of Pontiac car we'd hired had been recalled as there was a risk of fire caused by it back firing through the carburettor. Our hire car had obviously missed the recall.

We needed somewhere to live in Dallas so set off to look for accommodation. We were fortunate to find an apartment which suited us perfectly. Standing on the balcony we could look down at a fast-flowing stream which babbled over rocks and was fringed by trees. Once we'd moved in, I put food out to attract wildlife and had visiting squirrels and colourful Texan birds.

In the apartment complex there was a small kidney shaped heated swimming pool surrounded by lush vegetation and bright hibiscus flowers. As an enthusiastic swimmer the chance of swimming all year round was amazing. The pool was also a good meeting place for the young residents of the complex. I started talking to wives and found they loved listening to my English accent.

Our apartment was only basically equipped but the young Texan wives at the pool were quick to offer to lend us appliances. It seemed they all had two of everything. Soon we had a kettle, coffee maker, blender, iron, ironing board, TV and stereo. Their generosity made us feel very welcome.

I still had my worries about violence and gun crime in Dallas, so when I went to the door of our apartment to find a large man of African descent filling the frame I was nervous. My nervousness moved up a level when he walked into our apartment uninvited and asked if I had a sharp knife. I searched for the bluntest knife I could find and after handing it to him kept my distance. It wasn't until he was in my apartment holding the knife that he revealed he was the apartment handyman and had come to repair some electrical wires. He turned out to be a delightful character and when I came back loaded with shopping, he was there to carry my numerous bags of supplies up the stairs and into our apartment.

Soon after we arrived, we bought an ancient Oldsmobile V8 station wagon in downtown's dubiously named Lemon Avenue. It was enormous and dwarfed the Volvo estate parked beside it in the complex. The bonnet, or should I say hood, was as big as a double bed. When we went to a drive-in cinema, we could watch the film lying on the bonnet. But its size meant it wasn't very good in icy conditions.

Icy conditions were rare in Dallas but one night the temperature dropped to below freezing and we woke up to sheets of black ice on the roads. None of my new friends were prepared to venture out, but I thought the ice would be a challenge so off I set to the supermarket in our Oldsmobile station wagon. I parked the car on a sloping parking lot outside the supermarket and then watched as it slid sideways down the slope. It should have taught me a lesson not to try things just for a challenge, but it didn't.

Once I'd settled into the apartment, I had to find ways of filling my day. I was invited by a group of young wives to join them for crochet mornings. They taught me the art of crochet and as I sipped iced tea from an enormous plastic tumbler I got to know my new friends. Being able to crochet came in useful when I found I was pregnant. I crocheted blankets for my baby's crib, then moved on to more complicated clothing. I crocheted a blue bonnet with matching jacket and booties and a pink dress. In those days the sex of a child was unknown until birth, so there was a 50/50 chance our baby would be a girl and need a dress. I looked forward to the crochet mornings and the other wives' company.

One of the wives invited my husband and me to join her and her husband for Christmas at her husband's parent's home. They had a 4-seater plane, and we flew to an airstrip near the parents' house. I found the flight exciting, but a bit scary. I'd only ever flown in commercial aircraft so taking to the air in a 4-seater light aircraft was a new experience.

On arrival we were made very welcome, but we quickly discovered that tragically the brother of my friend's husband had recently been killed in Vietnam. There was an underlying feeling of sadness in the house. The parents had kept the brother's bedroom exactly as he'd left it when he was drafted to Vietnam. Over Christmas his presence in the house was palpable.

Our 6-month posting to Dallas was extended to a year and we started to settle. I signed up for oil painting and golf lessons and swam in the heated pool every day. We explored Texas, New Mexico and Arizona in our Oldsmobile station wagon, sleeping in the back and cooking on a camp stove. Our ancient Oldsmobile became our second home.

In New Mexico we visited Carlsbad Caverns. It was the most extensive limestone cavern system I'd ever explored, and still is. It was full of the most magnificent stalactites and stalagmites, some delicate and beautiful and others massive and impressive. It took 1½ hours to make the full tour of the caverns. There was even a restaurant below ground where you could stop for coffee or lunch. It was like a strange underground world. We walked in semi darkness on a narrow slippery path to the sound of dripping water. Beautiful unearthly shapes surrounded us eerily lit with spotlights and reflected in pools of water. It was a spectacular and new experience.

We drove on to the Grand Canyon in Arizona which was awe-inspiring. No postcard could ever do it justice. The sheer size of it can't be imagined, or appreciated, from looking at a photograph. At first sight the width of the canyon was even more impressive than the depth as the Colorado River running through the bottom can only be seen from certain viewpoints. We heard it was possible to walk down and stay overnight in Phantom Ranch, but as I was 6 months pregnant it was out of the question on this trip. We vowed one day to return and stay the night in Phantom Ranch.

As we continued our tour of Arizona we had a lucky escape. We had winter tyres on the Oldsmobile, but we were travelling on roads which were hot; so hot you could have fried an egg on them. I noticed bits of something black passing the window as we were overtaking an 18-wheeler truck. Pieces of rubber were shredding off one of our tyres which eventually burst. My husband controlled the station wagon with amazing skill, and we came to a stop. We'd been lucky. In our naivety we hadn't realised it would be dangerous to drive on hot roads using hefty winter tyres. How careless the young can be with their lives in the belief that they are immortal.

One day a member of the crochet group of friends invited me to coffee but when I arrived, I found her living room packed with my new friends from the complex. They'd arranged a baby shower for me as a surprise. I was overwhelmed. It was a very American party brimming with extravagance. A tall cardboard stork stood on the table and all the cardboard plates, and napkins were decorated with baby motives in blue and pink. In the corner was a large pile of presents. They were anxious for me to start unwrapping the presents straight away. I took the paper off slowly to keep the sheets intact, but they encouraged me to rip it off American style. There were so many presents to open and some of the presents were big. I was given a car seat for the baby and a plastic seat with an inset potty. Such friendship, kindness and generosity were so unexpected and quite overwhelming.

The summers in Dallas were hot, very hot. Heavily pregnant they slowed me down. In May when I was nine months pregnant, we visited a state park. The temperature was 101 degrees centigrade, and I can remember just managing to walk from one picnic table to the next before having to sit down.

Our son was born in Baylor University Hospital in Dallas, induced 3 weeks after my due date. Husbands weren't allowed to be present for births at Baylor, which saddened me. The first my husband saw of our son was when he was whisked past him in an incubator while he was sitting outside the delivery room. There was absolutely nothing wrong with our baby, it was just standard practice to put every newborn baby in an incubator for a while.

I phoned my mother in England soon after our baby's birth. She was thrilled but it made me feel a long way from friends and family. My husband wasn't given any paternity leave so when I left hospital three days after giving birth I was on my own. He did do the shopping, but his choice of produce was sometimes rather unusual. When I asked him to buy vegetables, he bought a prickly pear cactus to cook as he said he thought it looked interesting. He was certainly a lateral thinker.

At birth our son automatically became an American citizen, and he still has an American passport, although as dual nationality is allowed, he also has a British passport.

We chose Alexander as his first name. Then we realised that with Calvert as our surname we only had to give him a middle name beginning with an S and he would be named after the Advanced Scientific Computer, usually referred to as the ASC. My husband had spent a year overseeing the ASC's development, so we thought this was a fun idea. We chose Scott for him as a middle name, and our son and his initials became a permanent memento of our posting to Dallas. When he was an adult, we told him why we had chosen Scott as his middle name. I don't think he was very impressed!

The crocheted blankets I made were perfect for Alexander's borrowed wicker crib and he wore the crocheted blue bonnet, jacket, and booties. The pink crocheted dress remained unused.

When our new baby was only 3 weeks old, we were told to start packing. It was time to leave Dallas and return to Holland.

CHAPTER 4
Returning to Holland

When Alexander was 5 weeks old we left Dallas. Flying long distance with a new baby was a challenge, to put it mildly. When we changed planes in New York I walked around the airport holding Alexander propped up against my chest so that he could see over my shoulder, and someone asked if my baby was newborn. That was certainly how it felt to me. But moving at inconvenient times was all part of living the expatriate Shell life. Wives were not a major consideration when a career move was required for the husband. Wives, it appeared, fell in the same category as personal effects. Whatever the family circumstances they were packed up and moved to another country, along with their husbands. This wasn't something I dwelled on much as expatriate life was exciting and full of variety and challenges. It was just a fact of life.

After arriving in Holland, we checked into the Europa Hotel in Scheveningen for the second time in my husband's career with Shell. But hotel living with a very young baby wasn't easy. Shell thoughtfully offered us temporary accommodation in a flat, believing it would make life easier, but they were only partly right.

The flat was on the 5th floor of a block of flats, and I had a baby in a pram to cope with. To reach the car I had to go through the front door of the flat, pushing the pram with one hand while heaving open a heavy door with the other. I then had to wheel the pram along a concrete balcony and repeat the pram manoeuvre through another heavy door. Once back in the building I had to squeeze into a lift with the pram and after an awkward turn out of the lift I reached the front door of the building. But my ordeal wasn't over yet. I had to bounce the pram down a short flight of concrete steps before I was finally at ground level and in the road. By the time I reached the car I had little energy left to load the pram and baby into it. One day I was so exhausted I gave up on the idea of shopping and went back to the flat.

A house rather than a flat seemed to offer the solution to my struggle so we set off to find a house we could afford to buy. But the only house within our price range was an end of terrace house in urgent need of renovation. We only spent six more weeks in the flat before the house was ours and we moved in. It was wonderful to be in our own home at last; I could push my baby out through the back door and straight into the garden. Gone was the almost impossible daily struggle with the pram. From this point of view life had become easier but there were home improvements to be made and a great deal of decorating to be done. The struggle wasn't quite over.

I got started on the decorating straight away. Holding my crying baby in one arm I painted window frames with the other; it was a tricky procedure. The kitchen was in a poor state, so we gutted it, and our bedroom doubled as a kitchen. With no furniture we lived at floor level, and I cooked on a camp stove. It was a means to an end, and I couldn't wait for it to end.

Once our new home was renovated, we felt more relaxed and started to settle into the neighbourhood. We'd chosen to live in Rijswick not realising there was no British expatriate population there. I hadn't met a single British person since we moved in. The Hague and Wassenaar was where the British expatriates lived but I didn't discover that until after we'd bought the house in Rijswick, so I needed to meet the Dutch neighbours in the hope of finding new friends.

This turned out not to be difficult as the Dutch are very curious. One after the other our neighbours called to find out who had bought the house at the end of the terrace. One of the neighbours who called lived with her husband in a house behind ours with only a footpath separating our back gardens. She was delightful and offered to teach me Dutch in exchange for English lessons. She also took great interest in our house renovations and assertively instructed me on what colour to paint the walls. This wasn't quite so welcome, but it came as part of the package. We passed two very pleasant afternoons a week together giving each other lessons and I became fluent in Dutch. In addition, she fell in love with baby Alexander and was always pleased to baby sit. It was like having my mother living close by. This lovely neighbour was called Anne Dee and she asked if Alexander could call her Grandma Dee, which he did. She almost became part of the family.

Making friends after moving to a new country is an important part of settling in and being happy. I was lucky to find such a good friend in my Dutch neighbour. I was also fortunate that the friends we'd met in the leaking Victorian theatre, were still living in The Hague. By then they too had started a family and had a baby daughter. My friend, Liz, and I played at being mothers together. We'd walk in the park pushing our babies in their prams and never stop chatting and comparing notes on caring for our babies. We drank coffee in each other's houses and the infants played together. From time to time, we'd take it in turns to look after both babies and give the other one a taste of freedom for an afternoon. Having a good friend when coping with a baby in a foreign country was vital to my happiness and it was a perfect friendship.

With a new family, our activities became less adventurous, and we took to our bicycles at the weekend.

Holland is a wonderful place for cyclists with so many flat, dedicated cycle paths. Riding a bicycle is part of the Dutch way of life and consequently there's a large selection of child bicycle seats available to choose from. There were bicycle seats you could attach to the handlebars, some designed for a man's bicycle crossbar and plenty for the back to choose from. It was quite a common sight to see a mother with a child on both the front and back of her bicycle. We bought a seat for my husband's bicycle, and we became a bicycle mobile family. One of our favourite cycle rides was to Delft, the home of Delft pottery. We always knew we were nearly there when we started to smell the gin factory. Delft made a pleasant day out and a Dutch traditional pancake house made a great cycle stop for lunch. The Dutch don't put lemon and sugar on their pancakes as we do. There was a long list of possible toppings, but you could ask for practically anything on your pancake from onions and mushrooms to chocolate and bananas. Cheese and bacon were probably the most popular toppings.

One day we were invited to lunch by one of my husband's colleagues who lived with his family in a windmill beside a canal. It was fascinating to see how rooms could be fitted into a six-sided windmill. They were small, unusually shaped, but cosy. We were served a typical Dutch meal of a U-shaped smoked pork sausage, mashed potato, and gravy with onions. Pudding was Hopjesvla, Dutch coffee custard, served with a dollop of cream. It was delicious and so good to be served traditional Dutch fare.

Our host took us on tour of his windmill. He demonstrated how the top of the windmill needed to be rotated so that the sails faced the wind. He unfurled the sail cloth to cover the naked framework of the sails and then they were set in motion. With a whoosh the sails were off. We were delighted to have the opportunity to learn more about the traditional Dutch windmills we'd seen dotted around the landscape.

On New Year's Eve we were preparing to give a party when at the last minute my husband was invited to play a game of squash with a friend. He accepted which niggled me as there was so much to do before our guests arrived. He left for the sports hall, and I continued to work away preparing for the party, hoping his game of squash wouldn't last long. When my husband did finally return, later than I'd hoped, I noticed he was limping. He just said, "I've hurt my ankle". Our guests started to arrive, and he hobbled around serving drinks although he was clearly in a lot of pain.

The next morning his ankle was no better and we went to the hospital. A snapped Achilles tendon was diagnosed, and he was told he needed an operation to repair it. He'd been so brave the night before carrying on as normal despite being in considerable pain, even if he had been thoroughly annoying, accepting to play squash when there was so much to do. As I said earlier, personal comfort for my husband was low on his list of priorities and I admired him for that. His Achilles' tendon was repaired and when he was finally discharged from hospital his entire leg was sheathed in thick white plaster of Paris from his foot to his groin. There was nothing else for it but to cancel our skiing holiday booked for February.

We'd also been about to try for another child so that had to be postponed, too. It was months before he was free of his plaster cast and life could return to normal. As a result, there was a bigger gap between our children than we'd planned. It's interesting how a small single decision like accepting to play a game of squash can have a much bigger knock-on effect in life. I'd set my heart on having 2 years between our children but after the ankle incident there was a 2½ year gap between our sons for ever more.

Having a small child slowed us down a lot so our 2 years in Holland with toddler Alexander was quiet compared to all our other Shell postings. We loved being parents, and parenting was our priority, but we missed our active life.

We'd cancelled our first planned skiing holiday so the following year we tried again. My youngest sister, Marilyn, came with us to share the childcare. We drove to Crans-Montana in Switzerland in our old Volvo saloon, with red walled tyres, and attached chains to the wheels for the high snowy passes. It was a great adventure. We took it in turns to ski in pairs, leaving one person to care for Alexander. It worked very well, and we felt lucky to be able to ski together and get back to one of our much-loved activities.

The last summer we spent in Holland we had a camping holiday. It was 1974 and I was 5 months pregnant. In those days it was possible to put your car on the train in London Euston station and, after a night in a sleeper, drive your car off the train in Edinburgh. We'd seen photos of the Isle of Skye which looked beautiful, so we headed there from Edinburgh. When we arrived the weather was glorious, perfect for camping, and we pitched our small ridge tent. Unfortunately, the midges enjoyed the fine weather, too. They appeared in clouds at dusk looking for a meal. We were easy targets in a tent and there was only one way to solve the problem. We ate supper before dusk and went to bed at the same time as Alexander. It was the only solution. Apart from the midges the holiday was perfect and 2-year-old Alexander loved camping.

Our life in Holland this time was very different from those carefree days when we arrived in Holland for the first time. I very much wanted to have children, and certainly never regretted it, but the days of youth, freedom and an endless supply of energy were over. Freedom returns when your children fly the nest, but youthful energy never does.

Life was soon to move on to another chapter for us. My husband came home from work one day with news of our next posting. It sounded exciting. We were going to live in Borneo, in the small town of Miri in Sarawak. As I was 6 months pregnant, we needed to leave quickly or travelling could be a problem. I thought back to the game of squash the day of our party and pondered. If it hadn't been for my husband's sudden decision to play a game of squash our family would probably have been complete. It made me realise every choice we make in life can have a far-reaching ripple effect.

We found a tenant for our house and booked packers for our shipment to Borneo. But by the time we were ready to leave I was in the late stages of pregnancy. I was determined this time that my husband could be present at the birth of our child, so I resolved to go to Borneo with him. My eldest sister thought I was being irresponsible, but I'd been assured there was good provision for giving birth in Borneo, so I felt happy with the arrangement.

CHAPTER 5
Life in Borneo

By the time we left Holland I was 8 months pregnant. Commercial airlines had a 7-month limit for flying when pregnant but somehow, I managed to slip through the net. It wasn't easy to pack up the house and take a long flight in my condition, but it came with a perk; Shell arranged for the whole family to travel 1st class. We flew from Heathrow to Singapore, then on to Miri, in Sarawak, Borneo. The first leg was on a Pan Am Boeing 747, a Jumbo Jet. It was 1974 and in the 1970s the upper deck of 1st class was set up as a lavish bar with luxurious lounge type seats. I enjoyed exploring my opulent surroundings and playing at being wealthy. However, I wasn't the most popular passenger in 1st class. Our active 2½-year-old son was keen to do some exploring of his own which must have been an irritation to the rest of the first-class passengers and the flight attendants. On her way down the aisle the air hostess came across him inspecting the aisle on all fours. But instead of picking him up and returning him to me she just moved him out of way with her foot. I was filled with indignation. I didn't think that was the way to treat a first-class passenger.

The beautifully presented meals on the Jumbo jet were impressive. Our trays were laid with fine white bone China and included a pretty China salt and pepper pot. I think they were what impressed me most. Champagne flowed and as drinking when pregnant in those days wasn't considered a risk, I enjoyed quite a few glasses of champagne.

Singapore was hot. We had a few days there and I didn't enjoy myself at all. Sightseeing at 8 months pregnant in high temperatures and humidity just added to my jet lag exhaustion. I was relieved when we boarded the Douglas DC-6, a propeller plane, bound for Miri.

A taxi met us at Miri airport and took us to the Shell Piasau camp. When we reached the camp, the taxi stopped on a road which appeared to cross an expansive lake incongruously dotted with bungalows. The new part to Piasau camp was in the process of being built on a marsh. Unfortunately, the construction company hadn't worked out a drainage system before starting to build. To be fair it was October, which was when the monsoon arrived. It hardly stopped raining for a month.

To reach our bungalow we had to walk on boards. Fortunately, I thought this was all part of the tropical experience and embraced the challenge, and it certainly was a challenge. Walking on narrow, unstable boards with water each side when 8 months pregnant and top heavy was no easy task.

We opened the front door of our new home to be greeted by more water. There was a large puddle on the terrazzo tiled floor inside the door, produced by a poorly fitted air conditioning unit. We stepped over the puddle and set off to look at the rest of the bungalow. The bedroom held another surprise. There in the middle of the floor was a large rat with its throat torn out. This I did find a bit alarming. My husband was not so much concerned about the rat's presence as to what might have killed it. There was a gaping hole in the wall left ready for an air conditioning unit providing free access for rats or any other fair-sized wildlife.

Sarawak Shell had a tradition that as soon as a new couple arrived all the neighbours came to greet them; all at once that is. The fridge had been filled with drinks for the occasion. People flooded in through the door and told me who they were and where they lived. I heard what they were saying but registered nothing. All I wanted to do was to lie down in the bedroom with just the rat for company.

The bungalows remained islands in a lake for some time. Each morning the bachelor in the bungalow opposite left for work with his trousers rolled up carrying his shoes and his briefcase, with a towel over his arm. He waded through the water until he reached his car, which he'd parked on the road, then he dried his feet and put his shoes on. Watching this "playlet" each morning was an event I looked forward to.

A month after our arrival my due date was approaching so we needed to make plans. There was a hospital in Miri, but it wasn't used by the Shell expatriate community as it was basic, not air conditioned and reported to be somewhat fly infested. Our nearest air-conditioned hospital was in Brunei. Shell employees and wives used the company plane to visit Brunei. It flew from Lutong airstrip near the camp, but as my delivery was imminent, I wasn't permitted to fly. The only other way to reach Brunei was to borrow the company's 4-wheel drive Toyota and drive.

We left our 2½ year old son, Alexander, with some dear Shell friends, Jackie and Malcolm, who we'd met when we first moved to Holland. Once my small case was stowed, I heaved myself up into the higher than usual passenger seat of the 4 × 4 ready to start our long and challenging journey to Brunei. After the village of Lutong the road became a narrow track through the jungle. On one side was a long horizontal pipe where monkeys sat and watched us go by. Then the track petered out totally and we drove along a broad stretch of sandy beach for a while. When the track reappeared it brought us to the wide Baram River which had to be crossed by ferry.

Eventually we came to the border between Sarawak and Brunei. There we found a small wooden customs hut, occupied by some rather officious custom officers. Once they were satisfied that we weren't carrying contraband we were released to continue our journey. Soon after crossing the border, we reached the town of Kuala Belait. The Shell Panaga Camp where we would be staying was between the towns of Kuala Belait and Seria. The Shell run hospital, where I was planning to give birth, was close by.

Instead of waiting for our baby to arrive when it felt like it, we opted for an induced birth. For most Shell couples living in Miri this was the only choice available. A friend who was pregnant at the same time as I was didn't drive up to Brunei early enough and her baby was delivered in her bungalow in the Piasau camp. The morning after the birth she was flown with her baby to Brunei by helicopter. This wasn't something I wanted for myself and my new baby.

In the early hours of 26th November 1974, we welcomed our second son to the family and named him Andrew James. My husband was allowed to be present at the birth which was wonderful. Giving birth in Panaga Hospital, a wooden one-story building, was a different experience from the high-tech sterile environment of Baylor University Hospital in Dallas, where our first son was born. It was more painful, too.

As Brunei doesn't give its nationality to children born to foreign parents my husband had to drive over 60 miles to Bandar Seri Begawan, the capital of Brunei, to register our son's birth at the consulate. Soon afterwards he drove the 4-wheel drive Toyota back down the track to Miri and returned to work leaving me with our new baby in the hospital.

I stayed in hospital for 3 days, with no visitors. Then I was driven to the airport to take the company 12-seater plane to Lutong airstrip. The plane was delayed. I began to feel anxious. The airport wasn't air conditioned and I waited for what seemed like hours. Concerned about my 3-day old baby in the heat and with no one to talk to I felt very alone, exhausted, and close to tears. The plane finally took off and baby Andrew started crying and cried continuously throughout the 40-minute flight. The pilot tried to comfort me saying it was good if babies cried during the flight as it helped to clear their ears.

We landed in Miri, not Lutong as scheduled. The plane had to be diverted as the grass airstrip in Lutong was waterlogged. It had been a difficult flight, but I suspect the train of events was not unusual. As I walked down the steps from the plane carrying our newborn baby our adorable 2 ½ year old son came towards me clutching a bunch of flowers. It was a joyful moment. My struggles from earlier that day were forgotten. It's moments like that you never forget.

Only a matter of days after I arrived home, we opened the door to find a Shell employee we'd never met before clutching a tiny puppy. He'd found the puppy beside the road, and someone had told him we were looking for a dog. I don't remember that being true but this small, rather moth-eaten looking puppy we were being offered looked so pathetic we said we'd keep it. Miri locals often left their unwanted animals, either in the Shell camp, or close by, hoping someone in the camp would take pity on them.

We now had another new member of the family. As it was Friday that is what we named the puppy. We took him to the vet who told us he was only about 2 weeks old. He had worms and was in a bad way but in time he grew into a healthy dog resembling a small Alsatian. Friday and Andrew started life at the same time and grew up together. He became Andrew's loyal friend and seemed always to be at his side.

Piasau camp was laid out with no divisions between houses which gave the boys a lot of freedom to roam. Perhaps I should have kept a closer eye on them, but I didn't think they could come to much harm. As they were boys, they had a good go at putting my assumption to the test.

One day I was chatting happily to a friend on the veranda when Alexander, who was then three years old, appeared covered in tar from head to foot. Unknown to me a pile of molten tarmac had just been delivered in preparation for road building. I put him in the bath, but the tar stayed put. I needed a solvent, so I went to the fridge and found some margarine. I rubbed it all over him and this removed the tar from his body, but the tar and margarine mixture created a thick black tide mark round the bath. I was still learning about being a mother. I returned to having a chat with my friend, but not long afterwards our son reappeared on the patio. He was again coated with tar from head to foot. This time it was in his hair and that really was difficult to remove.

After 6 months in our Type 73 bungalow, we moved to a Type 70. This in Shell language was an upgrade to be proud of. A Type 70 was larger and provided accommodation for the more senior staff. Our new bungalow had just been finished and was at the edge of the camp. We had dense jungle behind us and the warm tropical sea to one side. We thought it was a great location, but it had a downside. The amah, our maid, refused to move with us. She was of Chinese origin, young, very pleasant, hardworking and was a great loss to the family. She was afraid to live in the amah's quarters of our new home, as they were at the end of the bungalow open to the sea and jungle; I could understand she might feel vulnerable living there. We worked through several amahs in our time in Miri but never found an amah that suited us so well.

We employed a lovely young Malaysian girl whose home was nearby, but she wasn't with us for long. Her father forbade her to see her boyfriend on religious grounds. She was so upset she attempted to take her life. While we were out one evening, she drank bleach, and we returned to find her gasping in front of the television. My husband drove her to hospital, and she survived but her throat was damaged, and she didn't return to us.

Most amahs we employed had uneventful stays, but they didn't stay long. Eventually we found an amah married to a policeman. They liked the accommodation and moved in.

She also spoke good English which was a bonus. They had no children, although they wanted a family, so when a relative's baby was orphaned, they were happy to give him a home. As sometimes happens, soon after she started to care for the baby she found she was pregnant.

Not long after that she came into the house carrying her adopted baby and handed him to me saying "there's something wrong with my baby". I gently took her baby from her but immediately realised it was dead. My husband took them to the hospital where the baby's death was confirmed. There was no inquest so I will never know the cause. Perhaps I shouldn't try to guess. I was only in my twenties and still learning about life. I met many events that shocked me as I progressed up the steep learning curve of life.

We loved living near the jungle and close to the sea. There was an openness about our surroundings which appealed to both of us. We were living in what was called the "new camp". The original camp, known as the "old camp", was made up of wooden bungalows surrounded by mature casuarina trees. It was a personal choice as to which you preferred.

I had my reasons not to choose the large Piasau wooden bungalow, known as a PWB. They were romantically tropical with large verandas and highly polished wooden floors, but the master bedroom was at the opposite end of the bungalow from the children's bedrooms. We heard that it took 4 minutes for one of the wooden bungalows to burn to the ground. To me a bedroom close to the children in a concrete bungalow seemed the sensible choice, although not the elegant or romantic one. During our time in Miri one of the bungalows did burn to the ground but fortunately no one was at home at the time.

When I said our surroundings were open it was a bit of an understatement. There was absolutely no vegetation at all in the "new camp". It was built on a marsh filled with sand which turned to a lake when the monsoon started. Bungalows were built on the featureless plain of sand and gradually linked by tarmac roads. Only then were roots of creeping grass planted around the houses. Fast-growing casuarina trees were planted, dotted around in the sand to break up the featureless landscape. I love gardening so I was quick to plant hibiscus, and bougainvillea bushes each side of our drive, and I made a flower bed, which I filled with pineapple plants.

The soil was light and sandy, and I thought my new plants would appreciate some manure to nourish them. So, I bought a large bag of chicken manure from a local farm, brought it home and tipped the bag out onto the garden. As I watched the pile of chicken mature started to move and then ran off. Almost all the manure in the bag had been eaten by cockroaches which had bred unchecked in the wonderfully nutritious bag of manure. I hadn't bought a bag of chicken manure; I'd bought a bag of cockroaches!

Having an amah gave me tremendous freedom during the day and having a babysitter permanently available in the evenings was perfect. From this point of view living in Borneo while we had young children was ideal. However, as I was only in my late 20s, I did find life in an isolated camp, surrounded by jungle rather restricting. I felt cut off from the rest of the world and everything I believed it had to offer me. There were no newspapers, or magazines available, very little TV and BBC World Service was intermittent and tended to peter out. I stopped trying to listen to the afternoon play as reception usually failed before I could find out how the play ended.

The temperature was about 80F all year round and the humidity close to 90%. Most of the day it was too hot to be outside. The time to go shopping was early in the morning. When I shopped, I left at 7.30 a.m. to drive the 7 miles to Miri town, leaving the two boys with the amah.

In the 1970s Sarawak was what we used to call a "third world" country, now known as economically developing. There were few processed or frozen foods available. Food was either dried or fresh. There was a daily market with fresh produce; fish caught a matter of hours earlier, fresh chicken and a good supply of meat from the local pig farm. There was also a good spread of locally grown fruits and vegetables.

When I first arrived in Sarawak one of the Malaysian wives took me to the market to introduce me to the art of shopping in Miri market. We bought vegetables and then she asked me if I liked fresh chicken. That sounded good to me, so I said "yes". She requested hers first. The assistant reached into a cage, took out a chicken and tied its legs together, making a loop so that it could be carried easily and handed it to her. The poor chicken hung upside down and flapped its wings in desperation. I was horrified. I quickly told her I'd changed my mind and didn't want to buy any fresh chicken after all.

There was a halo of flies around the fresh meat, but I thought if I washed and cooked it there should be no problem. The fillet of pork was excellent, both tender and tasty. The fresh fish was good, too, and there was a wide variety to choose from. Long barracuda fish with their teeth bared looked aggressive but tasted delicious. Prawns would appear from time to time piled high in enormous heaps.

Fruit was plentiful. Every day we had a plate of fresh pineapple, papaya, pomelo, bananas and rambutans on the table at both breakfast and lunch. The durian fruit was popular with the locals, so we bought one to try. It smelt like rotting flesh and didn't taste much better. We gave it to friends who also wanted to try it, but instead of eating it they put it in their freezer. Unfortunately, the smell was so pervasive it flavoured the entire contents of their freezer. They had to throw everything away. It may be good to try new foods, but this fruit turned out to be a culinary hazard.

There was no fresh milk. Milk came in a large tin and was powdered. A Shell wife, experienced in tropical living, showed me how to mix it up and store it in jugs in the fridge. She also demonstrated how to sieve the flour to remove the maggots. There was a lot to learn.

Once I'd adjusted to my new tropical lifestyle, I started to look for something to occupy my time. With an amah to do all the housework, washing, food preparation and some of the childcare I had time on my hands. There was a sailing club in the camp, and as I'd acquired a liking for sailing while working in Fowey I applied to join. I was told that before a member could sail one of dinghies a test was required to show competence.

The captain of the sailing club offered to test my capabilities, and we put to sea in one of the club's 470 sailing dinghies. Unknown to me the test involved a surprise capsize to test my survival skills. I'd never capsized a dinghy before but I'm proud to say I managed to right it and passed my test. After that I took part in dinghy racing every Sunday. I was also opted in by the captain of the sailing club as club secretary. He didn't ask me first, just appointed me after the meeting had started. It was satisfying to be involved, and I remained club secretary and took part in the Sunday racing throughout our time in Borneo.

I did experience a couple of mishaps during my Sunday racing. A gung-ho male Dutch sailor hit my boat while I was sailing over the start line. It was my right of way, and he should have held back. I called out to ask him if there was any damage to the hull and he assured me there wasn't. But the boat started to respond strangely to the helm, and I realised we were sinking. The air cavities in the hull were gradually filling with water. There was no rescue boat, as it had broken down so I headed for the shore. The bows kept disappearing below the surface mimicking a submarine. My crew and I shifted our weight to the stern to keep the bows afloat. Eventually the water was shallow enough for us to stand and we got out. The dinghy sunk. We only just made it.

Another time my mast toppled over, and the sails ended up in the water. My crew and I managed to gather them in and balance the mast down the centre of the dinghy. There was no sign of the rescue boat, as usual, and we drifted down the coast. The white capped waves were large and were gradually bringing us closer to the shore. The danger was that the boat would get side on to the waves and a breaking wave would turn it over. I used the tiller to hold the boat at right angles to the waves and with my heart in my mouth the boat surfed beautifully and rapidly up the beach. My big regret was that no one saw me carrying out such a skilful manoeuvre. By the time we finally made it to the shore we were on a remote beach and there were no witnesses. I must admit to being secretly very chuffed with my achievement.

Sailing took care of Sundays, but I needed something to do during the week. I suggested a book club to the other wives but couldn't rustle up any enthusiasm. I did slightly better with my batik class suggestion. I hired a local teacher, and we met once a week in our bungalow. This went well until I tired of doing all the clearing up after everyone had gone home. I tried the same with tie and dye but that didn't last long either, although I did make a turquoise and pink double duvet cover with matching pillowcases.

Coffee mornings seemed to be the most popular activity for the camp wives. I've never been a great fan of coffee mornings as I'd rather do my chatting while achieving something. I didn't show up at many of the coffee mornings and was criticised for it.

Living next door to us was a Japanese couple. I enjoyed chatting to the wife from time to time and we became friends. I brought up the subject of not attending coffee mornings and being criticised. She had some words of wisdom for me. "No one needs everyone to like them," she said, "all anyone needs is a few good friends. And," she added, "if some people don't like you, it's of no consequence". I've remembered her words to this day, and they've been useful.

Both my husband and I joined the Hash House Harriers and met the HHH group in a clearing in the jungle on Tuesday at 5 p.m., in the comparative cool of the evening. The men started work at 7.30 a.m. and finished at 4 p.m. so they were home early each afternoon. A paper chase was laid in advance, using disused cardboard computer cards, and we all followed the trail. It was noncompetitive and we ran at different speeds. My husband was always in the group at the front of the hash, whereas I came along with the group at the end. It was a good way to explore the jungle. We ran through pineapple plantations, encountered pig and chicken farms, and splashed our way through streams. We finished with a cold beer served from a van and went home sweaty, wet and covered in mud.

We always stepped in through the front door and shed our mucky clothes, leaving them in a pile for the amah to pick up and wash. I felt bad about this later. It was a thoughtless and presumptive act, and I regret not picking them up and putting them in the utility room.

Hashing was a good regular activity to take part in and an excellent way of keeping fit. Carrying out a demanding activity in a group and having a cold beer afterwards produced great camaraderie.

Sarawak Shell Berhard wanted the expats to integrate with the local population, so they didn't build a club with a swimming pool in the camp. Instead, they took over the running of the Gymkhana Club, GMC, in Miri. It had a well-maintained pool but was a 7-mile drive from the camp. Consequently, trips to the pool were an expedition. The large Shell camp in Brunei had a club in the camp with a big swimming pool, which was the envy of the Sarawak Shell staff and wives in the Piasau camp.

On one of our visits to the pool there was an expat family from Africa using the pool. The children were seeing how long they could hold their breath underwater. I noticed one little girl was lifeless when she surfaced. We pulled her out of the water and put her in the recovery position, but she was unresponsive. An expat wife was quick to act and started to give her mouth-to-mouth resuscitation. The child's mother was beside herself with terror. She tried to intervene and totally lost control. I did my best to calm her down, and to our great relief the child recovered. The Shell doctor arrived half an hour later having driven the 7 miles from the camp. He would have been too late to help. It was the expat wife's prompt action that had saved the child.

Not long afterwards the child's mother came to our house bearing a gift for me. It was an ornate pewter plate engraved with her words of thanks. I felt embarrassed as I'd done very little towards saving her child's life, but I did think it was a wonderful expression of gratitude. Gratitude is something we all welcome and occasionally we feel disappointment when it's missing. This time I was being shown more gratitude than I deserved.

The Miri Amateur Dramatics, MADS for short, met, rehearsed, and put on performances at the Gymkhana Club. MADS was an active group made up of talented and enthusiastic people from the expat community. The wife of an oil palm plantation manager drove for two hours on a dirt road full of potholes to join the group and played an active part. Maggi was a very talented producer and was active most of the time we lived in Miri.

I tried my hand at auditioning and to my surprise was given the leading role in the production. Learning my part and rehearsing became a large part of my life during our time in Borneo and I loved it. I found it easy to learn the script and very much enjoyed acting. I played in 3 performances a year: two plays, and a pantomime at Christmas. Some productions were more memorable than others.

During my time in Miri probably the most memorable performance, for both the actors and the production team, was Habeus Corpus by Alan Bennett. I think we all felt we pulled it off remarkably well. I played Murial Wickstead, whose large bosom was a vital part of the plot, so my bust had to be generously padded. I sent photos home after the performance and my mother's comment surprised me. She asked if I was pregnant. I wished I had been but when I suggested to my husband that we have another child he said two children were enough to cope with on flights around the world. I had two lovely sons, so I had to be grateful.

The Secretary Bird by William Douglas-Home was another memorable production in which I played Liz Walford. In the old-time musical production, I sang a solo, "In the Shade of an Old Apple Tree", and in the pantomime, I played the principal boy one Christmas, and the princess another. I had found a new talent and happily embraced success. I just hope I didn't behave like a Deva. I did rather expect to be given the leading role in every production.

Our youngest son, Andrew, loved playing in the sandpit and one day, when he was about 2 years old, he was in the sand playing while I was typing up the minutes of the boat club meeting in the sitting room. Our dog, Friday, as usual, was by Andrew's side in the garden. Friday came in through the open door and sat at my feet whimpering. Once he had my attention he walked to the door, then came back, sat at my feet and began to whimper again. He repeated this time and time again. I remember thinking if this was a film he'd be trying to tell me something.

Finally, I thought I should get up and follow him. He led me to the sand pit where Andrew was stuck under his big plastic lorry crying. I was amazed that Friday knew to come to me for help and he'd worked out a way to communicate with me. Having never had a dog before I knew little about them. Friday had just taught me how loyal, clever and understanding dogs can be.

Not long afterwards I was walking in long grass in the sand dunes when I heard a faint mewing coming from somewhere in the long grass. I hunted until I found the source of the mewing. It was a tiny black and white kitten that would have fitted into my pocket. I picked it up. It had beautiful markings, and I immediately fell in love with it. The problem was that my husband disliked cats, but despite this the tiny kitten was going home with me.

Friday took the kitten under his wing as another charge for him to look after. When my husband came home from work,

I gently broke the news to him that we had an addition to our family. He wasn't exactly ecstatic with joy, but he said he was happy for the kitten to stay, much to my relief.

Annual leave was a time we all looked forward to and spent many hours, probably days, planning. It was a 2-month holiday every 12 months. The fare home was paid by Shell, and we could choose our route. As Borneo is so far east of the U.K., we could travel one way round the globe and return the other, for the price of a normal return fare. The trip needed a lot of planning, which usually started as soon as we returned to Miri from the last leave. It was a chance to see the world and I had every intention of taking advantage of the opportunities it offered.

We were in Borneo for 4 years and we circumnavigated the globe by air 3 times. We often had 3 month's leave as my husband had courses which added to the leave. We spent about a month travelling home, a month in the U.K. and a month travelling back to Borneo.

We didn't keep a base in the U.K., so we relied on staying with friends and family. I worked on the premise that every stay should be no longer than 3 days. It worked well. When we arrived, people were delighted to see us. The next day was spent catching up and taking a trip of some kind and the following day we left after breakfast.

As we were travelling with young children, when we weren't in the U.K., the standard of accommodation was important, and we always selected 4-star hotels. But unfortunately, this didn't prevent us from getting ill from time to time. We stayed in New Delhi for a few days before flying to Kashmir to spend a week on a houseboat. I was longing to see the Taj Mahal, particularly as I'd been given an alabaster model by a friend when I was a teenager. To see the actual Taj Mahal would be a dream come true. We tried to book the train to Agra but there were no train tickets available at short notice, so we had to find another way of reaching it from New Delhi. We approached a taxi driver who agreed to drive us the 130 miles to Agra to see the Taj Mahal and return the same day.

The taxi was an ancient rusty Morris Oxford. The 130-mile journey at 80 m.p.h. on poor roads was the most terrifying drive of my lifetime. I remembering praying we wouldn't hit something. It was a relief when we stopped for a break. After some refreshments we rode an elephant. That felt safer than the scary drive.

We reached the Taj Mahal safely and it fulfilled all my expectations. It was impressive and fabulous at the same time. With its ivory-white marble domes, minarets and bright semi-precious stones inlaid into the marble, it couldn't have looked more beautiful. It's elegant perfect symmetry and its position perched on the bank of the river Yamuna made it an awesome sight. I was thrilled we'd found a way to reach the Taj Mahal, although the return trip to New Delhi in the ancient rusty Morris Oxford was still to come and likely to be just as terrifying as the journey out.

From New Delhi we flew to Srinagar in Kashmir where we'd booked to stay in a houseboat on the Dal Lake. The houseboat was luxurious, the setting stunning and the staff wonderful, but my husband and I developed a bad case of "Delhi Belly". The staff on the houseboat insisted that we'd picked it up in New Delhi but if we did it took a long time to develop. Anyway, we were very ill and struggled to enjoy what should have been a dream holiday.

When we felt better the houseboat staff took us on an outing to Gulmarg, in the Himalayan Mountains. A white tablecloth was spread on the ground and set with silverware and silver dishes for our picnic lunch. We sat round the tablecloth and ate in style. It was like a flash back from the time of the British Raj.

Every man in the Gulmarg village seemed to own a horse and every one of them wanted to rent his horse to us. In no time we all found ourselves sitting on a horse, including our 3-year-old son Andrew, who was hoisted up and perched on the saddle of a large horse, despite our protestations. In single file, slowly and sedately, with a boy leading our 3-year-old son's horse, we climbed up into the mountains.

The scenery was magnificent and when we dismounted, we were surprised to find a heavily wrinkled old man quietly sitting cross legged smoking a hooker. Alexander and Andrew were fascinated by the old man and his hooker. Likewise, he was fascinated by two very blond small boys who seemed to have appeared from nowhere. It proved to be a unique experience only marred by our bad bout of Delhi Belly.

During one of our trips around the globe we hired an impressively large silver Buick in San Francisco and drove south visiting the red woods, Yosemite National Park and Death Valley. We planned to take a tour of the Paramount Pictures Studios before returning the car to the rental company in Los Angeles.

I photographed our small boys standing at the foot of a Giant Redwood and in the beautiful Yosemite National Park producing enchanting photos for the album.

Death Valley was impressive. It was like nothing I'd ever seen before; it was so very hot and barren. While driving through Death Valley my husband decided he wanted to experience the heat, so he turned the air conditioning off and wound down the windows. This mad plan didn't last for long. By a majority vote of 3 to 1 the windows went back up again, and the air con went back on.

We visited the Devil's Golf Course, gnarled terrain left by an ancient, evaporated lake with crystals of pure table salt. Andrew was amazed to find a golf ball lying amongst the salt pinnacles of the Devil's Golf Course.

We drove on towards Furnace Creek and as we approached, we saw green trees. It was such a contrast to the landscape we'd been driving through. There were lawns with cool sprinklers rising like fountains. Furnace Creek is a geological phenomenon. It's a natural oasis at an elevation of 190 feet below sea level and fed by springs arising in the Amargosa Mountain Range. We spent the night in Furnace Creek Ranch which was a lavish hotel. The contrast with the desert was so unexpected. It gave the oasis a dream-like quality as if we were floating in a mirage.

While we were in Borneo, socialising amongst the expat community, mostly took place in the camp. We had endless parties: cocktail parties, dinners and fancy-dress parties. Anything to amuse ourselves as there was nothing else to do in the evening. We drank a lot. It was not unusual to go to a drinks party and then go on to a dinner party.

We dressed formally and by the time I left Borneo I had 32 long evening dresses. We couldn't buy anything in the shops larger than a size 10, as the population were small in stature, but dress makers would make any garment we designed or copy one we already had. Fabric was available, and if we stopped in Bangkok enroute home we could load up with silk, so there was no problem in finding fabric.

Inevitably there were illicit affairs in the camp. Being thrown together in a confined area with few distractions had a good deal to do with it. Many of the ex-marital affairs were obvious to the rest of us as we spent so much time in close proximity to each other. Two people would disappear from a party for some time and then reappear through different doors. We all put two and two together. Most of the camp affairs came to nothing and probably only happened as some people felt they wanted something to spice up our rather isolated life.

My husband was always looking for something to spice up his life, but it usually took the form of a new challenging activity. This time it was scuba diving. There was no scuba diving club in Miri, but Sarawak Shell had the equipment needed. We'd both done part of a Padi scuba diving course in the U.K., but never qualified. We had a basic knowledge of Scuba diving so my husband felt confident that we could start diving in Miri.

We didn't start with an easy dive, as would have been wise. We set off in an open motorboat bound for one of the oil rigs wearing clothes to protect us from the sun and jelly fish stings once we were in the water. When we arrived at the rig we jumped overboard and laden with heavy lead weights around our waists gradually descended. We kept close to one of the metal legs of the oil rig as we dropped towards the seabed. The oil rig legs looked massive and unreal, almost threatening. Fish swam in and out between the legs and seemed to have accepted them as part of the environment. We continued our descent until we reached the bottom which was 100 ft below the surface. It was a new and exciting experience, but a bit daunting.

We'd taken a friend with us who wasn't a diver, and my husband was looking after him. Somehow, I became separated from the two of them, and I found myself without a dive buddy, and alone. I started to surface but noticed that fish seemed to be swimming round me in circles. Something wasn't right!

From my training I remembered it being necessary to stop from time to time when ascending to prevent decompression sickness known as "the bends". So, every time the fish seemed to be swimming round and round, I stopped until they stopped. I didn't panic but I was extremely worried and very relieved when I surfaced. On reflection, our gung-ho approach to a dangerous sport was not impressive.

We did eventually find a colourful reef at 30 ft which made for a more comfortable dive and was certainly more suitable for me. While I was diving in Miri the best part as far as I was concerned, was getting back safely and talking about the dive in the Boat Club over a drink in the bar.

I didn't fancy every dive my husband planned, so sometimes he dived with a friend. One Saturday he and a friend left for a dive in the motorboat after breakfast. Time ticked by but they didn't return. I started to worry as they were usually home by lunch time. I went to the boathouse and looked out to sea but saw nothing. I started to contact friends, and the news of the missing divers rapidly swept around the camp. One couple took me to their home and plied me with brandy in an effort to alleviate my worry.

Shell management got to hear of the missing men and a boat went out to look for them. It was reported that they'd found the boat, but no one was in it. I became desperate as there was a good chance there'd been a fatal accident. The deputy manager's wife must have thought the same as she started to make up beds in her bungalow for me and for my children, imagining I might have been widowed and would need support.

The Shell helicopters were alerted but were delayed, and by the time they were ready to go it was too dark to make the search worthwhile. The tugs which service the rigs were alerted. They arranged to position themselves in a line, each one further out to sea than the last. It was up to the crews on the tugs to scan the water with their eyes as the search light swung from right to left and left to right.

I asked if I could join the search and was allowed to board one of the tugs. As the search light scanned the sea the captain and crew watched from the wheelhouse. This concerned me as they were travelling at speed, and I felt they'd be unable to spot something in the water before they ran it down. I went to the bows of the tug and lay down, hanging on as tightly as I could, so that I could follow the arc of the search light as it moved from right to left and back again.

Eventually, I picked out the outline of a small boat just before the search light lit it fully. I shouted to the crew to slow down. I could see two figures standing in the boat and relief flooded through me. We'd found them!

I thought they'd be elated to see us, but they gave us a mixed reception. They said when the tug appeared and headed straight for them at speed, they thought it was going to run them down. They were standing up in the boat getting ready to jump overboard. They were exhausted having drifted for hours unprotected from the blazing sun. The outboard engine had broken down before they'd had a chance to have a dive.

On the Monday morning the two divers were summoned to the Shell manager's office. Sarawak Shell were not happy. The search had cost the company thousands of dollars. They were severely reprimanded and told to take a spare outboard with them next time.

Living in, what some people might imagine a tropical paradise, we thought we'd have lots of visitors, but we only had three during our time in Borneo. My elder sister, Sally, came out for 2 weeks and later my parents-in-law came for 6 weeks.

We borrowed the company 4-wheel drive Toyota to collect my sister from the airport in Bandar Seri Begawan which is at the northern tip of Borneo. She experienced the day long drive south through Brunei and into Sarawak as soon as she arrived. With a drive through jungle, a trip across the Baram River and a drive along a beach she'd already had a taste of life in the tropics by the time we reached our bungalow. She was awestruck by the tropical paradise her little sister was living in.

During my sister's time with us we took her to see the Niah Caves. It's an impressive large limestone cave system in Gunung Subis mountain, a 2-hour drive from Miri. After we parked the car, we crossed the Niah River by boat and then had a long trek to the caves of about an hour on board walks through dense primary rainforest. When we finally reached the cave, we noticed a cloud of bats whirling around the cavernous mouth of the Great Cave. The cave entrance is 60 metres high and 250 metres wide like a gaping hole in the jungle covered hill. Thousands of roundleaf bats and black-nest swiftlets live within the vast darkness of the caves. The swiftlets feed on insects in the jungle during the day and at sunset return to roost in the cave in a similar number to the bats.

We needed a torch each to explore the remarkable interior of the caves. Long interlinked bamboo poles reached up to the ceiling and men harvesting the black-swiftlets nests for bird's nest soup scaled precariously up them to reach the roof, where the swiftlets built their nests. The birds create their nests by securing gummy threads of their own saliva to the ceiling, which hardens in the air. The entire nest is edible. One name for the swiftlets is Edible-nest Swiftlets. Bird's nest soup is a delicacy in Chinese cuisine, and they believe eating it will help them maintain youth, as well as have a long life and a strong body.

Guano, accumulated bird and bat excrement, is dug from the cave floor to be sold as fertilizer. We watched guano collectors working by the light of paraffin lamps filling great sacks of guano to sell. Unfortunately, human disruption and interference within this fertile wildlife habit and the harvesting of birds' nests is causing the population of swiftlets and bats to gradually diminish.

We took my parents-in-law to Niah Caves during their visit, too. A visit to the caves was a must for all Shell camp visitors. As they had a 6 week stay with us we had time to take them to Sabah in northern Borneo as well. We flew to Sabah on one of the Chinook helicopters used to transport workers to the rigs. It left from Lutong airstrip, just outside the camp, and landed at Kota Kinabalu.

My parents-in-law weren't fit enough to climb Mount Kinabalu, but we enjoyed exploring the park. It was my first encounter with leaches. If we stood still on the path, we could see the leaches making their way towards us, attracted by our body heat. We carried a pack of salt to sprinkle on them to make them drop off; a lighted cigarette works as well. I didn't attract any leaches, but my mother-in-law collected quite a few.

We did everything we could to give my husband's parents a memorable holiday and included them in our socialising, so I was gutted when a friend came to tell me that my mother-in-law was saying unpleasant things about me to my friends. She was telling them that I wasn't a nice person, I only ever thought of myself, and had married her son for his money. I found it hard to believe she could accept our hospitality and then try to blacken my name. My husband said he would reprimand his mother, but I thought this would make the remaining weeks unbearable for all of us, so I asked him to say nothing to her.

When the in-laws returned home to the U.K. my mother-in-law wrote, not to us, but just to my husband to thank him for having them. Since I had suggested we paid their fare to visit us as they seemed a bit down, I thought this was mighty unfair. There are many mother-in-law stories told by daughters-in-law, but I think my mother-in-law from hell took the biscuit.

Flying around the world every twelve months was an amazing experience, but occasionally our travels didn't work out quite as we'd hoped. We planned to spend a week diving in the Maldives, which is well known for its excellent coral reefs. Unfortunately, our aircraft was delayed, and we missed the weekly flight from Sri Lanka to Male. We couldn't wait a week for the next flight, so we found a taxi driver, who agreed to take us on a tour of Sri Lanka for a week, instead. When he realised, I liked gemstones he arranged for us to visit several sapphire mines.

I was told that cornflower blue sapphires were the most sought after, which was a surprise, as when my husband bought my engagement ring in the U.K., we had been told that dark blue sapphires were the most valuable. I bought three cornflower blue sapphires, at three different mines, and had them set in a ring. I've since learnt that velvety blue to violetish blue sapphires command the highest price, not cornflower blue sapphires, or dark sapphires.

During some of our travels it was the flights that were memorable. We were flying from Kuching to Hong Kong in a jumbo jet when we met turbulence. I was walking down the aisle of the plane with 3 ½ year old Alexander coming along behind me when the plane suddenly dropped. I managed to hold on, but Alexander was thrown to the floor. I couldn't reach him as the turbulence was so bad and felt distraught watching him struggle unable to help. A passenger scooped him up, put him on her knee and held on tightly to him until the plane was stable again. I felt very emotional at the time and still do, writing about it. I was so grateful to her.

After 4 years in Borneo, we were posted to the U.K. I was quite happy to be going home, but sad to be leaving our loyal 4-year-old dog, Friday, and our cat. We found them new homes but felt bad about leaving them.

Living in Miri and seeing so much of the world had been quite an experience. I'd learned a great deal about life, and the world, and I was no longer the naïve, pregnant young women who had arrived in Miri 4 years earlier. In many ways, it had been an easy life. We lived under the protective umbrella of Sarawak Shell, which was always there to look after us. They even changed the light bulbs when needed. But it had been a restricted life living in a Shell camp in a remote part of the world. I was looking forward to a normal existence in the U.K., in the real world I'd grown up in, and being close to my family.

It was nearly Christmas when we flew home. We decided to take a direct flight to the U.K. from Bandar Seri Begawan so that we could be with my mother and stepfather on Christmas Day. The flight from Bandar to London was a direct flight and scheduled to take 12 hours. But the flight was delayed and when it finally took off it only flew as far as Damascus and then landed. We were just told the flight had been terminated. We weren't told more than that.

We milled around the airport not knowing what was going on and what would happen next. Then there was an announcement, "There's a plane on the tarmac bound for Paris with a few spare seats and the first to reach it will be given a seat". We managed to board the plane in time, but there were only single seats available. Somehow, with no shared language, I managed to ask several Arabs in their long flowing robes to move seats so that I could sit with our two small boys. It was remarkable how amenable they were and how it happened so smoothly without any fuss. I was so very grateful.

We reached Paris and took a flight to London which arrived late on Christmas Eve. It had taken 36 hours, instead of 12, but we'd made it to the U.K., and we were in time for Christmas with the family.

CHAPTER 6
Posting to England

So here we were in the U.K. ready to start a normal English life, if such a thing exists. It was what I'd been longing for, so now it was up to me to get on with it. When I left the U.K. for Holland in 1969, I'd been married for only 3 months and my husband had been a student during that time. My lifestyle then included boiling ham bones and adding vegetables to create a nutritious supper. Now it was 1978, nearly a decade later, and much had changed. We had a family, and my husband was a successfully employed geophysicist working for an international oil company. I'd travelled the world and been used to having a full-time servant. I was going to have to adapt to a very different lifestyle in this next chapter of my life.

I took stock of the changes I'd need to make. We were in the country of my birth but I hadn't lived there for 7 years and my circumstances had changed dramatically. A new location is always a challenge whether you move from Borneo to the U.K. or to the next county. I'd not only changed countries, but climate and we were now on our own, not being looked after by Shell. We'd been used to being spoon fed for 4 years.

We were lucky that we already had somewhere to live. During our last leave from Borneo, six months earlier, we'd bought a bungalow near Guildford as an investment. The idea was to let it while we were living abroad. But before equipping it for tenants we'd contacted Shell Head Office in London and asked if there was any chance, we might be posted to the U.K. in the near future. They assured us that there was no likelihood whatsoever of us returning to the U.K. any time soon. So, we bought Ikea furniture and furnished our bungalow, 'Key West', cheaply and basically. We registered details and left keys with a letting agent. But just before we were about to leave to return to Borneo, we were told our next posting would be to the U.K., in 6 months' time.

Now we'd returned to England we were looking forward to living in our bungalow. We drove up the drive and there it was looking like the January's photograph on a wall calendar. Long icicles hung from the gutters, some nearly a foot long. Seeing the icicles made me feel happy to be back in England. I could look forward to having four seasons once again. The prospect of spring coming soon was exciting. I'd plant daffodils and in early spring the weeping willow in the front garden would be coming into leaf. Life in the U.K. was going to be good.

But I was surprised to find I experienced something of a culture shock not long afterwards. When I was an expatriate living in a third world country, I was amongst hardy, although indulged, people who loved to travel and party. But the expatriate lifestyle I'd been used to in no way resembled the British way of life. It was poles apart. I found my neighbours weren't the slightest bit interested in where I'd lived, or my experiences travelling around the world. They seemed more interested in how many pints the milkman had left that morning, or if the dustbins had been emptied. I had to reboot my way of thinking; I'd have to rethink not only my lifestyle but my expectations as well.

Our shipment from Borneo was delivered three months after we arrived. A massive lorry backed up the drive carrying two large wooden crates. It unloaded its cargo, and cardboard boxes were piled high in the drive. It was a daunting sight. I had to find room in our bungalow for everything in those cardboard boxes.

I started to unpack but we had a duplication problem. Our bungalow was already fully equipped, mostly with items from Ikea. Fortunately, we had a spacious loft. We wrapped up everything we'd purchased for the tenants, filled one cardboard box after the other, heaved them up the ladder and stored everything we'd bought in the roof. Only then were we ready to unpack. Alexander and Andrew, now 6 and 4 years old, were delighted with the goings on; they dived into the pile of empty card boxes on the drive and played happily. That kept them occupied and safely out of the way.

With our house sorted, finding shops which suited us was next on the list, followed by schools for the children, new friends and leisure activities.

There was a village school for Alexander and a play school for Andrew, so schooling was easily fixed. There were shops in the village with a greengrocers and butcher so no problem there. But there's no quick way too find new friends. The neighbours were friendly and welcoming but not bosom friend material. I decided to just wait and see what, or rather who, would turn up.

Not long afterwards I went into a hardware shop and made enquiries about buying firewood. It was January and we were cold after living in Borneo. We had an open fire, so logs were needed. Another customer in the shop kindly told me where I could buy logs and asked if I was new to the area. I explained I'd just moved back to England from Borneo. To my surprise and delight she immediately invited me to her home for a coffee. A sherry appeared, too. We enjoyed each other's company and like me she had two young children. A friendship developed quickly and I'm still in contact with Jane to this day. As the Japanese neighbour in Borneo so wisely advised me, "You only need a few good friends". I'd made a great start as I now had a friend.

Next, I needed something to achieve during the day while the boys were at school. I signed up for both a writing and a touch-typing course. Then I found a guitar teacher as I wanted to improve my guitar playing so that I could accompany myself when singing country music. We had a sizeable garden, and I knew once spring arrived, I'd enjoy working outside in the fresh English air. Life in the U.K. was going to be fine once we settled, but very different from life in Borneo.

Leisure activities gradually evolved. I joined an aerobics class and jumped around to music wearing a tight top, tight leggings and brightly coloured leg warmers. It was all the rage in those days.

My husband wanted to learn to sail. He'd patiently cared for the children every Sunday for 4 years while I raced 470 sailing dinghies in Miri, and now he wanted to try sailing himself. We bought a Toppa, a single-handed sailing dinghy we could put on the roof of the car. It was a perfect choice as one of us could sail while the other one looked after the children. It took only fifteen minutes for my husband to pick up the rudiments of sailing and ask if he could put me ashore. He was a remarkable man, highly intelligent and able to pick up anything at the drop of a hat.

We sailed at Frensham Ponds, near Farnham, and the boys played in the sand while one of us sailed. Our time sailing the Toppa was simple and satisfying, but it wasn't long before my husband became tired of sailing such a simple craft and suggested we bought a yacht. This was no surprise; he always pushed the boundaries of every sport we took up to the limit and often beyond. We bought a 32 ft Westerly Berwick yacht which was stable and, although slow, was a good family boat. We moored it in what was then called Chichester Yacht Basin.

My husband's interest in sailing had been ignited and from then onwards we sailed almost every weekend throughout the year. We also spent every summer holiday on the boat. One year, on New Year's Day, as we left Chichester Yacht Basin, we noticed we were creating a trail of broken ice behind us. We had a Calor gas heater to keep us warm and oil lamps to light the boat in the winter evenings. Despite an element of discomfort, we usually enjoyed our all weather, all season, sailing weekends.

My husband continued to pursue his interest in sailing avidly and took a navigation course. Predictably he couldn't wait to put his newfound knowledge to use and soon afterwards set out to cross the English Channel. Alexander, Andrew and I, with some reluctance, took on yet another challenge.

The weather was key to our enjoyment of our sailing expeditions. We had some enjoyable crossings and rather too many bad ones. Probably the worst crossing was the one when we hit fog mid channel while navigating the main shipping lanes which run both ways. We couldn't see a thing, just a wall of white. The guide on a cruise we took to the Faroe Islands recently aptly described this situation as "watching the fog from the inside". It was a good description.

While making our foggy crossing I was sent up to the bows of the yacht to listen and look for ships. My instructions from my husband were to launch the life raft if I saw a ship bearing down on us. What a scary possibility that was. I peered into the fog praying that I wouldn't see anything at all and fortunately I saw no ships, but I did smell them as they passed close by. I sat on the bows of the yacht for 5 hours. When I asked my husband if I could return to the cabin for a cup of coffee and a warmup my request was firmly denied.

Sailing across the channel took 13 hours and in thick fog the passage seemed endless. Finally, although we could still see nothing but fog, my husband announced that his calculations showed we were close to the entrance to Cherbourg outer harbour. The words were barely out of his mouth when we saw the shapes of towers on the harbour wall looming out of the fog. My husband's chart navigation had been brilliant; we were sailing through the entrance to the outer harbour.

Only then was I allowed to make my way back from the bows of the yacht to the cockpit. I went down below into the cabin and caught sight of myself in the mirror. Each hair on my head was adorned with tiny water droplets and water drops glistened on my eye lashes. So much for my longed-for normal life in the U.K!

We often sailed on to Guernsey after Cherbourg and loved the island, but there was a downside. My husband preferred to moor away from the crowd. Instead of berthing in the marina like any normal sailor we dropped anchor close to a massive stone wall which extended seawards towards the castle. To get ashore we had to take the rubber dinghy to the bottom of a ladder, tie it up, then climb up a long, narrow metal ladder to reach the top of the wall. It scared me stiff. Coming down the ladder after dark was even more frightening. I'd loved to have tied up in the marina like everybody else.

We had many a scary trip on our yacht, which we called *Snowflake*, so named because it wasn't uncommon for snow to be falling on the deck while we were sailing.

One alarming experience took place in the Channel Islands. We were caught in a severe storm off the Isle of Sark. The wind was storm force 10, two levels higher than gale force on the Beaufort scale. We sought shelter in a bay and dropped anchor. Foaming spume seemed to be rising from the surface of the water vertically, like rain falling in reverse. The rubber dinghy tethered to the stern of 'Snowflake' was in a frenzy, repeatedly rising up from the sea's surface and trying to climb into the cockpit with us.

Our yacht bounced around, but the anchor held. A French boat in the bay wasn't so lucky. Their anchor was dragging, and they were getting closer to the rocks. Panic broke out amongst the crew and with terrified shouts they fought for what seemed like hours to keep the boat from being thrust onto the rocks.

Life in the U.K. had turned out to be far from dull but after a while I missed taking flights to far flung places. I watched planes flying overhead and imagined being on board flying somewhere new and exciting. Flying had been so much part of our lifestyle until we moved back to England, and I missed the thrill of going to places I'd never visited before. I longed to be able to stare in wonder at exotic and stimulating sights. That was all in the past now. We didn't take a single flight in the 5 years we lived in the U.K.

Occasionally we had a break from sailing and camped for long weekends with two families we'd met in Holland. These weekends were always a delight. Liz and Keith, who we'd met in the Victorian theatre when water drops started falling on their heads, had returned to live in England. Joan and Chris had been living in The Hague when we arrived and had returned to live in England, too. We enjoyed camping with them and as we all had children of similar ages, they had fun playing together.

We were camping in Wales one weekend when our happy band of children set off to explore. They came back with precious spoils from their trip in the form of sheep's bones and skulls. They each added their contribution to a pile of skeletal bits in the middle of the circle of tents. I thought this rather macabre collection of treasures might carry a risk of infection but fortunately not one of the children suffered illness as a result.

Once a year we had a break from our winter sailing expeditions and drove to France or Austria to ski for a week or two. My husband and I had started skiing while at college when one winter we took a train to Val d'Isere in France on a youth activity skiing holiday. It was a new experience for us both.

The train was shunted onto a cross-channel ferry and secured noisily with chains. The dormitory carriages were fitted with bunks three tiers high, and I was allotted the top bunk with no possibility of sitting up, but that was fine, I just stayed lying down. When I opened my eyes in the morning snowy mountains were flashing by. It was a glorious sight to wake up to.

After the Val d 'Isere trip we skied almost every year and introduced the boys to skiing at a young age. Alexander started when he was 3½ years old during our first leave from Borneo. We checked him into a ski class for very young children and at the end of the morning went to pick him up. We found the ski class, but Alexander was nowhere to be seen. The instructor denied having any recollection of him ever being there.

Looking for a small child who's gone missing in subzero conditions is a parent's worst nightmare. We didn't know where to start looking for him. In the end we decided to go to the kindergarten to enquire if anyone there had seen him. Outside the door we saw what looked like Alexander's skis, boots and poles. We went inside and there he was happily playing with the kindergarten toys. To say we were relieved doesn't express fully how we felt at that moment. The childcare assistant told us she'd wondered where the little blond boy she'd never seen before had sprung from. Alexander had felt cold and didn't like skiing, so he'd left the ski class. He'd asked someone at the door of the kindergarten to take his skis off so that he could go inside and warm up. We gave him full marks for ingenuity, but he'd given us an awful fright.

Andrew was 4 years old when he started skiing and took to it like a duck to water. With no ski poles he'd put his skis together at the top of the mountain and speed down the slope heading for bumps to liven up the run. I tried to take photographs of him, but he was too fast, I couldn't get ahead of him to snap the action. He's still a keen skier and goes skiing with his family every year. How different children from the same family can be.

Living in England I had the opportunity to use my teaching qualification once again. I applied for a part-time job teaching maths to a remedial class of 12-year-olds. I went for an interview and got the job. Afterwards I went out to lunch with friends to celebrate and suddenly it dawned on me that I'd tied myself to a job 4 mornings a week. I'm not sure I'd thought it through, or perhaps I didn't think I'd get the job. The teaching went reasonably well, and I quickly slotted back into teacher mode but although I liked teaching maths the children, mostly boys, were difficult to teach as they had absolutely no enthusiasm for learning the subject.

At the end of the year, I gave in my notice and applied to work as a supply teacher. This was much more enjoyable. I'd be phoned up out of the blue at 8 a.m. in the morning and given the address of a school to report to. I wasn't told what I'd be teaching until I got there. One morning when I arrived, I was told I'd be teaching French. I had no qualifications as a French teacher but that didn't seem to worry the headmaster. He told me which page in the textbook they'd reached, and I was expected to just take it from there. Another time I was told to teach football all day. As I didn't know the rules of the game this proved difficult.

Then I struck lucky. I was offered a job teaching full-time in a private school for a term. The children were very polite and well mannered. Each child was asked to bring a napkin ring from home to put on their napkin at lunch time. I was impressed.

But taking a full-time job for a term didn't go down well at home. My husband said he didn't want me to work, and we didn't need the money, which was true, but that wasn't the point. I wanted to work. He told me that if I worked full time, he would do no more in the house than he did already. I wasn't sure what he did already, so I went ahead and took the job.

The teaching was enjoyable but by the end of the term I was drained of every ounce of energy I possessed. I had attempted the impossible. Running the home and ferrying the boys around, in addition to teaching, proved incredibly exhausting. To make matters worse every Friday after school I had to pack everything needed for a weekend at sea on our yacht. The moment my husband came home from work on

Friday evening we loaded the car with the provisions I'd organized and drove down to Chichester Marina. We didn't get home until Sunday night. It was the last straw. I was young and fit, but I couldn't take the pace. At the end of the term, I made a resolution never to take on full time work again.

Instead, occasionally, I taught on supply in a private girl's school; filling in when there were staff absentees. It was great, the perfect job for me. I enjoyed the stimulation of working and had time to run the home, and enough energy to pack provisions and sail every weekend.

But one morning the headmistress phoned to ask me to teach when I already had plans to make Alexander's birthday cake for his party that day. The boys' birthday cakes weren't two sponges stuck together with jam and cream, but a major construction job. They would request anything from a railway engine to a rocket on a launch pad. I told the headmistress I couldn't teach that day as I was making my son's birthday cake. She didn't phone to ask me to teach ever again. I was punished for being honest. If I'd said I was going to an aunt's funeral I would still have had a job.

It wasn't the first time I'd run into difficulties for being honest. It often happened and still does. If I am asked a question the questioner gets the truth, even if they really didn't want to hear it. Somehow my parents had taught their five daughters to be honest. I'm not sure how they did it, perhaps by only expecting and accepting the truth. I'm pleased to say my sons grew up to be truthful, too. I know lies can get you out of a hole, but I find it impossible to make up stories to get me out of trouble; it goes against the grain. The way my parents reared me had the effect of setting all my standards for the rest of my life.

I loved being a mother and was proud of my two fine sons, but being a mother had its moments. The boys fought, as all boys do. They were having one of their fights in the sitting room one day when Andrew, the younger of the two, pushed Alexander into the glass coffee table. I heard a crash and rushed to see what had happened. There were sharp shards of glass everywhere and some very dangerous looking large, jagged pieces, too. I grabbed Alexander and checked every inch of him but didn't find a single scratch. I was terribly relieved and not in the least bit cross as both boys had survived what was an accident. We replaced the glass with safety glass, ready for the next time.

The boys' fights weren't normally serious, but if they did get heated the best way to stop the fight was for me to stand between them. I knew they wouldn't touch me. The moment I moved into place the fight came to an end. The respect these two small boys showed me then, and still do, was and is remarkable, and very gratifying.

Each day the two of them dreamt up things to do. They were full of ideas. One day they each built a house out of cardboard on the lawn which they played in all day. When evening came, they said they wanted to sleep outside in their houses. I didn't like to put a damper on their enthusiasm, so I agreed. I got very little sleep that night, as I paid frequent visits to the lawn to check on them, and on one visit found Andrew's house had collapsed and he was sleeping in the open. I picked him up and carried him to the car, carefully putting him on the back seat without waking him. In the morning the two of them drank milk from the bottles left by the milkman and called it their breakfast. They had such a wonderful time. I was very relieved they'd come to no harm and that I'd had enough courage to allow them to have a memorable adventure in the back garden.

Sometimes I had to act calmly when inside I felt terrified for the boys' safety. It was lunch time, and the boys were nowhere to be found. For some reason I glanced up and there at the top of two tall evergreen trees, twice the height of the bungalow, were the boys swaying backwards and forwards holding onto the spindly tops. I felt like shouting at them and telling them to come down at once, but something warned me that this might be a dangerous thing to do. Instead, I simply said "It's lunch time, can you come down now please?" I watched with my heart in my mouth as they climbed back down the trees and returned safely to me.

As a mother you never quite know what to expect next. There's no training for motherhood. We mothers must do what we think is best at the time. I did make mistakes but in later life realised there was no point in beating myself up about them. When a mother or father make a decision, they believe to be the best decision at the time that has to be good enough.

My mother had a wise maxim. She said, "you should always be two steps from danger". Meaning more than two things had to go wrong before you were in danger. I remembered my mother's words of wisdom as my sons were growing up and tried to apply them, but it was difficult with two small, very adventurous boys. I have, however, thought about them frequently throughout my life and passed her wise maxim on to my husband, my children and my grandchildren.

The boys started to grow up. Our eldest went to prep school and our youngest moved to the village school. Then the inevitable happened. We were posted. We could have been sent anywhere in the world but to my disappointment we were told we were going back to Holland. We'd lived there twice already. I'd hoped when my husband joined Shell, as international staff, I would see the world, not keep returning to Holland. I was far from delighted. I don't mind uprooting myself and disrupting the children's lives to move to a country we'd all find exciting and stimulating, but going back to Holland didn't warrant the disruption it would cause.

There was an international school in The Hague, but its academic reputation wasn't great. Leaving the U.K. would mean the boys would have to board at a prep school if they were to stand the best chance of passing the common entrance exam when they were 13 years old. So, decisions had to be made. Alexander was already at Aldro prep school so boarding there wouldn't be too much of an upheaval for him, but Andrew was still at the small village school. He would have to not only move schools, but start to board.

My husband was needed in Holland in January, but winter didn't seem the best time for the boys to start boarding. We moved Andrew to Aldro, as a day boy, in preparation for the move, and I sat down with my husband to discuss our choices. I was relieved when he generously offered to move to Holland by himself, look for a house to buy and for 3 months come home for the weekend every fortnight. This would mean the boys could start to board at the beginning of the summer term. Then, once they were settled at boarding school, I planned to let the house and join my husband in Holland.

We visited Holland to choose a house from the three my husband had found. The first one was a town house on three floors with no direct access to the garden from the living area so that was struck off the list before we looked inside. The next one we turned down largely because the owner had Indian music playing loudly through speakers throughout the house as we walked from room to room during the viewing. We couldn't get out fast enough. Like Goldilocks we chose the third house.

Alexander and Andrew started the summer term as borders at Aldro School and I took the ferry to Holland to join my husband. It was difficult leaving the boys behind, but necessary. A new chapter in my life had begun and I needed to give it my best shot. I knew it wasn't going to be easy. I'd have to adapt to a new lifestyle without my children—well, in term time anyway.

Before I left, I had a photographic portrait taken. It seemed a good idea as I was nearing my 40th birthday and in those days when you were over 40 you were considered to be past your best. A portrait of me taken before I was 40, would, unlike Oscar Wilde's Dorian Gray, preserve my young looks for the record and make a good keep's sake.

CHAPTER 7
Back in Holland

It was 1984 and here I was back in Holland for the third time. Was I ready to face the challenges the move would thrust upon me? How soon would I be able to adapt to a new lifestyle, settle and feel happy? I was about to find out.

We were lucky we'd bought a house already, but we couldn't move in as the house was empty. We'd chosen to buy in Wassenaar this time where there was an enclave of British families living, I was excited about that. The first house we'd bought was in Rijswick where there were very few expatriate families. When I discovered this, I was so very disappointed. This time we'd made a more informed choice, and I was full of optimism.

Our house, however, was rather too close to a busy arterial road named "Wittenburgerweg". There was a service road in front of the house but the road noise from Wittenburgerweg was intrusive. When we viewed the house, the previous owners had assured us the road noise didn't bother them, but it bothered me. With so much road noise I realised gardening would no longer be a pleasure and it would be impossible to open any of the windows at the front of the house. Well, you never do get everything you desire when you buy a house do you? I decided I'd just have to accept the noise and get on with life.

There was one aspect of the house's location I loved. On the other side of the main road was an expansive field backed by trees. Standing on the balcony of the master bedroom I could watch horses, cows or sheep in the field. This was an uplifting sight and a taste of the countryside in an otherwise built-up area

I liked most of the house layout. The sitting room was at the front of the house with a lovely bay window. It linked with the dining room and they both linked to a large sized hall. But the kitchen was small, in fact it was very small.

We gradually furnished the house, left the hotel and moved in. Only then did I cook my first meal in the kitchen. As I moved around preparing the meal tears rolled down my cheeks. I felt restricted and cramped. There was a depressing view of a small yard and shed out of the only kitchen window. I felt upset and a feeling of desperation overtook me. Our kitchen in England had windows in all directions. Outside one window there was a big apple tree with woods beyond.

I missed my lovely leafy view. This Dutch kitchen would take some getting used to and for me was a real downside to our move.

Fortunately, a visit to Wassenaar town centre was a treat. The main street was pedestrian only and full of up market shops. In those days you dressed up to go shopping. The clothes shops were superb, and my wardrobe expanded. A shopping trip usually included a coffee in one of Wassenaar's cosy cafes. At the start of our posting to Holland it was only my visits to Wassenaar town that cheered me up. They were a delight and delights were rare.

I missed Alexander and Andrew terribly. I wrote to them every single day and received letters from them once a week. Letters were delivered to a box perched on a wooden stake at the end of our narrow garden path. I took the boys' letters out of the box and opened them immediately and as I walked up the path to the front door I started to read them. By the time I reached the front door I was usually in tears. I shed a lot of tears when we first moved to Holland.

Alexander adapted to boarding school well and was fine. It was Andrew's letter which brought me to tears. He was only 8 years old and a sensitive child. He hated boarding school and was very unhappy. We thought about moving him to the International School in The Hague, but it wasn't set up to prepare children for the common entrance exam which was a problem.

Andrew was bright but his schoolwork didn't reflect his potential. We felt he needed teaching geared towards passing the common entrance exam. We planned for both the boys to board at Charterhouse from 13 to 18 as we could be sent to live anywhere on the globe at the drop of a hat. I've spoken to Shell wives since who regretted sending their children to boarding school, but it was something we all accepted as necessary at the time. I hope we did the right thing.

We imported some furniture from the U.K. and went shopping for furniture in Holland to equip our empty house. My husband fell for a very heavy Dutch oak table with a top that was at least 5 inches thick. It came with six very heavy carved oak chairs which needed two hands and a hard tug if you wanted to pull them out from under the table. The dresser, which was part of the set, was equally hefty. In the sitting room we had some rather beautiful English reproduction oak furniture which we'd bought new and shipped.

Everything imported had to be listed and declared to Dutch customs. My husband's somewhat quirky attitude to life led him to slip "One yacht" into the list of cutlery. I don't think the Dutch customs officers appreciated the joke, if it was a joke.

One day I looked out of the window to see two uniformed men walking round and round the Volvo estate car we'd brought with us from the U.K. They seemed to be examining it. The two men knocked on the door and when I opened it I realised they were Dutch customs officers. They asked to come in and I sat them down at the hefty Dutch oak table. They'd come to interrogated us about what we'd imported.

The Dutch have very strict rules and make sure everyone adheres to them. They said the car had come into the country several times through Hoek van Holland before I officially arrived to live there. That apparently was an offence but I'm not sure to this day why. I was dispatched to get our passports. One customs officer was pleasant and the other one decidedly unpleasant. The pleasant one picked up the passports and flicked through them, in theory looking for stamps confirming my entry into the country. The stamps were there but he didn't mention them and put the passports down saying, "that's okay". I was so grateful to him and felt sure he'd grabbed the passports as he knew what would happen if the unpleasant officer had picked them up.

Our furniture was then put under scrutiny. As the customs officers were sitting at the ridiculously heavy table which screamed Dutch furniture, they commented that we'd obviously bought our furniture in Holland. Fortunately, they didn't look in the sitting room which was full of new English furniture. It was a tense hour of interrogation, and I heaved a sigh of relief when they left. I'm sure it was the list with *12 teaspoons, one yacht, 12 forks,* etc. that had made them suspicious. When we sailed the yacht to Holland later that summer, we had no problem importing it. We had to plough through a large amount of paperwork, but that's what we'd come to expect. The lesson here is always to be straight with customs officers and never think for a moment that they share your sense of humour.

At the end of the school summer term, we collected Alexander and Andrew from school and took them to Chichester Yacht Basin to board *Snowflake*. We needed to get our yacht to Holland, so we decided to do that with the boys at the end of their first term boarding. I'm sure they just wanted to go straight to their new home in Holland, but they were used to their father's outward-bound approach to life and didn't complain.

We sailed towards Dover, crossed to Boulogne then started to make our way along the French coast towards Belgium, and eventually Holland. The trip went smoothly, and the boys took it in good spirits. In Boulogne they were amazed by the number of dogs poos on the pavements. Children seem to be fascinated by poo, and they enjoyed their new game of dog poo spotting. From then onwards all poo was called "a Boulogne".

We berthed the boat in Scheveningen Harbour on the west coast of Holland and took a taxi to our home in Wassenaar to spend a week recovering from the first leg of our trip. We all needed a break. We still had a long sail from Scheveningen to Hindeloppen Marina, in the IJsselmeer, ahead of us.

After a week we returned to Scheveningen and started to sail northwards up the west coast of Holland towards the IJsselmeer. For hours on end the coastline didn't change. All we had to look at were long sandy beaches and sand dunes. Eventually we reached Den Helder, at the northerly tip of Holland. We motored through the lock in the dyke and finally into the IJsselmeer. Hindeloppen Marina was only a short sail from the dyke and once we were safely moored, we packed our bags and caught a train home. Alexander and Andrew had taken the trip in good spirits. I was proud of them.

The boys had regular exeats, long weekends, while they were boarding at Aldro Prep School, and I went backwards and forwards to the U.K. on the Hoek/Harwich ferry to be with them. We stayed with my mother in Wootton Bassett and only now do I appreciate how much she did for us.

She was always welcoming and fed us well, but she wasn't a great cook and sometimes food was a little overdone. One evening my mother served chipolata sausages for high tea. The boys usually loved sausages, but Alexander left his. My mother, as always, was understanding saying, "don't worry I'll give them to the birds". Alexander looked at her, his face full of concern, and said, "But I don't want the birds to break their beaks". Children take a while to learn how to conceal their true feelings so as not to offend. Fortunately, my mother was very tolerant of her grandsons, even when they played cricket in the garden bowling towards the conservatory.

I was just settling back in Holland after yet another trip to England when the doorbell rang. I opened the door to find a lady I'd never met before standing on the door mat. "I've come with a request", she said. "Would you consider being chairman of the British Women's Club Youth Activities?" I was amazed. I'd never heard of the *British Women's Club Youth Activities* and wondered why she was asking me if I'd be chairman. She went on to tell me that the BWC arranged activities, during the holidays, for children who were away at boarding school. At present she was chairman but as she was leaving Holland soon, she needed someone to replace her.

She seemed convinced that I was the right person for the job. I could only assume none of the present committee members wanted to do it and someone had suggested she asked me. But I was concerned as to how the members of the committee would feel when someone they didn't know, and who knew nothing about the workings of the Youth Activities Committee, suddenly became chairman.

With Alexander and Andrew away at school during the term they needed activities to keep them occupied during the holidays so taking this on seemed the perfect solution. I agreed to start right away. I took up my position at the first meeting and the committee showed no animosity towards me, which was a relief.

My new job turned out to be a blessing. I'd found something to do with my time and it helped our social life to blossom. I met expat families from companies other than Shell and families of staff at the British Embassy. Alexander and Andrew found new friends and enjoyed the activities.

I had a committee of 10 ladies all with different talents and qualities and I loved finding the right activity for each of them to organise. One committee member was nervous of being in charge of an activity, but I found she was fine arranging trips to a candle factory where the younger children could make candles under the factory staff supervision.

During each school term the committee dreamed up more activities. We arranged for the children to play squash and tennis, to go on wind surfing courses, to skate at the ice rink, to swim and to take part in many other activities. I was chairman of the Youth Activities Committee for the entire time we were in Holland: it became central to my life and made me feel fulfilled.

There were other pursuits I found to keep me occupied while the boys were away at school. I sang in an international choir, which I loved. We had a brilliant conductor and gave several concerts a year. I particularly enjoyed the Christmas concert when we sang all the well-known carols and others that weren't so well known. I formed many friendships with members of the choir and always found the practices uplifting. I also swam with a group once a week and worked towards Dutch swimming medals. We had coffee afterwards and developed friendships. I also played squash and tennis.

During our time in Holland, I developed two lifestyles which I alternated between. While the boys were away at boarding school, I filled my time with my own pursuits, but as soon as they came home, I stopped everything I was doing and made them the focus of my attention. It worked well.

The year after we arrived in Holland, I turned 40. It was an event I was determined to celebrate. We bought 21 bottles of different champagnes and arranged a blind champagne tasting party. Our 19 guests were each given a small glass and a scoring sheet. Champagne was poured with the label concealed and our friends had to mark each champagne out of ten. At the end of the evening, we had a clear winner. Veuve Clicquot Rose had the highest score, a score far higher than any of the other champagnes. The party was a great success. I promised myself I would celebrate every birthday for the rest of my life by drinking at least one glass of champagne and to date that's what I've done.

We gave a lot of parties during our time in Holland. One of the highlights of the year was our New Year's Eve party. The adults had a party on the ground floor and the boys had a party on the third floor. Just before midnight the two parties came together for fireworks let off in the road outside our house. It was something many Dutch families did on New Year's Eve; except those that lived in an area with thatched roofed houses where fireworks were forbidden.

While in Holland I developed an interest in photography. Parts of Holland were very photogenic, and I started to photograph some of the attractive scenes around me. I often took a train to Amsterdam and wandered round the streets photographing bicycles, bridges, canals, trams and anything I saw which would create a good photograph. I loved my trips to Amsterdam. There seemed to be something to photograph in every direction I looked.

The Keukenhof, an impressive and well-known bulb garden, was a wonderful place for photography too. Every spring the gardens are vibrant with tulips, hyacinth and daffodils. There are cherry trees covered with beautiful pink blossom, and at the end of April and beginning of May they all bloomed together to create an awe-inspiring spectacle. I used to leave home early and be first through the gates when they opened. By doing this I could get scenic shots of the bulbs without crowds of people in my photographs. Once the coaches arrived around 11 a.m. I could no longer photograph general scenes, so I changed to taking close-ups of individual flowers.

Photographing windmills in Holland was a must. In Stompwijk there were three of the traditional Dutch windmills in a row beside a canal. Sunrise was the best time for it as they created a stunning picture as the sun came up, particularly on a frosty morning. One morning I was lucky to find a pair of swans floating on the canal in a patch of clear water surrounded by broken ice. As I watched, one swan spread its wings and I caught the action. The photo came first in a competition, and it was this success which made me decide to try to market my photos.

Selling photos for postcards seemed a good place to start. I found the name and telephone number of postcard publishers printed on the back of every postcard I looked at. I bought a selection of postcards published by different companies and made three appointments. With a portfolio of named and numbered slides in my briefcase I took the train to Amsterdam. I was thrilled when every publisher I visited retained a selection of slides. After each appointment I went to Amsterdam Central Station Cafe and re numbered all the slides while drinking a cup of coffee. By re numbering the slides I kept my portfolio looking fresh for each publisher.

Soon afterwards my photographs started to appear in postcard racks all over Amsterdam. It wasn't a great money spinner, as I only received 5 cents for every postcard sold, but it was a lot of fun and satisfying to see my work for sale. Whenever I visited Amsterdam and came across a postcard stand, I'd move all my postcards to eye level to help promote my sales. Recently I found some of my postcards published in 1988, for sale on *eBay*. I've also noticed *Art Unlimited* are selling my postcards on their website.

I started to have prints made from my slides and a few were displayed for sale in a cafe in one of the Stompwijk windmills. They were also hung for sale in the Hindeloppen Marina cafe. I cut the cardboard mounts for each photograph in an art shop in the Hague and one day the owner of the shop asked if I could put together a solo exhibition of my photos to launch the opening of his new art gallery. That was a surprise. I was thrilled to have my work recognised as good enough for a solo exhibition.

On the evening of the opening, I served champagne and canapes. It was an ego boosting occasion for me and I sold quite a few framed photos. Unfortunately, my photos didn't continue to sell after the opening night as the gallery was unknown and not easily spotted by passers-by. I called in one day to find the gallery empty of customers. But after my exhibition I had enough requests for photos from friends to make me continue to believe in my photography.

However, there was a downside to my exhibition. There often seems to be a downside to success and this was mine. At an International Club lunch, I'd sat next to a Russian woman. We'd got on well and I thought she might be lonely, so we arranged to meet up a few times and I invited her and her husband to my exhibition. I also invited several diplomats from the embassy. The diplomats met the Russians.

Soon afterwards I was visited by one of the diplomats, with his armed bodyguards in tow, and questioned. They'd discovered the Russians were spies. He wanted to see anything the wife had given me; perhaps he was looking for bugs. Anyway, we were never invited on board British naval vessels when they docked in Amsterdam ever again. We were clearly held under suspicion. It was such a shame as I'd enjoyed being formally welcomed on board visiting vessels by the smartly dressed crew. It made me feel special. So much for being compassionate and befriending someone I thought might be lonely.

My plight wasn't improved when Shell asked my husband to go to Russia to help them with their oil exploration. I was invited to accompany him. The British Embassy staff got to hear about our forthcoming trip to Russia and I was taken to one side at a party and warned not to meet up with my friend while I was there. I hadn't kept in contact with her and didn't intend to see her again, but it was a bit spooky being warned not to meet her.

Our flight to Moscow was on Aeroflot and we were brought champagne throughout our 3-hour 40-minute flight. When we arrived in Moscow we were treated like royalty. We were met before passport control and escorted to a waiting car.

While in Moscow my husband was busy every day, so I took buses to sightsee and shop for souvenirs. I bought a rather fine Russian fur hat. While travelling on the buses I tried not to look conspicuous and wore simple clothes and a head scarf in an attempt to look Russian. My disguise was obviously convincing as I was talked to in Russian wherever I went. I just nodded in reply. The only time I did have a problem was when the sun came out and I put my oversized sunglasses on. Someone shouted "American" at me, so I removed them very quickly!

We were wined and dined every evening and served large amounts of caviar. Vodka was in free flow, but I managed to avoid having to drink any. After a week we were given an escort and taken to St Petersburg by train. We slept in a plush carriage and were brought tea in the morning in a glass with a silver holder. I was very impressed.

St Petersburg was so different from Moscow. I'd found Moscow rather austere, apart from the Kremlin and St Basil's Cathedral, which were beautiful. The architecture in St Petersburg was charming. We visited the Winter Palace, Hermitage Museum, which was fascinating. I've never seen so many stunning exhibits. It would have taken a week to look at them all. One day we were walking out in the city when we heard music coming from a church. The congregation were singing, and it was such a beautiful sound. I fell in love with St Petersburg.

Back in Holland once more we got on with life. Spring was a favourite time for friends and relatives to visit Holland and there were plenty of places for us to show them. There were the magnificent Keukenhof gardens to visit, and fields bright with rows of bulbs. We took them touring the bulb growing areas where from the road you could catch glimpses of multicoloured stripes in the fields created by rows of colourful hyacinths and tulips.

Visits to Amsterdam were always appreciated by our guests whatever the time of year. They involved a boat trip on the canals with a continuous commentary about the different types of houses beside the canals, the picturesque bridges, and the busy port of Amsterdam. The art in the Rijksmuseum delighted our guests. It could easily take most of the day to see everything. There were so many fascinating paintings by Dutch masters and the vast *Night Watch* painting by Rembrandt to enjoy. My mother visited when there was a solo exhibition of Rembrandt's work at the Rijksmuseum. To go from room to room and see nothing but Rembrandts was a real treat.

Delft made an excellent visit for friends and family, too. If our guests were feeling energetic, we'd climb to the top of the church tower in the square. New Church, *Nieuwe Kerk,* has the second highest tower in the Netherlands at 108.75 metres. Climbing up the 376 steps could only be attempted by our young or very determined guests.

Shops around the square were full of Delft pottery with intricate blue patterns. Some beautiful pieces were handmade, hand painted and expensive. Delft pottery in the souvenir shops tended to be machine made and the decoration was printed. These pieces were much cheaper. There was also a shop with a pottery attached where you could watch the artists at work painting plates and vases.

We always stopped for coffee; every Dutch town seemed to have at least one cosy cafe. A *speculaas* biscuit usually came with the coffee but my favourite addition to a cup of coffee was apple pie with whipped cream. The Dutch *appelgebak met slagroom* was special. I've never had such good apple pie and cream anywhere else in the world.

A trip to see the magnificent sight of 19 windmills at Kinderdijk, built in 1740 as part of a water management scheme to prevent flooding, was also a must for our guests. It was granted the status of a UNESCO World Heritage Site in 1997. Of all the postcards sold in Holland a view of the windmills at Kinderdijk must be one of the most popular.

In summer we took our guests to Alkmaar to see the cheese market. Enormous round cheeses were laid out in rows the length of the square. Traditionally dressed men, the carriers, loaded eight cheeses at a time onto berries and carried them across the square to the weigh house to be weighed. Each cheese weighed 13 kilos so eight must have been quite a weight to carry. I always enjoyed the spectacle as much as our guests did.

We found plenty to do while living in Holland. We sailed almost every weekend in spring, summer, and autumn. In winter the IJsselmeer froze, and the boat was lifted out of the water for 3 months to prevent ice from damaging the hull. That gave me a welcome break from sailing every weekend, but it didn't mark the end of outdoor activities. As soon as the canals froze, we took up ice skating.

Our sailing weekends started on Friday evening when we drove from Wassenaar to Hindeloppen, which took 2 hours. We left the marina as soon as we'd loaded the boat with our weekend supplies and sailed north to Makkum, a town on an inlet close to the dyke. We'd tie up for the night and have a beer with a Bols Genever, Dutch gin, chaser. This always marked the start of our weekend sail. It's interesting how the habit of having a particular drink at a particular time and place can become so special and enjoyable. Drinking a beer with a Dutch gin chaser wasn't something we did at any other time.

On Saturday morning we'd go through the lock and sail across the Wadden Sea to one of the Frisian Islands. Texel is the largest island, more urbanized than the others, and as there's a car ferry it can easily be reached by car from the mainland. For this reason, it wasn't our favourite island.

Vlieland is the next Frisian Island in the chain. It's rural, beautiful and car free. There's a ferry three times a day from the mainland but only for foot passengers. We frequently visited Vlieland; we'd tie the boat up on a wooden pier on arrival and hire bicycles. There was a network of cycle paths winding through the dunes, and we loved the freedom of cycling close to the sea, surrounded by nature.

It was a great place for birdwatching. There was a wide variety of different species of birds nesting there, oyster catchers, curlews, eider ducks and many different species of wading birds. The oyster catchers created a flash of colour on the beach and filled the air with their shrill call. We'd have lunch in a pancake house eating pancakes covered with ham and cheese in true Dutch fashion. We loved our weekends on Vlieland as they were peaceful and gave us a chance to unwind and relax.

We also visited Terschelling, Ameland and Schiermonnikoog which are the last three Dutch islands in the chain, and again we always hired bicycles. We needed a long weekend to visit Schiermonnikoog as it was the furthest island from the Ijsselmeer and two tides were needed to reach it. The *Waddenzee* is very shallow and the passage to Schiermonnikoog dries out at low tide. As a result, all the boats en route for Schiermonnikoog go aground halfway across. When we crossed to Schiermonnikoog we had to wait for the tide to turn and water to flood back in again before we could continue our journey. *Snowflake* had bilge keels, two small keels instead of one deep one, so she could sit comfortably on the bottom when we ran out of water. We would climb down onto the sand and enjoy being on our own remote sandy island until the tide came in again. Our two boys loved this part of the adventure.

In the 1980s the Dutch canals and lakes froze in winter and every weekend *tochts* were organized. These were planned skating routes across linked lakes and canals ranging from 15 to 60 kilometres in length. The *tochts* were advertised each Saturday in the newspaper and we could choose which length *tocht* we'd like to do; we usually chose *tochts* of about 25 kilometres.

The Dutch have a fondness for official stamps and once we'd signed up for a *tocht* we'd be given a card which needed to be stamped along the route to prove we'd followed the route correctly. There were refreshment stalls on the ice provided by people who had houses backing onto the canals. You could get a much-needed coffee, hot chocolate, cold drink or a snack. At lunch time a hot bowl of *erwtensoep*, a traditional Dutch split pea soup containing smoked sausage, served with a crusty piece of bread made a welcome break and was always included in our *tochts* adventures. The Dutch have a reputation for wanting to make money selling things, so this was a perfect opportunity for them to set up their stalls on the ice. It was also a wonderful, and much appreciated service to the skaters.

One day my husband decided it would be a great idea to do a 60-kilometre *tocht*. I usually complied with his desires as, if I didn't, his disappointment made life difficult. Fortunately, the ice was like glass that day, smooth and shiny with hardly a ripple. We set off with a male friend wearing our long bladed Noren skates and swept along at a good pace, eating up the kilometres. But 60 kilometres is a long way. The men were fine, but eventually I began to feel tired and needed a sugar fix. "What I really need" I said, "is a Mars bar". I continued but with ever decreasing energy and enthusiasm for this 60-kilometre tocht we'd signed up for. Then the friend came alongside me and handed me a Mars bar. Aren't some people lovely? He'd taken on board my plea and the next time we passed a refreshment stall he'd skated off and bought one for me. I managed to pick up speed a bit after that.

But it was getting late, and the official finishing stamp was still some way away. The *tocht* had to be completed by

5 p.m. so I was forced to pick up more speed. I knew I'd be very unpopular if I prevented the men from getting their medals. As we approached the finish, I was close to collapse, but we did get the final stamp needed and were able to hand in our cards fully stamped. Despite having doubts about the wisdom of attempting a 60-kilometre *tocht* I was proud to have completed it and chuffed when my medal arrived. I still have it, somewhere. My husband often pushed me to my limits, but I was always pleased when I achieved the challenges, he set me, well—almost always.

While we were in Holland Alexander moved from Aldro, his prep school, to Charterhouse. Andrew was still at Aldro but fortunately their term dates coincided, so they were able to fly out together. They joined us for their half terms as well as their long school holidays. Time with them was precious and we made the most of it.

We bought the boys Noran skates, and they joined us on *tochts*. We did a 20-kilometre *tocht* with the boys at Kinderdijk, where we skated on the Alblasserwaard polder, surrounded by 19 windmills. With the beautiful windmills and people skating, the scene reminded me of paintings by famous Dutch masters that portray similar scenes.

One summer my husband decided we should sail our yacht *Snowflake* to the Baltic. He'd recently spent a few days there and said the weather was fantastic. We set off in the rain and hopped from one Dutch Frisian Island to the next and then sailed east to the German Frisian islands. From there we headed north to Heligoland. It continued to rain.

As we approached the island of Heligoland it looked like a rock sticking out of the sea. But when we landed and started to explore it turned out to be a fascinating island with a small population of a about 1,000 citizens. If a cruise liner was visiting it teamed with people but when the ship left it was practically deserted. Once the streets were empty the feeling of remoteness and isolation was overwhelming.

From Heligoland we headed towards the Elbe estuary with Cuxhaven as our destination. This leg of the trip did not go smoothly. We needed the tide to be with us when sailing up the Elbe, so we killed time going round and round in circles waiting for the tide to change. When we finally thought the tide was in our favour we made our way up the Elbe, only to discover it was against us. The sea was rough and the journey to Cuxhaven seemed endless. Huge waves built up behind *Snowflake*, threatening to break over the stern of the boat, but then subsided. My husband kept telling his increasingly nervous crew that Cuxhaven was round the corner, but it didn't appear for a very long time.

It was getting dark by the time we sailed into Cuxhaven harbour. We anchored and as the sky turned blueberry blue fireworks lit up the night sky. There were laser displays and continuous exploding fireworks spraying the sky with colour. We'll never forget this magnificent, unexpected firework display. It made our visit to the illusive Cuxhaven worth the struggle.

The next morning, we entered the Kiel Canal and started motoring. Towering ships bore down on us one after the other, stealing our water and driving us into the bank. It was rather an unpleasant journey, particularly in the rain. The great weather my husband had promised had not materialized. Every morning, we woke up to the sound of heavy rain hammering down on the roof of the cabin. It continued to rain every day for the entire month. My white pleated skirt hanging in the wardrobe remained unworn and when I pulled it out of the wardrobe at the end of the trip, I found a black line of mould running down each pleat.

Tempers became frayed amongst *Snowflake's* crew. We needed time away from each other. So, when we stopped for an overnight stay in Rendsburg, I suggested we spent the day apart from each other exploring on our own. My husband left, then one after the other the boys left. At last, I had the boat to myself, which was wonderful, but I thought I'd better leave, too. After a few hours, one by one, *Snowflake's* crew returned to the boat. We felt refreshed and relieved to be back in the relative comfort of *Snowflake*. Having a much-needed break from each other had worked.

By the time we reached the town of Kiel we were experiencing high winds in addition to torrential rain. It was impossible to continue to sail. We moored *Snowflake* in Kiel and set out for Copenhagen, travelling first by ferry and then by train.

The city of Copenhagen lightened our spirits with its street players and endless cafes. It was heaven sitting comfortably outdoors eating dinner and watching jugglers, fire eaters and playlets performed. Quite a treat after the endless days of continuous rain and daily challenges we'd been coping with on *Snowflake*.

Our trip home was no better than the trip out. When we got home, I announced that from then onwards we would not be taking our summer holidays on *Snowflake*. Instead, we'd be renting a yacht in the Mediterranean, where good weather could be guaranteed, or so we thought.

The following summer we drove to St Tropez and had the most idyllic holiday sailing along the mediterranean coast. The difference was unbelievable. We swam, relaxed, and ate out. It was stress-free, warm, and wonderful. Alexander jumped off the yacht into the clear turquoise water and when he came up, he called out to me, "This is the life", and so it was.

The next year my husband wanted to do something more exciting, which was invariably what happened. We drove down to St Tropez and boarded our rented yacht, but instead of sailing peacefully along the coast swimming and eating delicious meals in restaurants, we set sail for Corsica.

We calculated it would take 36 hours to make the trip. This meant sailing for two days and a night. The days were okay, but the night wasn't much fun at all. We needed to take 4-hour shifts, in pairs for safety. I sailed with Alexander who was 14 at the time and my husband sailed with Andrew who was only 11 years old. In the night we hit a submerged log which removed the speed log from under the hull. That alone was enough to put me off night sailing.

Once we arrived in Corsica we spent one night in Bastia harbour, then headed south along the Corsican coast. The weather deteriorated, and we were forced to turn round and head back to the comparative safely of Bastia harbour. We dropped anchor and there we stayed as the storm raged.

We couldn't all leave the boat at the same time in case the boat dragged anchor, so we had to go ashore in pairs. I was on anchor watch with Alexander when we noticed clouds of smoke billowing up from the forested hinterland. The drama increased when planes flew in to fight the fire. One aircraft after the other swooped down over the sea scooping up a cradle of water which they released over the blazing forest. It continued for hours. Although we couldn't go ashore, we had plenty of drama to keep us entertained.

Despite this interesting interlude the holiday wasn't turning out to be much of a success. The high winds didn't abate, and we were forced to stay anchored in Bastia harbour for a week, with occasional trips ashore. At the end of the week, we headed back to St Tropez. The storm had abated but the sea was still very disturbed and choppy. Our passage back to

France was rough and uncomfortable. Alexander and I sailed the yacht from midnight until 4 a.m. We were both being sick and there was nothing to eat. The French stick we'd thought might sustain us was lying limp on the floor of the cockpit in 2 inches of sea water. I remember saying in my distress, "Beam me up, Scotty". I wanted to be anywhere but where I was.

It was pitch dark, we were soaked in spray, black water looking like moulten tar was swashing around the hull and we were both feeling ill. There was nothing we could do to make things better, we just had to stick it out until 4am when my husband and Andrew would take over.

During our sail to Corsica the beautiful weather we'd imagined to be guaranteed in the Mediterranean didn't materialise. It was more of an ordeal than a holiday. It did, however, provide us with experiences which we've laughed about ever since.

We were back home in Holland, when, after supper, I was making coffee in the kitchen while my husband watched TV with the boys in the living room. I was carrying a tray of cups full of coffee through the kitchen door when I looked up to see a large ball of light coming down the stairs. I screamed but somehow managed not to drop the tray. As I stared in disbelief at this weird moving mass of light it turned the corner and went into the living room. According to the male members of the family watching TV it disappeared into the TV and turned it off. They turned the TV back on again and continued to watch their programme. It was left to me to climb up two flights of stairs to the attic to see if the ball of light had set fire to anything on its way down.

I discovered the phenomenon we'd witnessed was rare ball lightning. This can appear from a pea sized ball of light to one 100cm in diameter. As ours seemed to fill the width of the staircase it must have been close to the maximum size. In my research I discovered only 5% of the world's population have seen this phenomenon so I felt quite privileged having experienced it.

We'd had 5 years in Holland, a long posting by Shell's standards, and I knew we'd be sent somewhere else soon. I just hoped it would be to a country where we could be as happy as we'd been in Holland. Our lifestyle had been packed with activities. We also acquired a wide circle of friends, from companies other than Shell, and from the British Embassy. Being youth activity chairman had been a blessing; it had made me feel fulfilled and opened paths to new friendships which had broadened my experience. My interest in photography was blossoming and it looked as if it was developing into a hobby which might provide me with pocket money. It had been a good five years.

The posting to Holland which had brought me to tears several times when we first arrived eventually turned out to be one of the best postings we had while my husband was working for Shell.

CHAPTER 8
Life in Calgary

Life as an expatriate wife with a husband working for an international oil company was happy and stable until suddenly everything changed. On one very normal day while I was cooking supper during our posting to Holland my husband arrived home from work and came into the kitchen. He was emitting an air of tangible excitement. I knew he had news for me, and I was getting more than a hint of an idea that the news was good. "We've been posted," he said, "and our posting is to Calgary". It certainly was good news. We both loved skiing and the prospect of being able to ski every weekend during the winter made Calgary a most attractive posting. New horizons and lots of fun were coming our way.

With our two sons at boarding school the move would be straight forward. We just had to let our house and pack. Royal

Dutch Shell made packing very easy. They named the day, packers arrived and packed anything and everything. Once, when we unpacked on arrival, I found an apple core carefully packed in a dish! Shipping personal effects was paid for by Shell and free if your possessions were within the shipping allowance capacity.

Belongings are easily transferred, but unfortunately lifestyle isn't. You really do start again when you move to a new country. While I'd been living in Holland I'd sung in a choir, we'd played badminton with the International Club, and we'd enjoyed sailing to the Dutch Frisian Islands in our yacht *Snowflake*. This hobby certainly wasn't transferable, and the rest weren't as transferable as you might think.

I also had my blossoming photographic business to consider. I was supplying photos to postcard printers in Amsterdam. My photographs of Amsterdam, the bulb fields, windmills, and general views of Holland, sold as postcards, and could be found on postcard stands all over the city of Amsterdam. I'd had a solo exhibition in a gallery in The Hague and started to sell framed prints. Selling my work in Holland was going well. But if I wanted to continue my photographic business in Canada, I'd need a work permit. I hoped that wouldn't be too difficult to achieve.

We let our house easily, sold our beloved yacht *Snowflake*, said our farewells to our wide circle of friends and left to start a new life in Canada.

As soon as we'd landed at Calgary International Airport, we rented a car and drove to the hotel Shell had booked for us. Flying west there's a seven-hour time change and the time in Calgary is 7 hours earlier than in the U.K. So, the next morning we were up before dawn ready to explore our new surroundings. We headed out on Highway 1 to Banff in the Rocky Mountains while it was still dark.

My first sight of the mountains at dawn filled me with awe. I'd skied in the Alps surrounded by mountains, but the Rocky Mountains were different. Individual mountains looked more massive and appeared to rise straight up from the ground. Castle Mountain rose majestically from the wide valley where the Bow River meandered. Rundle Mountain towered over the town of Banff. I was impressed. We decided from then onwards trips to the Rocky Mountains every weekend would be part of our new lifestyle.

Our rented car was a rather large Chevrolet saloon. We both had to take a driving test when we arrived, and I took mine in the Chevrolet. As I'd been driving in the U.K. and Holland for the last 22 years, I didn't think I'd have a problem. When I took my test I was particularly careful when driving on black ice as the large Chevrolet didn't handle well on ice. I failed. The examiner explained why. "There are two types of bad drivers", he said, "those who drive too fast and those who drive too slowly. You drive too slowly so you've failed". I was shocked and mortified. I thought I was a good driver.

We went house hunting and found an unusual, whitewashed house with Spanish Style arches to rent. It had a built-in BBQ, complete with chimney, in the kitchen. The only furniture was a waterbed which Andrew put his name on. We grew to love our spacious Spanish Style house.

A four-wheel drive car was a must to cope with snowy conditions, so we bought one and handed back the oversized Chevrolet. The 4 x 4 purchase was a sensible decision, but we then chose a blue convertible Pontiac Firebird as my husband's company car. That was a fun decision but not a sensible one. It didn't hold the road well in snowy and icy conditions and breaking on ice required a special technique. The art was to start breaking long before the traffic lights to allow for skidding time.

Once we had the four-wheel drive car, I took my test again and this time I passed. When I arrived home, I drove the car into the garage and when I stepped out of the car, there at my feet was a tissue. I followed a trail of tissues which led to our youngest son, Andrew, sitting on the sofa in the living room. Andrew had laid the trail in preparation for me coming home in tears. His empathy for me was touching and very endearing. Even at an early age he must have been aware of my sensitive nature.

Shell company employees never seemed to complain about difficulty transferring their jobs from one country to another. Presumably because even if they're in a different country, they're still working in a Shell office. Expat wives, on the other hand, had to fit into a new community and discover ways to fill their day after they'd fulfilled their wifely chores. Very few wives worked in those days. But I wanted to work, selling my photographs. I applied for a work permit and was granted an interview. I put together a portfolio of my work to take to the interview and proudly presented large, printed examples of my photography asking for permission to sell them in Canada.

The interviewer looked at my work and then he looked at me. "You're an entrepreneur," he said with a perceptible element of disgust. "We don't like entrepreneurs". The interview and my dream of a future for my photography business ended right there. I remember those harsh words clearly to this day.

As I expected my application for a work permit was turned down. I packed up my prints and as I walked out of the office clutching my portfolio, tears rolled down my cheeks. Sadly, for me tears often accompanied my struggle to adapt to a new lifestyle. Being sensitive probably helped make me a creative photographer but it didn't help with the disappointments I experienced when trying to settle in a new country.

I joined a choir. Singing in a choir in Holland had been a joy and I'd met some delightful people. But the choir I joined in Calgary wasn't the same as what I'd been used to. The sopranos in the choir were cliquey and didn't welcome me. Rather unkindly they shifted me out of the pew I was sitting in saying, "We need your seat for a friend". One evening I was driving into Calgary for a choir practice when I realised, I wasn't looking forward to singing with the rather hostile sopranos. I firmly believe that there's no point in doing what you don't enjoy if you don't have to do it. I made a snap decision, and that evening told the choir organiser I would be leaving.

Badminton with the International Club in The Hague had been such fun, so we were keen to start playing in Calgary. We'd played with a small group of people in a church hall in Holland. There were low beams which the shuttle cocks frequently bounced off, causing peals of laughter. The games were casual and very enjoyable. Afterwards we all went to a pub for a drink.

We joined a badminton Club in Calgary. In contrast the Calgary club met in a purpose-built sports hall. All the players were competitive, and we were not first choice when players were selected for a match. We ended our membership when we found neither of us enjoyed playing badminton anymore. Once again, my motto "never continue what you don't enjoy if you don't have to do it" kicked in.

In Canada it was skiing which took over our lifestyle. From late September until early May we left Calgary every Friday evening and drove to the Rocky Mountains. We started with downhill skiing. Then friends suggested we tried cross country skiing. They recommended wooden skis which we bought. We tried them out skiing from the top of the Sunshine Ski Resort cable car down to the town of Banff. There was no marked trail, just a steep snowy slope. Both of us tumbled down the slope laughing all the way. Then we went out and bought metal edged backcountry skis.

We quickly learned that ski gear for backcountry skiing was very different from downhill gear. Multiple layers with a waterproof top layer were needed. Layers had to be easy to shed as our bodies heated up when the going got tough.

Our backcountry ski trips took us to remote log cabins in the mountains. My favourite was Skoki Lodge. It was an 11-kilometre trek to Skoki which started from Lake Louise Ski Resort.

We had a standard packed lunch for our outward journeys which consisted of a sandwich, dark fruit cake with marzipan, bought at Christmas then kept frozen, and a drink of orange juice in a small cardboard carton with a straw. We packed skins to cover our skis which were essential for climbing steep slopes and mountains. We strapped a shovel to our back packs in case we had to dig ourselves out of an avalanche. I wasn't certain a shovel would be enough, but it might help.

The trail to Skoki Lodge took us over Deception Pass. This pass was aptly named as when climbing the mountain, you thought you were about to reach the summit three times before you did. It was a tough climb. My husband mastered telemarking, a type of skiing which is used to descend steep slopes when backcountry skiing. But I didn't; my mastery of backcountry skiing didn't match his. Instead, I tumbled down most of the slopes we encountered. Once at the bottom of Deception Pass, we crossed a vast frozen lake. Then, finally, we'd see smoke curling up from the Skoki Lodge log cabin chimney. It was such a wonderful sight. We knew then we were nearly there.

Liz and Keith, who we'd originally met in Holland, in the Victorian theatre with a leaking roof, joined us for a skiing holiday with their daughter, Becky. They were downhill skiers, and I was surprised when they agreed so readily to ski to Skoki Lodge with us. They hired backcountry ski equipment and off we set with our standard packed lunches.

It was snowing hard and there was no visible trail. The virgin snow was soft, powdery and very deep. Alexander and Andrew went ahead and set a trail, of sorts, which we followed. That helped a bit, but Liz, Keith and Becky struggled to make headway. I followed our two sons but the 3 adults quickly got left behind. My husband stayed with our friends to help them up when they fell off the trail and had to dig themselves out of deep snow.

When I reached our lunch spot, I sat under a bush trying to shelter from the driving snow and started to eat my lunch. I was just sucking up the last of my carton of juice when my husband and our exhausted friends arrived. "I will never forgive you for this, Rosemary," my usually placid friend, Liz, exclaimed. With Liz's desperate reprimand ringing in my ears, I finished my juice and continued the journey alone.

When I saw smoke curling up in the distance, I was more relieved than I usually was. It had been a tough trip. Gradually the cabin came into view and when I arrived at Skoki I found Alexander and Andrew comfortably settled in. The large, blackened kettle steamed over the fire, and I was given a very welcome mug of tea.

Not long afterwards the door to the cabin flew open and a flurry of snow blew in. This was followed by the rest of our party. My dear friend Liz almost fell through the door practically collapsing from exhaustion. Alexander and Andrew removed her snow encrusted coat, sat her down and gave her a mug of tea. Seeing my sons caring for my friend made me feel a proud mother. I wasn't quite so proud of myself. How could I have subjected my precious friend, Liz, to such an ordeal? She said no more at the time and continued to be my friend despite me failing to look after her. It was years later when Liz and I were reminiscing about the ski trip to Skoki that she said, "I wouldn't have missed it for the world".

Old friends who go through life with you and share your experiences become part of the framework of life and can never be replaced. Later Liz and I went on to share more tough experiences and during these we supported each other. We remain firm friends to this day.

Skiing every weekend in the winter was something I looked forward to and in addition there was plenty to photograph. I was continuing with my interest in photography, despite being unable to sell my photographs in Canada.

While I'd been living in Holland, I'd achieved one of the Royal Photographic Society distinctions, an Associateship, ARPS. The next award was a Fellowship, FRPS. I had an idea. During our back country skiing expeditions, I'd noticed beautiful natural patterns created by snow and ice. Photographs submitted for a Fellowship distinction must be "a distinctive body of work". An artistic collection of winter patterns could fit that description perfectly; all I needed was 12 outstanding photographs. That couldn't be difficult, could it? I started to photograph natural winter patterns every time I went on a backcountry skiing expedition. I collected patterns created by frost covered trees, snowy humps, frost covered seeding grasses, snow covered trees, icicles and ice patterns on windowpanes. I had more than enough prints, so I displayed them around the house and tried to work out which ones had the most impact.

I was able to be in England on the day my photographs were to be judged in the Royal Photographic Society headquarters in Bath. Once again, I stayed with my mother in Wootton Bassett. She was keen to come with me to see my photos assessed but it was something I needed to do alone. I couldn't bear the thought of my mother sitting beside me if I was to face rejection and failure.

I sat in the auditorium all morning waiting for my panel to be displayed on the stage. Each time a new panel of photographs was carried in and displayed it wasn't mine. I ate lunch by myself, and my nervous anticipation grew, then I returned for the afternoon session to watch and wait. A couple of hours ticked by, but my panel still didn't appear.

Finally, the penultimate panel was brought in and displayed. It was mine. In silence the judges examined each photo. I waited not knowing what they might say. There was no way of telling how they were reacting to my photos as they slowly picked each one up and looked at it. Eventually they started to speak. They were full of praise. All the judges loved my photographs. It was unanimous. I had produced a panel of photographs worthy of a fellowship. A wave of relief flooded through me; I had succeeded.

The judges left the auditorium and as they walked past me, they invited me to join them for coffee. One of the judges asked if I would give him the photograph of ice ferns I'd taken on a windowpane as he loved it so much. Achieving a Fellowship of the Royal Photographic Society was one of the highlights in my life. I sang in the car all the way back to my mother's house in Wootton Bassett.

Sadly, however, once I've achieved something and the thrill has worn off it becomes wallpaper in my life and ceases to remain exciting. Reaching for something which may remain beyond my grasp is the exciting part. I should imagine this is true of many of us.

When sons Alexander and Andrew came out to Canada for their long summer school break, we tried to arrange a family holiday tailored to their interests and ages. We'd heard about a trip you could take whitewater rafting through the Grand Canyon, run by *Canyoneers*. This sounded a promisingly exciting experience and the perfect holiday for teenage boys, so we booked it for the first summer we spent in Calgary.

Visas were needed to visit the U.S. from Canada, so we went with the boys to the U.S. consulate. We wrote down our passport details which included our place of birth. When they came to Alexander's place of birth, which was Dallas, Texas, they said, "we don't give our citizens visas, we give them passports". Alexander was asked to swear an "Oath of Allegiance". He said, "Yup," and was given a passport. "Yes" would have been more in keeping with the occasion but no one seemed to worry.

We flew to Flagstaff where we all bought Teva sandals in an outdoor clothing shop for the rafting trip. Our Teva sandals were fabric with rubber soles. They were the perfect footwear for whitewater rafting and a memorable purchase. We lived in them for the entire week, and we still talk about how amazing they were to this day.

We boarded an inflatable raft pulled up on the beach at Lees's Ferry, below Glen Canyon Dam. It was a large craft which took 20 people, 18 passengers, a cook, and the captain. We each had a locker for our personal belongings and were given a life jacket and sleeping bag. We made ourselves at home and waited in anticipation.

We set off down the Colorado River and ran one rapid after the other. Alexander and Andrew loved sitting in the bows of the raft feeling the full force of the spray as we plunged through each rapid. The passengers sat along the perimeter of the raft as we travelled down the river, then when we were about to enter a rapid the captain shouted "down", and we all slipped down onto the seat below us.

I found the rapids exciting but what I really enjoyed were the nights. We slept in sleeping bags under the stars. I never sleep well so, while I was awake, I could watch satellites making their way across the wonderfully clear sky and look for shooting stars. Our nights were blissfully peaceful. We'd been told to check our shoes for scorpions in the morning but there was no place for scorpions to hide in our Teva sandals so once again they proved the ideal footwear.

At mile 61.5 the fast-flowing Little Colorado River joins the clear Colorado River in a flurry of muddy water. Despite its mud content the Little Colorado provided us with an additional highlight to the thrilling rapids. We walked up the bank of the river each carrying a tyre inner tube, waded into the water, and sitting in the ring were spun round and round at speed down the Little Colorado River back to the Colorado River. It was easy to get stuck in whirlpools and often we had to rely on someone else floating by to give us a push to release us from the whirlpool we were trapped in. We walked back up the Little Colorado and enjoyed the thrill of being swept down in its swirling waters as many times as we could, before we had to return to the raft.

The rapids in the Colorado River are rated from 1-10. Lava Rock Rapid scores a 9, but those with a rating of 7 or 8 are quite thrilling enough. At mile 98.2 we reached Crystal Rapid, which is rated 8. The captain beached the craft and led us up to a viewpoint from where we could look down on the rapid. We all stood there and looked, having had no explanation as to why we'd climbed up just to look at the rapid. Then we returned to the raft.

We ran the rapid; our raft hit a hole, was almost bent double and one of the passengers' spectacles were whipped off his head by the force of the spray, but we made it through to calmer waters. It was then that the captain explained why he had taken us to view the rapid before running it. He said, "I needed to work out a safe passage as last time I turned the craft over". He explained that it was a particularly hazardous rapid as there are several large holes and a dangerous rock garden mid channel. I'm glad he waited until we were safely on the other side of it before he told us.

We were relieved to hear that no one was injured when our captain flipped his craft, although some passengers were trapped under the raft and had difficulty getting to safety. When the craft capsized numerous black plastic bags full of various items were thrown into the river and everything had to be collected up and lifted out by helicopter. It's mandatory for all waste to be carried out of the canyon, so some of the plastic bags contained daily waste, including portable loo waste, from the last 98 miles. The rescue team had to open every unmarked plastic bag before they could discover what each contained.

We didn't feel bored for a moment during the 280-mile trip through the Grand Canyon to Pearce Ferry in Lake Mead. The scenery was constantly phenomenal, and we ran 110 rapids, 45 of which were rated higher than 5. Whitewater rafting through the Grand Canyon made a brilliant family holiday and I would certainly recommend it to a family with teenagers.

As soon as there was a good fall of snow in the Canadian mountains we started skiing again. We continued challenging adventures into the backcountry, some of which were only enjoyable on reflection. My husband liked to break away from the normal trails and explore. I often struggled to keep up, but there was usually a good tale to tell when we got home.

One weekend he decided we'd leave from Lake Louise and climb to Lake Annette, via Paradise Valley, a trip of 17km. When we arrived at Lake Annette it was snowing hard, so we sheltered under a bush to eat our packed lunch. Looking across the lake I could see avalanches of snow rushing down the mountain slopes. It made me feel very unsafe. Once back in Lake Louise we called in at the ski equipment shop, as we often did, and told the owner we'd just skied up to Lake Annette. "No, you must be mistaken," he replied. "No one goes to Lake Annette in winter; it's far too dangerous". Well, we did!

My husband continued to push the boundaries of backcountry skiing, I think in a quest for excitement and challenge. We took to using helicopters to ski in areas inaccessible by road. We booked a backcountry skiing holiday in Mount Assiniboine Provincial Park, a beautiful UNESCO World Heritage site only accessible by helicopter in winter. It was snowing hard when we boarded the helicopter. We started to gain height, but then descended rapidly and landed, aborting the flight. Not a great start.

We took off a second time, but visibility was poor. I was sitting opposite our son, Andrew, who was about 15 years old at the time. Looking out of the window through the blizzard we could see we were flying very close to a sheer rock face. Andrew looked at me, perhaps hoping for confirmation that we were not in danger. I thought we were in great danger, but I smiled encouragingly at him. How duplicitous I was, but there was no turning back at that stage so that was the only option open to me.

We did arrive safely, much to my relief. Assiniboine Lodge, where we stayed, was picturesque, surrounded by towering mountain peaks. Snow conditions were fantastic, and we enjoyed a wonderful week backcountry skiing. It was certainly a memorable holiday and was the only time we took a helicopter with the boys to a remote mountain lodge.

But my husband and I continued to use helicopters to reach mountain ski lodges and huts while the boys were away at school. I always tried to make sure we were on separate helicopters to ensure that if the helicopter crashed our children would have at least one parent. On one occasion I boarded the first helicopter and asked my husband to take the next one. We were about to take off when they found there was one spare seat and called to the group waiting to let them know we could take one more passenger. Imagine my distress when it was my husband who came hurrying towards the helicopter.

My fears about the safety of helicopters were not unfounded. We flew by helicopter to a remote self-catering hut on a mountain side for a week's backcountry skiing. There was a makeshift helipad, a relatively small area of snow on the side of the mountain. It was up to the hut guests to keep the snowy helipad in good shape so that it was safe for the helicopter to land. After every new fall of snow, we all went out and stamped down the snow to create a firm landing pad. When it was time to leave the helicopter came to collect us and landed safely, dropped off the next week's guests to stay in the hut and took us back down the mountain. But when the helicopter flew in at the end of the next week it toppled over killing the passenger who was sitting in the seat I'd sat in two weeks earlier. It was a tragedy which shouldn't have happened, and it made me realise the danger we were putting ourselves in.

We often flew with a Swiss pilot who operated privately, keeping his helicopter in a hanger in his garden. I was so very sorry to hear, after we left Canada, that he'd been killed when his helicopter crashed. The mountain guide who had taken us on trips also died in the crash. We'd certainly been testing our luck with our life choices. These two events brought home to me that those who live to a ripe old age are the lucky ones as they've avoided being involved in a fatal accident.

With teenage boys we found a good way of spending Christmas was to go to the mountains for some downhill skiing. They enjoyed the speed and preferred it to backcountry skiing. It suited me, too, as we didn't have to face the risk of flying by helicopter to a mountain top. On Christmas Day we had the ski slopes almost to ourselves and in the evening enjoyed Christmas dinner in a hotel. It worked brilliantly for all of us.

But it's often very cold in the Canadian Rocky Mountains in December and January. When we were skiing at Lake Louise Ski Resort one year the temperature dropped to -20F, -29C, and we found our skis would stick on the piste instead of sliding smoothly down the slope. With the intense cold we could only tolerate one run at a time and had to dive into the cafe for a mug of hot chocolate to warm up between runs.

In Sunshine Ski Resort high above the town of Banff, the temperatures dropped even lower. One Christmas we were staying at Sunshine Mountain Lodge when the temperature dropped to -36F, almost -38C. The cable car from Banff was closed but the chair lifts in the mountains resort kept running for those staying in the hotel. I dropped a ski pole as I got onto the chair lift and the young man who climbed onto the chair behind me kindly picked it up for me. When he handed me my ski pole at the top of the lift, I noticed a large patch of white on his left cheek and realised he had frost bite. Taking my gloves off all I said was, "you've got frost bite" and gently placing my hands on his face I kept them there until blood returned to the white patch. Then I said, "You need to return to the hotel straight away". Nothing more was said, and he skied off down the slope. I was rather moved by this interaction between two total strangers. Helping each other had come so easily to both of us, without a second thought.

It was a privilege living near the Rocky Mountains and it provided me with some excellent photographic opportunities. Castle Mountain, which stands beside Bow River, rising in splendour from the valley floor, was a great favourite. We passed it every time we drove into the Rocky Mountains from Calgary on Highway 1.

We liked to arrive before sunrise and watch the snowy slopes of Castle Mountain become totally transformed. A mountain reflects rosy, pink light from the sun before the sun rises above the horizon; this pre sunrise pink light is known as alpenglow. The turrets of Castle Mountain would glow with a rosy, pink light, while the Bow River Valley below remained blue with the shadowy light of pre-dawn. The dramatic contrast between the two colours was magical.

One morning we stopped beside Highway 1 to wait for sunrise, but it was bitterly cold. With the wind chill factor it was -40 Fahrenheit, -40 centigrade. I kept my camera inside my thick down coat until I was ready to take the photo. At the last minute I attached it to my tripod. Once I'd finished capturing alpenglow on Castle Mountain I started to move away from my camera. I couldn't. My face was frozen to the tripod. I've never experienced such dangerously cold temperatures before or since.

The Rocky Mountains were also rich in wildlife. I loved sitting quietly watching the animals and then capturing their characteristic behaviour with my camera. Columbia ground squirrels would sit erect beside their holes squeaking warnings of danger. Chipmunks made good subjects as they were quite tame so easy to photograph in close-up.

One day I came across an elk peacefully grazing on a patch of grass in the town of Banff. I walked towards it until it filled the frame in my camera. I was about to release the shutter when it lowered its antlers and started to charge. With my heart in my mouth, I fled. I escaped but reminded myself to respect wildlife in the future as it is unpredictable.

My portfolio of photographs grew, and I was sorry not to be able to market them in Canada. However, I discovered there was a sizeable camera club I could join. Calgary Camera Club met every two weeks in a large auditorium in Calgary. I went along to a meeting and slipped into the back row of seats. It was an impressively large club with about 100 members attending each meeting.

The president addressed the members, then there was a photo competition judged by a guest judge. It seemed a well-run club, but I was sad that at the end of the evening I left without anyone speaking to me. At least they hadn't asked me to move to make room for their friends, as had happened at the choir practice. I continued to attend the club meetings for several weeks and still no one spoke to me.

It was time for me to make a positive move, so I entered a photograph into the competition. To my surprise it won. It wasn't that my work was outstanding it was just different from any of the other photographs. My photos of Dutch windmills and other Dutch scenes did well in their competitions, and I won nearly every week. At last people started to speak to me. Not long afterwards I was flattered to be asked to join the camera club committee. Taking positive action had paid off.

A year later I was elected president of the club. The first thing I did was to enlarge the committee by one member. I appointed a new committee member responsible for welcoming all new members the first time they attended a meeting. Anyone expressing an interest in the club needed to be made to feel welcome.

Skiing came to an end at the beginning of May. Conditions really weren't very good by then, and I'm not keen on skiing on ice, rocks and grass. However, there was no interruption in our trips to the Rocky Mountains. We simply swapped our skis for our walking boots and camping gear and headed up a mountain on foot. We had some strenuous climbs carrying the most enormous backpacks but enjoyed camping beside glorious lakes in remote locations.

We didn't always have to climb a mountain to camp. We discovered beautiful Waterton Lakes National Park, south of Calgary, in the Southern Rockies where we could camp beside Waterton Lake, windsurf, and follow mountain trails.

One weekend we set off to climb Bear's Hump trail. It was a steep mountain path with tremendous views, but I noticed bear scats on the path and felt nervous as there was a possibility we could meet a grizzly bear. After a while I got tired. I'm not built for mountain climbing, but my husband said he wanted to continue the climb. I started to follow the trail back to the campsite by myself. Fresh bear scats were thick on the path, and I became frightened. At every corner I expected to meet a grizzly bear. The advice is to curl up in a ball, protecting your vital organs, and wait for the grizzly bear to go away. As I made my way down the mountain, I was continually alert waiting to curl up in a ball at a moment's notice. Fortunately, I didn't meet a grizzly bear and returned safely to the campsite.

Another form of wildlife which was a problem was mosquitoes. On one occasion we had to eat supper beside the lake wearing head nets. We posted our food into our mouths accessing our mouth via the bottom of the head net. Not the easiest way to eat supper. It did cause a lot of laughter, and we all remember that amusing lakeside supper.

Our family whitewater rafting holiday through the Grand Canyon had been a great success, and it was hard to find anything as exciting for the next summer family holiday. We decided that exploring the Rocky Mountains by road might be fun, so we hired a Toyota 4×4 to give us plenty of room for camping gear. We put bicycles on a rack on the back and windsurfers on the roof.

We headed west from Calgary on Highway 1 and before we reached Lake Louise took highway 93, Icefield Parkway, north towards Jasper. It was a scenic route passing numerous lakes and an impressive glacier. After Jasper we continued north through British Columbia and eventually reached the town of Hyder in Alaska.

Our holiday had morphed into a long drive with daily targets of places we wanted to reach. We stopped each night to camp but hardly used the bicycles and windsurfers. We drove 923 miles from Calgary to Alaska. We then started on our way back to Calgary. We drove 285 miles from Alaska to Prince Rupert, British Columbia, which was on the coast and put the car on a ferry for the 15-hour voyage down the inside passage to Port Hardy. The inside passage is renowned for its scenic beauty, so I was optimistic that I'd find plenty to photograph. At first, I really enjoyed the scenery, but I must admit that after about 12 hours it all seemed a bit samey.

Our drive back to Calgary via Vancouver was a further 890-miles. We'd covered nearly 2,100 miles in 2 weeks. It had been an experience and we'd seen some beautiful scenery, but I think the whitewater rafting trip made a better family holiday. I vowed to plan our summer holiday the following year more carefully.

I couldn't sell my photos in Canada, but I could give them away. I was approached by Donna von Hauff, who was putting together a book on Alberta parks to be called "Alberta's Parks, Our Legacy". She chose a selection of my photographs and used 38 in her book. My photos were used on both the front and back cover. The book was published in 1992 and is available on Amazon today for £229.70. I couldn't be paid for the photographs at the time, but I've got two copies of the book so perhaps I should sell one and make my profit now.

I was always on the lookout for exposure for my photographs, so I sent a selection to a monthly photography magazine to be considered for their *Show Case* feature designed to launch new photographers. They printed four pages of my photographs, and I was contacted by two photo agencies, one in Vancouver and the other in Toronto.

Son Andrew answered the phone to the Toronto agent and wrote the phone number down, but he wrote it down incorrectly. It was frustrating as I couldn't contact the agency. Some months later I came across *Focus Photo Agency* in Toronto advertised in a photo magazine and thought something looked familiar about the phone number. I checked it against the number Andrew had given me and by accident he'd switched two figures.

I flew to Vancouver and Toronto to see the agencies. The Vancouver agency wanted me to agree to supply 200 photos a month which I couldn't do. The staff in *Focus Photo Agency* in Toronto were delightful. They loved my photos and just wanted more. I explained that none could be sold until I left Canada, but they were fine with that. It was fortunate that I managed to contact *Focus Photo Agency* as soon afterwards it was bought by *Tony Stone Images* which was eventually bought by *Getty Images*. I've submitted to *Getty Images* ever since and have nearly 12,000 photos for sale worldwide on their website.

My original contact with *Focus Photo Agency* had gone from being a disaster with the wrong phone number to a way of making a good income for 32 years. In my life I've experienced many disasters which have made good eventually.

I was delighted to be asked to be president of the Calgary Camera Club for a second year and was looking forward to it. Unfortunately, Shell decided this was the time to uproot us from Calgary and send us somewhere else. I'd really enjoyed my year as president as it had given me a purpose and goals to achieve. It was upsetting not to be able to continue for another year. But looking on the positive side, once I'd left Canada my photographs with *Focus Photo Agency* could be sold. The black cloud created by being uprooted and moved to another country had a silver lining.

We'd enjoyed our posting to Calgary for so many different reasons. It had been a posting full of satisfying fun and we felt lucky to have had the opportunity to live in Canada for 3 years. But we're all familiar with the saying "all good things come to an end". Well, they did.

CHAPTER 9

Life in Houston

Our time in Calgary had come to an end and we'd been told of our next posting. We were being sent to Houston, Texas. In those days I was of the firm belief that International Shell had a world map and a pin. When they thought you'd put down roots in your present posting and were enjoying yourself they got out their pin and stuck it in their world map. Wherever it landed was your destination for the next few years. Yes, I was cynical but sometimes it just felt like that. We were loving life in Calgary and had no desire to leave.

When we told our Canadian friends we were moving to Houston they offered their commiserations. "Oh, poor you", some said, "Houston, the deep south, oh dear!" What did they know that we didn't? I thought it was just another place where we would take time to settle but once we'd settled, we'd be perfectly happy and contented. The reason for their sympathy would no doubt reveal itself in time.

Taking one of our cars with us and driving down to Houston from Calgary sounded a perfect plan. We packed the boot of our blue convertible Firebird with a small tent, camping stove, sleeping bags and just a few clothes. There wasn't much room for anything else. We'd already said goodbye to all the friends we'd made during the last three years while living in Calgary. Now we had to say goodbye to our neighbours and the lovely home where we'd been so happy.

We lived simply during our drive down to Houston washing out T shirts and shorts when needed. We ate easy meals cooked on our camp stove and dined out from time to time.

There were wonderful places to visit. We stopped off at the ancient cave dwellings in Mesa Verde National Park in Colorado, then went on to the massive stacks of wind-carved red sandstone in Monument Valley in Arizona.

A trip to the Grand Canyon was a must. We'd visited the south rim while living in Dallas, but at the time I was six months pregnant so we couldn't walk to the bottom. The opportunity to fulfil our dream of clambering down the steep path on the canyon side had arrived. We pitched our tent and camped in Grand Canyon National Park then started to plan our trip.

We decided to take Bright Angel Trail down to the bottom and South Kaibab Trail back up to the rim. It would be a 10-mile hike down taking about 4 hours and a 7½ mile climb back up taking about 7 hours. Staying overnight at the bottom of the canyon seemed a good plan. We made enquiries about booking a night in Phantom Ranch but discovered it was necessary to book a night's stay months in advance. This was devastating news. We'd so looked forward to walking to the bottom of the canyon and back up to the rim. It couldn't be done in a day, so we'd have to abandon our plans and move on.

But after making more enquiries we found there was a possibility a few places could become available through cancellations. We were told if we went to the visitor's desk at 7 a.m. the next morning we might be lucky. We were up early and joined the queue. As we came nearer to the desk our hopes soared. Our trip to the bottom of the canyon depended on there being space for us. We finally reached the desk. A space for a couple had just become available. We couldn't believe our luck. The news was music to our ears.

A coach took us from the visitors' centre to the start of Bright Angel Trail. We chatted to a couple on the coach, and they asked if they could hike down with us. With great enthusiasm we set off down the trail with Bob and Sue carrying plenty of water and a packed lunch each. There were loos at intervals on the trail and we were amused when Bob rushed off every time, we saw one saying, "My mother said I should never pass up a loo". It did slow us down a bit, but it was very amusing.

The views along Bright Angel Trail were breathtaking and the path easy to negotiate. We stopped for our picnic, then continued down. I'm better at going downhill than up and sped down the trail to the bottom of the canyon leaving the others behind. When I reached Phantom Ranch, I opened the door and found myself in a bar. Perfect I thought as my rapid descent had left me thirsty. I started to order a drink and then realised my husband had all the money. To my surprise someone in the bar immediately offered to buy me a drink. I shouldn't think that happens too often in a bar in the U.K. I was truly touched by this generosity. I found there was a tremendous sense of camaraderie amongst those who had reached the bottom of the canyon. There was a feeling that we were all in it together, fulfilling an ambition.

Yes, we'd all walked to the bottom of the canyon but the big challenge of climbing back up to the top was still to come. The next morning, we left at 5.30 a.m. to climb the South Kaibab Trail up to the rim of the canyon. The first 3 ½ miles were okay, but then the path started to rise steeply following a series of switch backs. Looking up I could see giant zigzags where the path went back and forth seemingly endlessly. The last 4 miles were a struggle. My husband urged me to keep going. He said if I stopped, I wouldn't be able to start again. I did manage to keep going, but I so longed to stop to catch my breath.

When I reached the top there was a restaurant, which was perfect, except I could hardly persuade my legs to climb up the steps to go inside. Seven hours of almost continuous climbing had taken its toll. It was days before I fully recovered.

With one of our ambitions completed we continued on our way to Houston. The distance from Grand Canyon to Houston direct is 1,290 miles, but we had plans for more sight-seeing, so our journey would be longer. We visited White Sands National Monument in New Mexico with its spectacular white gypsum sand dunes scattered with Yucca plants. The Yucca plants weren't in flower, and I resolved to visit again when they were in bloom.

Finally, we arrived in the outskirts of Houston. Giant billboards rose up from each side of the road. We felt very small. Eventually massive sky rise buildings took over. My heart sank. I'd enjoyed spending time photographing landscapes and wildlife in the beautiful Rocky Mountains in Canada. What on earth was I going to photograph, or even do here?

Shell Oil had booked us into a smart Hilton hotel and given us a month to find more permanent accommodation. I'd been tipped off that the best place to live was on the outskirts of Houston which was safer and quieter than the city itself. But to my disappointment my husband wanted to be within a few minutes' drive of the Shell office. We started to look at apartment complexes and condominiums in Houston.

The newly built gated complex the letting agent took us to was attractive and within a 15-minute drive of the Shell office. As it had only recently been completed very few of the condominiums were occupied. The agent assured us that most people renting the condos would be doctors, as it was close to a hospital. It was a compact condo complex built around a pool with palm trees and a waterfall at one end. It seemed to suit our needs.

I love swimming so the thought of a daily dip in the pool was wonderful. When we'd had a posting to Dallas, some years earlier, the apartment complex had a beautiful heated, kidney shaped pool surrounded by plants. In winter steam curled up from the surface invitingly and I had a dip every day throughout the year. If we rented the condo, I'd to be able to swim outdoors every day throughout the year again. With that in mind and it being close to the Shell office we decided we'd found the perfect place to live.

We chose the condo opposite the palm trees and waterfall. The refreshing sound of splashing water as it tumbled over the rocks was going to be our background music. By the time we moved into our new home, we were content that we'd made a good choice. There were electric gates to the complex and a high wall around it, topped with dangerous looking bladed electrified barbed wire. A bit over the top I thought, but it made me feel secure.

We moved in and the condo management called us in for an introductory presentation about living in the complex. They started with some tips. "Take one of your guns with you whenever you answer the door" they advised "and if you're a bad shot choose the biggest". This was unexpected and alarming advice. We didn't have a gun and wouldn't know how to use it if we did!

Houston did have, and no doubt still has, a reputation as a city with violent areas. Is this what the Canadians were warning us about? What we didn't know when we rented the condo was that there was a motorway bridge near the complex and across the bridge was a very dangerous area. Perhaps I should have spent more time researching the safe areas to live. But life is topsy-turvy when you first arrive in a new place, and I just wanted to sort everything out and get settled. Our hasty choice of accommodation taught me a valuable lesson. If you don't know a city, you don't know where the best place is to live, so do some research before you choose.

Our sons came out to join us during the summer holidays and we enjoyed the pool. So far life in Houston was okay. We all signed up for a scuba diving course in Houston and qualified. Once we were ready to put our newly acquired skills to the test, we put our names down for a dive trip to Cozumel in Mexico which was being arranged by the scuba dive shop. There was a direct flight from Houston International airport which only took 2 hours, so we were in the water testing our equipment the same day.

Most dives were drift dives. We were dropped off by the boat and drifted along with the current past beautiful coral reefs brimming with colourful fish and other marine life. At the end of the dive the boat picked us up. The whole dive was effortless. A Mexican beer at the end of the day with a twist of lime tucked into the top of the bottle was the icing on the cake.

Keen to dive in new places we signed up for a week on a dive boat leaving from Houston for the Gulf of Mexico. We settled into our cabin for four, with bunk beds. During the night I was woken by the sound of water sloshing somewhere. I thought it must be waves breaking against the hull of the boat, but it seemed too loud. It almost sounded as if the water was inside the cabin. I was on top bunk, so I climbed down the ladder. At the bottom of the ladder, I was expecting my foot to reach the floor but instead it entered water. Was the boat sinking?

No, fortunately not, but what I'd first thought was 6 inches of water on the floor was in fact sewage. A pipe had burst, and the contents of the boat's effluent tank had emptied itself into our cabin!

Our younger son, Andrew, was sleeping on one of the bottom bunks. The evening before I'd watched as he carefully stored all his clothes and precious electronic gizmos under his bed. I woke him up. He shot out of bed and started to delve under his bed for his belonging. His clothes were soaked with effluent and every one of his electronic gizmos ruined. He was heartbroken. I don't remember too much else about the dive trip. Compared to our fabulous experiences diving in Cozumel our diving expedition in the Gulf of Mexico was nothing short of a disaster.

Once the boys returned to the U.K. I found life in Houston took some getting used to. I felt lonely. Only a few of the condos were occupied and those that were occupied seemed to be inhabited by people who kept their curtains closed. With the Astrodome so close it was footballers who rented the condos, not doctors. The footballers were single young men mainly of colour and were only there when playing at the Astrodome. A footballer rented the condo next to ours and we were entertained to his taste in loud thumping music which was easily audible through the thin walls. Life in Houston was turning out to be very different from our wonderful three years in Calgary.

I enjoyed swimming in the pool and made it a daily routine. But as winter approached the pool seemed to be getting cooler. Steam failed to curl from the surface. I made enquiries as to when the heating would kick in. The news wasn't good. The pool wasn't heated. My swimming routine was about to come to an end for the winter.

I needed something to do so I started to write a book. My photos had been featured in 14 Photography Year Books, published by Fountain Press, and many of my photographs were used to illustrate "Alberta's Parks, Our Legacy". The owner of Fountain Press suggested I might like to write a guide to photography.

I got started and posted each chapter back to the publisher in the U.K. by registered mail. He told me my book was progressing well, so I continued until I'd finished. But my *Guide to Photography* failed to be published. I was naturally disappointed, but I'd enjoyed writing it and it had kept me busy, so it wasn't a complete waste of time. There's usually a positive side to most disappointments.

On 24th October 1993 I flew to Churchill, Manitoba to join a group of photographers to photograph polar bears. Even the flight from Winnipeg to Churchill was exciting. We landed in a blizzard in the middle of nowhere. A man ran out from a hut and handed a package to the flight attendants. There seemed to be nothing else there except a man and a hut. I got the feeling that anyone living there would be on the very edge of survival.

The town of Churchill was under deep snow. It looked beautiful, but it was difficult to get around. In our high, arctic snow boots with the hoods of our down jackets pulled up to keep out the blizzard we trudged through the snow to reach a restaurant for supper. It was my kind of holiday. I like extreme conditions, and I found the feeling of remoteness and isolation in Churchill exciting.

The next three days we spent driving around the shores of Hudson Bay in a tundra buggy. It had large tractor-like tyres, specially designed to keep us out of reach of the polar bears and to cope with the rough snowy terrain. Propped up beside the driver was a rifle for our protection. From the tundra buggy I had my first sightings of polar bears in the wild. They looked so powerful and impressive in their natural snowy habitat and made wonderful photographic subjects.

For the second half of the week, we were taken to a mobile bunkhouse parked on the shore of Hudson Bay. Linked units provided a lounge, dining room, dormitory and kitchen. We boarded the bunkhouse directly from our tundra buggy to keep us out of reach of the polar bears and stayed there for 3 days. When meals were being prepared the smell of cooking drew the bears to the bunkhouse and presented us with a perfect opportunity to photograph them.

On our last morning we'd packed away all our camera gear in preparation to leave before dawn, but the tundra buggies were delayed and didn't arrive as scheduled to pick us up. The sky was clear, and we could see there were several bears on the snow-covered tundra below the bunkhouse. As the sun came up, we realised we were about to witness an exceptional sight.

We hurried to unpack our equipment and waited. As the sun rose it back-lit the polar bears and with the sun shining through the tips of their fur each bear glowed with a halo of rosy, pink light. It was magic. Bulky polar bears stood on their hind legs and punched each other, play fighting. We'd been given a superb opportunity and just by chance.

My trip to Churchill had been wonderful, but I was soon back in Houston. Social life in Houston was scant and confined mostly to company dinners. American Shell employees' wives kindly invited me to join them to shop in the glamorous shopping centre of *The Galleria* and to finish with a light lunch. Unfortunately, dressing up to shop and eating light lunches with acquaintances didn't satisfy or fulfil me. I was at my happiest when I got home, shed my smart clothes and put my jeans back on. I shopped with the employees' wives many times and on one occasion bought a pink silk skirt. When I got it home, I tried it on again, but it simply wasn't me and I never wore it. Sadly, the shopping trips and light lunches did not bring me happiness.

I found I loved visiting the state parks in Texas with my husband. Every Friday night we'd pack our camping gear and drive to one of the state parks in our Ford Transit. It was a deluxe vehicle with tinted windows, plush velvet armchair seats and room to sleep in the back. There were so many delightful state parks in Texas and during our stay in Houston we camped in 25 of them.

The parks were well equipped with individual camp sites set amongst trees and well-maintained shower blocks. Each tent, or vehicle pitch, had a wooden table with bench attached and a charcoal BBQ. We'd get up before sunrise to enjoy the colourful Texan sunrises and watch wildlife feeding at dawn. One early morning I spent a long time observing and photographing a white-tailed deer grazing. It gradually became accustomed to me and allowed me to approach it for some close-up photographs. The trust the deer put in me fulfilled and satisfied me, unlike shopping and light lunches.

Our morning trips were peaceful and filled me with contentment. Breakfast was a simple meal seated at the wooden table with bench attached. Once the kettle had boiled for tea, we'd pour hot water over a packet of instant fruit flavoured porridge and give it a good stir. It was perfect and I loved it. The downside came when we drove back to Houston on Sunday evening. I could almost feel gloom descending upon me.

The summers in Texas were very hot, and walks restricted to the early morning and evening. From May until October the heat combined with 100% humidity limited activities. So, in May we started to visit the coast. We drove south to Galveston and Padre Island where we camped. The beach looked more like a car park during the day, but it was the way things were in Texas, and we got used to it.

Big Bend National Park was a wonderful place to visit but it was a 10-hour drive from Houston. Trips to Big Bend were restricted to long weekends.

Our first trip was on an Easter weekend. The 10-hour drive proved tedious. For mile after mile Texan countryside remained unchanged. We took it in turns to drive and each of us sat at the wheel with the van on cruise control for hour after hour trying not to fall asleep. Gradually we started to see more prickly pear cacti with large yellow flowers, the famed *Yellow rose of Texas*. The change of scenery was encouraging as it was a sign we were getting close to Big Bend National Park.

We drove into the park which was wild and beautiful. My husband always liked the challenge of a climb so soon after we arrived, we packed our tent and camping gear into our giant rucksacks and set off up a steep path towards the summit of Casa Grande Mountain. I think my husband would have loved rock climbing, but that wouldn't have worked for me. He was slim and of athletic build, whereas my very feminine build bore no resemblance to a mountain goat.

I always carried a camera in those days as I'd started submitting photos to Tony Stone Photo Agency in Canada and was on the lookout for marketable photographs. The view as we climbed was magnificent. Roads, trees, and buildings in the valley below grew smaller until they looked like a model. I composed a shot with the rugged rock face in the foreground, contrasting dramatically with the tiny detail of the park below in the background. It's still for sale worldwide on the internet through Getty Images. That made the climb worthwhile.

We pitched our tent, cooked a meal, and settled down early for the night as it was too cold and dark to do anything else. The next morning, we awoke after rather a chilly night; a hot cup of tea was what we needed. I unscrewed the top of a bottle of water and attempted to pour water into the kettle. Nothing came out. The water was frozen solid. It was a while before we could make that warming cuppa.

Back in Houston we traded in our blue Firebird for a new sleek looking dark green Firebird. I wasn't keen on driving the rather cumbersome Ford Transit van, so the dark green Firebird became my car. I really loved driving it and it was much admired.

One day, while it was still new, I drove to a jet wash. Naturally I was proud of my car and wanted to keep it looking pristine. The jet wash facility was made up of a row of about 6 bays with coin operated jet wash hoses. It was fully automatic and there was nobody in attendance. I started soaping my car.

I noticed a large, rather dilapidated car arrive. It didn't drive into one of the jet wash bays but parked across the end of my bay. Down went the windows and two heavily built black men stared out at me. This was not a good sign. I told myself not to panic or do anything quickly. This is where my bit of acting experience came in useful. I put on a show. I looked at the nozzle on the hose as if there was something wrong with it, then I gently laid it down on the ground and went round to my car driver's door. Opening the door in the most normal way I could, I jumped in and drove off. The two black men in the dilapidated car followed me. I was afraid to drive straight back to the condo complex in case they drove in after me when the electric gates were open. Instead, I drove around for a while keeping in built up areas and eventually lost them.

A few weeks later a woman was shot and killed for her car at that very same jet wash station. This confirmed to me that Houston was a dangerous place to live. I had a new ambition. My ambition was not to make my final departure from Houston in a coffin. It was a good ambition, and I stuck to it. I bought a pepper spray which I attached to my key ring. As I walked across the parking lot to my car after my weekly shop at the supermarket, I put my finger on the top of the pepper spray ready for action. I wasn't being alarmist. It made good sense.

As Christmas approached the radio programme I was listening to announced shopping tips for Christmas. I listened out for where to shop and ideas of what to buy. The shopping tips, when they came, were a bit of a surprise, "Drive in the middle of the road," was the advice. "This will prevent you from being run off the road". They omitted to tell us what might happen if we were run off the road, but it wasn't difficult to guess. The advice continued. "When crossing the parking lot walk in a determined way looking about you. Do not look uncertain". "Look under your car on arrival and in the back seat". Apparently, robbers would lie under cars and grab your ankles as you climbed in. If you left the car unlocked there was a risk an attacker would get into the back seat and attack you from behind. I reminded myself of my ambition not to leave Houston in a coffin.

Apart from the incident in the car wash there was only one other time when I felt my life was threatened. I went to the door one day at about 3 p.m. in the afternoon. There, filling the door frame was a tall and broad man of colour. He told me he was staying with a friend in the complex but had forgotten his key and was locked out. He said he needed to collect his car from a garage and would I give him a lift. Clearly the answer was 'no' but I wasn't sure of the outcome if I just said "no". I had to think quickly. I said, "I'd be delighted to give you a lift but I'm afraid my husband is due home any minute and I must be here when he arrives". He seemed to accept this as a good reason and left.

The next day we found a leaflet in our letter box. On the leaflet was a photo of my caller. The leaflet read "This man is wanted by the police. If you see him contact the police immediately. Do not approach". My ambition to stay alive was working.

Sons Alexander and Andrew were due to fly out for the summer holidays and we had to dream up a family holiday which would interest them. So far, the whitewater rafting through the Grand Canyon had proved to be by far the best North American trip we'd had. The challenge was to find a holiday equally as exciting for this year.

I found a kayaking trip in the British Virgin Islands which looked as if it might suit teenage boys. We'd start from Tortola and kayak from island to island for a week, camping each night. That was about all we knew about the holiday. It sounded like fun, so I booked the trip.

When we arrived, we were given double kayaks. Alexander and Andrew shared a kayak and made a great team. I sat behind my husband in another double kayak and did my best to follow his forceful strokes. We camped on uninhabited islands and meals were prepared by the two organizers who accompanied us in the safety boat. Each morning, we were given a plastic bottle of water to put in the kayak. That was our day's water supply. Unfortunately, the bottle heated up quickly in the kayak and we drank warm water with a plastic flavour every day for a week. We kept clean by swimming in the sea. There were no freshwater showers, so a residue of salt built up on our skin. With the sun beating down on us all day we developed rashes on our arms and legs. I won the prize for the most virulent rash covering the greatest area of my body.

But despite the discomfort the holiday was a success. The boys loved camping on remote islands and kayaking long distances in the open sea. The best part for me was the freshwater shower at the end of the week when we booked into a hotel.

The second week we rented a yacht and had an idyllic time sailing, swimming, eating, and having freshwater showers. The boat had a shower in the stern so we could shower the moment we came out of the sea after a swim. It was sheer heaven.

The next summer we went back to the British Virgin Islands, but this time we didn't kayak, we rented a yacht for 2 weeks. We took our own scuba diving equipment with us and rented compressed air tanks. Sailing and scuba diving in the clear, warm waters of the Caribbean made the perfect holiday for our teenage boys. I'm pleased to say I enjoyed it, too.

My favourite road in Houston became Interstate Highway 45, the freeway which led to Houston International Airport. I took a flight home for 3 weeks every 6 months to see our sons, my parents, my sisters, and to get away from Houston. I also signed up for some organised photo shoots with Joseph van Os Photo Safaris. They were well organised and always exciting.

On one of the safaris, we photographed exotic animals which were privately owned and used in photo shoots. A shoot was set up with a tiger running along the beach. It ran backwards and forwards as we took photos. The tiger was doing another lap when a jogger appeared running along the beach towards it. He stopped in his tracks with a look of total disbelief and horror on his face. His expression would have made a more compelling photo than the tiger.

The wild animals we photographed were trained and tamed, although, there is no such thing as a tame wild animal. We were taking shots of a cougar when it suddenly sprang up and pounced on its keeper throwing her onto the rocks. We were standing behind our tripods but not a single shutter clicked. We were all far too shocked.

We took it in turns to photograph a male lion. It was a beautiful beast. When it was my turn, I lay on the ground in front of it and using a wide-angle lens took its head in extreme close-up; my head was only inches from its mouth. When I stood up the keeper said, "I could never be a photographer". "Why is that?", I said. "I could never take a risk like the one you've just taken," he replied. I had no idea I was putting myself in danger.

I joined several photo trips during my time in Houston and enjoyed photographing wildlife and landscapes with the *Joseph van Os* groups. Over dinner each evening we were free to talk about technical aspects of photography without the threat of boring the other dinner guests. I relished my photo trips. I was also very happy to escape from Houston.

After joining a group of photographers to photograph the aspen trees in golden autumn colour in Colorado I took a flight home. There was no refreshment on the flight as it was under 2 hours. I'd had nothing to eat or drink for hours and couldn't wait to get home and have a cup of tea and something to eat. As the taxi sped along my favourite airport freeway, although admittedly going in the wrong direction, the driver gave me some recent news. "See that bridge," he said, pointing to the one crossing the freeway near our complex, "did you hear what happened there last night?" He gave me the news whether I wanted to hear it or not. "A pickup truck was travelling with men in the back carrying guns" he said, "they spotted a red Mercedes saloon driving in the same direction which they fancied so they shot the driver. But he car didn't stop as the driver was in cruise control. The red Mercedes crashed."

This wasn't something I wanted to hear, particularly as it was after midnight and I was returning home to an empty house, as my husband was away on business. When the taxi dropped me off, I felt anxious and couldn't wait to be safely inside our house. I put the key in the front door and turned it, but the door didn't open. I had no idea why, but I appeared to be locked out. What was I going to do?

The reception desk was closed and most of the condos were in darkness. I pressed a few doorbells where I could see lights, but no one answered the door. I went through my options. Our garage was remote controlled and had no key so there was no access to my car. With no car I couldn't drive in search of a hotel and to walk out of the complex on foot would have gone against my ambition not to leave Houston in a coffin. So, no solution so far.

At night our complex was checked every two hours by armed security officers. I thought of contacting them when they arrived but there was a risk that I might be mistaken for a burglar and shot on sight. Seeking help from a security guard would only work if I picked one that wasn't trigger happy. If I lay down on a sun lounger I could be mistaken for a vagrant, so I would have to stay out of sight. I found a poolside lounger and pushed it as far as I could into the bushes and lay down to try to get some sleep. The giant Texan mosquitoes found me and as the saturated air-cooled dew fell and I began to get wet. I emptied my suitcase of clothes and covered myself with the contents as best I could. I was hungry and thirsty, but I had nothing with me to eat or drink. I watched as security guards made their way round the complex with powerful torches, the mosquitoes continued to try to eat me, and I got increasingly wet and cold. I didn't get much sleep.

At 6 a.m. a light went on in our neighbour's house. The footballer had moved out and a charming young Irish doctor and his wife had moved in. He was working at a hospital, the one the letting agent had told us about. The sight of a light in the next-door house so early filled me with hope and relief. I rang the doorbell, and the doctor came to the door. I told my story between sobs of frustration, fear and relief. The young doctor was quick to work out how he could gain entry to our house. I had the key to the backdoor, but access to the back door was blocked by the garage. There was a high wall between the two condos but if he scaled the wall he could reach our back door.

Without hesitation he nimbly climbed up the wall and let himself into our house through the back door. He found the front door had been locked from the inside. We later discovered that son, Alexander, had left the house to return to university and in his thoroughness had locked the front door from the inside as an extra security measure. He'd gone out through the back door, then left through the garage setting it automatically to close behind him. The house was impenetrable.

Our posting to Houston had more than its fair share of difficult times but my favourite airport freeway, Interstate 45, gave us easy access to the International Airport and flights to wonderful dive locations. My husband and I went to the island of Bonaire in the Caribbean where the diving was superb. The coral was remarkable, and I especially remember a tall coral structure lying at about 70 feet that looked like a giant purple vase.

We also flew to Belize in Central America to scuba dive. It was a primitive place, but the diving was remarkable. There were golf carts for hire to be used to explore the area. We hired one and set off along a sand road through the jungle. We had to keep up quite a speed to outrun the cloud of mosquitos that gathered round our heads. The sand road was full of potholes, so I carefully put them between the front wheels of our golf cart. But however hard I tried to miss the potholes we seemed to go down with a bump. The golf carts coming towards us seemed to be doing okay. When we returned to the golf cart hire centre, we got out of the vehicle, and only then did we discover what the problem was. Although all the carts coming towards us had four wheels our golf cart only had three. We'd hired a three-wheeler! It's funny the things you remember about a place. The diving was good, but the golf cart drive was far more memorable.

While living in Houston we continued to celebrate Christmas in a ski resort. Once Alexander and Andrew were home from university, we'd take my favourite freeway to Houston airport and fly to Salt Lake City in Utah where we'd hire a car. We always stayed in the same rented apartment in Park City and skied Alta, Park City Mountain, Solitude and Deer Valley. One Christmas Day, in Deer Valley Resort, we were almost the only skiers on the slopes. Deer Valley was, and still is, a ski-only resort, no snow boarders are allowed. The slopes were peaceful to ski without the threat of being mown down by snowboarders and it became our favourite resort. Skiing was the perfect way to spend Christmas with teenage boys. Leaving Houston for a couple of weeks and spending time playing in the snow with the family was sheer joy.

When we next visited the dive centre, we found they were organising a scuba diving trip to the Great Barrier Reef. I was keen to go and delighted when my husband agreed. The idea of diving on the Great Barrier Reef seemed like a dream. Up until then it had only been something I'd read about. We booked the trip.

We arrived in Australia and started to explore Sydney. It felt more like home than Houston and I loved it. We then flew up to Cairns where we boarded a dive boat to scuba dive on the Great Barrier Reef for a week.

I was surprised to find, where we were diving, that the coral and fish weren't as colourful as I'd imagined they would be. The coral reefs we'd explored in Cozumel, Belize and Bonnaire had been vibrant with colour which was what I loved about them. The fish that inhabited the Great Barrier Reef weren't colourful, but they were bigger than anything I'd ever seen before. Giant cod fearlessly approached us opening their massive mouths. The squid were enormous too which made them easy to photograph. My 35mm camera in bulky underwater housing was cumbersome so I appreciated some easy subjects.

A dive with sharks was planned for the next day. It sounded a bit scary, but I thought if I didn't go, I might be sorry to have missed the experience. I left my camera gear behind. I was going to keep an eye on the sharks and that wasn't going to be through the lens of my camera.

We were instructed to make a descent until we came to some rocks and then to hold onto a rock. We were warned that it was essential to stay perfectly still once the sharks arrived.

I found a rock and with difficulty hung on but felt nervous and started to breath rapidly. I could see from the dial on my tank that I was using up air quickly. A mass of fish bones was attached to the ship's anchor which was thrown overboard. Sharks swam in from all directions and tore at the fish bones. I noticed that one shark was much larger than the others and behaved differently from the rest. It swam from one diver to the next appearing to look each one in the eye as it passed. I started to breath even faster.

Finally, the sharks left, and we were allowed to ascend and climb back on board the boat. There was great chatter and concern amongst the dive leaders. The arrival of the large shark was unexpected. I believe they said it was a Tiger shark, although I can't be sure. My dive with sharks was one of those dive experiences that is far more enjoyable in the telling than it was at the time.

After the dive boat returned to Cairns a chain of events began which disrupted, and at times shattered, my life for years. We were given a free day to spend as we chose so we thought we'd hire a car and see something of the Cairns area. We'd met a very nice Texan couple and decided to invite them to join us on our exploratory trip. But before we could ask them a young Texan woman heard we were hiring a car and asked if she and her husband could join us for the day. It was hard to refuse as we hadn't already asked the couple we'd hoped would be able to join us.

During our day of exploration, I noticed my husband and the young Texan woman were getting on well. They were laughing and having fun together. There was clearly an attraction between them, but I thought nothing of it as she had only been married for a year. How little we know of our future. I later learned that she'd fallen out with her husband before they left for Australia. Presumably that was why her attention was focused on my husband. Gradually my dream trip to the Great Barrier Reef morphed into a nightmare. My husband's chance meeting with a young Texan woman changed the course of my life.

After we returned to Houston, I went back to England to visit our sons, my parents, and sisters for 3 weeks. When my husband picked me up at Houston Airport on my return, I was pleased to see he was looking very happy. This I interpreted as him being pleased to see me. But I was wrong.

He came home early from work one day. Except it wasn't work he'd come home from. He'd been with the young Texan woman, and he'd rushed home to make a confession. He told me he'd been seeing her while I'd been in England. Her husband had found out and was about to phone me. It was shocking news, a brutal bolt out of the blue. I loved my husband with all my heart and trusted him. I was still reeling from the news when the phone rang.

The woman's husband asked to speak to me. He said, "I thought you were a nice couple and now your husband is having an affair with my wife". I felt almost as if he was holding me partly responsible. What was happening seemed surreal.

While I was in England the young woman had phoned my husband at his office. The dive centre had supplied a list of Great Barrier Reef dive participants listing both office and home phone numbers. She had been handed the means to contact him without fear of me picking up the phone. She'd told my husband she was upset as her marriage was breaking up and needed to be comforted. He told me she'd taken her clothes off and offered him sex. He had been unable to resist temptation. My husband assured me that the affair was over which was a relief. Men can be weak when tempted by the offer of sex, so I forgave him. I hoped we could put his brief lapse of faithfulness behind us. I loved him, and I knew he loved me.

The young woman's husband, on the other hand, was incensed and showed no signs of forgiving his wife, or my husband. He threatened to shoot them both if he found them together. The young Texan woman phoned to tell us of the threat and said we should report it to the police. Apparently in Texas when someone threatens to kill you it's important to let the police know so that the threat can be recorded. Quite how this prevents the crime from happening I'm not sure. It didn't prevent me from fearing for my husband's life.

We needed to leave Houston, and quickly. Fortunately, our posting had come to an end which was perfect timing. But unfortunately, this meant there were lots of farewell parties and dinners to go to so that everyone could say goodbye to us and wish us well in our next posting. One party was held on the evening of the day my husband had told me about his affair. The last thing I felt like doing was going to a party where we would be the centre of attention. I had to muster all the courage I possessed to get ready for that party. I dried my eyes, put on my party clothes and fixed a false smile on my face for the evening. It wasn't easy.

Our time in Houston had come to an end and I still hadn't developed a taste for shopping at the *Galleria* and doing lunch. Life in Houston had been difficult, sometimes dangerous, and sadly it had ended very badly. During a farewell dinner a Houstonian asked me how I'd enjoyed my time there. I replied, "It was a total waste of 3 years of my life". Rather a harsh thing to say, particularly to a Houstonian, but it was the way I felt at the time. When we'd left Calgary three years earlier to drive to Houston, I had no idea what was in store for us.

Instead of flying directly to Holland for our next posting I suggested we went first to Alaska for a holiday. This, I thought, might take my husband's mind off the dreadful ructions which had occurred in our lives and give us time to return to our happy relationship. He loved remote places and mountains, and we had enough air miles to pay the fare. It seemed the perfect solution. As I boarded the plane to Alaska my spirits lifted. I had achieved an important ambition. I was leaving

Houston for good, and I was still alive. I had succeeded in not making my final departure from Houston in a coffin. Ironically, and sadly, it was my husband who left Houston in a coffin some years later. How unpredictable life can be.

As it turned out Alaska didn't provide the perfect solution to our marital problems. I damaged my knee badly carrying boxes of books down the stairs while packing and when we arrived in Alaska there was no way I could climb mountains with my husband. He became frustrated and I felt useless.

My husband's frustration at my inability to be active mounted until he suddenly got out of the car and said, "I'm going for a walk". Later I discovered he used the time to buy a necklace for his mistress and post it to her. I only know about the necklace because when we reached Holland she phoned to tell me.

While my husband was away making his secret purchase, I wandered the streets of Anchorage and found an interesting rough sleeper to talk to. The homeless man had been employed laying gas and oil pipelines in the extreme north of Alaska. He had become an alcoholic, lost his job, his home and as a result, his wife. One life choice, or weakness, had ruined his life. Was I in danger of the same happening to me? Was my husband's weakness in not resisting temptation about to change the course of our lives?

For colour photos use QR code for www.rosemarylairdauthor.co.uk

A Life in Pictures

CHAPTER 10
Marriage Breakup

When my husband told me he was leaving me I saw a blank white sheet. It was a strange sensation. What I was looking at, I realised, was my life from that moment on. Both my husband and the life I'd known for 26 years had disappeared, been deleted, and the future I'd anticipated for both of us had been deleted with it.

Life as an oil company employee's wife had been full of fun, change and challenge. I loved my husband, and he loved me. We shared a wonderful partnership. He went to work and earned lots of money and I did everything else. It worked well. Now I'd been fired. I'd embraced life as a dedicated Shell wife and given it everything, but my experience was no use as a qualification. I was soon to be alone and with no career to fall back on.

We'd moved back to Holland after our 3 years in Houston and were staying in a hotel when my husband gave me the devastating news that he was leaving me. I'd thought his dalliance with the young Texan women was behind us and I looked forward to being happy again. We'd buy a house and probably another sailing boat. We'd loved spending weekends sailing to the Frisian Islands in *Snowflake* and now we had a chance to buy another boat, start sailing together again and have more fun.

But fun wasn't coming my way anytime soon. We'd been followed. The Texan woman had jumped on a plane to Amsterdam shortly after we'd arrived and contacted my husband. He was flattered and found her commitment to him irresistible. He didn't hold back when telling me of his feelings towards her. He seemed to have entered a state of euphoria. "She loves me", he said, "she makes me feel alive. I feel as if I've won the lottery". His words were like sharp arrows piercing my heart.

Distraught and heartbroken I cried for days. I looked terrible. My eyes looked like those of a dead fish on a slab in the market. But I knew I had to accept the situation. It's impossible to force, or even persuade, your husband to love you. It's not the way it works. He'd moved on and had new loyalties. He'd given his heart to another woman. I've observed in life that men have an ability to make a quick change when it comes to love.

But to my surprise the young Texan woman got back on a plane and returned to Houston. My husband said he believed we could have a good life together. I was filled with joy. Life had turned a corner to reveal a life I thought I'd never have. My distress evaporated and I felt happy and blessed. I could laugh and smile again. I'd thought my happy life with my husband had come to an end but here we were making a new start. We moved to a Shell flat as a stepping stone to buying a house.

I made a few changes to my underwear draw. I needed to freshen up my attraction if I was going to keep my man. I also bought a short black leather skirt, suspenders and stockings and a few low-necked blouses. He seemed to like the changes, and we settled back to our happy life together.

One evening after work my husband went for a run, which he often did. Hours passed but he failed to return. It had been dark for a while, and I was becoming increasingly anxious. I wondered at what point I should phone the police. I waited and I waited. It reached midnight .Shortly after midnight my husband returned. He seemed amazed to find me up, fully dressed and in an anxious state. He seemed rather annoyed to find me waiting up for him and said he'd been for a long run.

Of course he hadn't. His mistress had flown back to Holland and was staying in a nearby hotel. He'd spent the evening, and part of the night with her. I was devastated. The chance of a future with my husband seemed to have flown out of my reach again. The Texan woman had a hold on him which I couldn't match.

The idea of taking my own life sneaked in as a way forward. I couldn't face life without him. There was a large carving knife in the kitchen drawer and looking at it scared me. What if in a fit of pique I took it and ended my torment. I had to prevent this from happening. I took the knife and put it in a box. I put the box right at the back of a shelf in a cupboard and locked the door. I took the key and hid it from sight. Now I could no longer grab the knife in a moment of madness. I hoped that during the time it would take me to reach the knife my sanity would return. Perhaps my mother's wise words that you should always be "two steps from danger" had subconsciously helped me. It was the only time I nearly toppled off my foundation rock created by a secure childhood.

Our elder son, Alexander, arrived for Christmas. He was studying for a PhD. at Cornell University in the U.S. at the time. He was aware of the marital problems, and I'd asked him to come home for Christmas to give me support. The last update I'd given him was that his father's affair was over, and we were moving forward with our life together and putting it behind us. He arrived thinking all was well, but soon after his arrival my husband gave us a further update. He told us he would only stay until we'd had Christmas Day together and then he would leave us.

Our youngest son, Andrew, arrived from the U.K. He was studying at Durham University. We all met him at the airport and drove back to the flat. As he walked through the front door of the flat, he said, "It's so good to be home".

"But you've never been here before" I said.

He looked at me lovingly. "Wherever you and Daddy are is home".

My heart went out to him, and I was filled with sadness. Not for myself this time but for our sensitive younger son. What he had always regarded as home was about to be torn apart.

My husband asked Alexander and me not to tell Andrew he was leaving after Christmas Day. He said he wanted to break the news gently to him himself. I'm not sure how he intended to do that as there's no gentle way to tell someone you're abandoning them. Time ticked by and he didn't tell Andrew. Alexander and I couldn't bear Andrew being unaware of the situation any longer so we told him about his father's affair and that Christmas Day would be the last day he would have with us.

I can remember so clearly the poor boy's face when we gave him the devastating news. His expression was one of total disbelief. He knew the Texan woman. She'd befriended him at a party and talked exclusively to him all evening. When it was time for us to leave the party, she'd suggested he stayed, and she'd offered to take him home later. We insisted he came with us. I didn't trust her, and neither was I sure to whose home she might be intending to take him.

Christmas Day dawned. It had snowed during the night and the view from the bedroom window was beautiful. With a thick dusting of snow over everything the scene was one of total serenity. I looked at the scene and a mixture of awe and desperation ran threw me. I was gazing at a view that was calm and very beautiful but within me my heart was being torn apart and full of sadness. What would be the final day of our happy family life had begun.

We exchanged Christmas presents. Mine from my husband was a long box. As he gave it to me, I said in jest. "I should imagine this is either a screwdriver or a vibrator". They were just the items I thought he might think I needed for my single life. I took the wrapping paper off and opened the long box. There lay something I'd never owned before in my life but there was no mistaking what it was. It was indeed a vibrator.

I don't remember lunch on Christmas Day. I should imagine I cooked turkey with all the trimmings. It's what I did. I would have gone through all the right motions despite the fog I existed in and my internal desperation.

After Christmas lunch we went for a walk on the beach. There was a good covering of snow which was perfect for snowballing. It was a forceful game. Snowballs from our sons and myself all flew in the same direction. My husband commented that he seemed to be the main target. Should he have been surprised?

Boxing Day arrived. This was the day my husband was due to go to his woman. However, he had an alternative suggestion. He offered to drop me off at my mother's house in the U.K.

That obviously seemed sensible to him as then I'd be catered for, and he'd be able to remain in the flat and keep our only car.

Alexander was incensed. "If anyone is leaving," he said "it's you". I was right to ask him to come home to give me support. "And before you go", he added "you'll transfer some money into my mother's account". He escorted his father to the computer and stood over him. Our son at 6ft 3in dwarfed his father at 5ft 11½in. Alexander didn't take his eyes off the screen as £200,000 was transferred from my husband's current account into mine. Then Alexander stretched out his long arms and enveloping his brother and me in a hug, he told his father to go.

I'd never thought of my children as my protectors. I had always been theirs. How the tables can turn when children become adults. To me they would always be my children who, as a mother, I was designed to protect. Had I been blind to the fact that they had become young men?

My husband had another change of heart. He didn't leave. He said he would stay. We all went out to celebrate. There was laughter and love abounding as we ate a hearty meal at our sons' favourite restaurant *The Argentinian*. When we got home, we continued in our exuberant mood, but my husband remained strangely silent. Then he finally spoke. "She's heartbroken," he said, "I'll have to go to her". He'd phoned his mistress to tell her he'd decided to stay with his family, and she'd understandably been upset. But he didn't go to her, he stayed. On reflection I feel sorry for the poor man. He was so torn between his family and what I now believe to have been a temptress practicing more than a hint of emotional blackmail.

Our sons returned to their universities and life got back to normal. My husband and I went out together to celebrate New Year's Eve and we both agreed that we were very pleased to say goodbye to 1995. It had been a terrible year; one of uncertainty for him and heartbreak for me. We both looked forward to embracing 1996 together.

I joined a swimming group and started to play tennis and badminton. While swimming one of the ladies in the group who knew we were house hunting told me of a house for sale in Wassenaar. My husband and I went to see it. It was perfect. It had French windows opening out onto the patio and a beautiful garden which was south facing. It fulfilled my dreams. There was a large kitchen with room for a good-sized family table. The master bedroom had a view of the garden and an ensuite bathroom. Four bedrooms were exactly what we were looking for. We put in an offer, and it was accepted. The sale went through and to make sure I felt secure my husband put the house in both our names.

It took a while for our personal effects to arrive from Houston, so we stayed in the flat. Life returned to normal, and we continued our happy life together. Finally, we were given a date when everything would be delivered to our new home. The crate containing our belongings arrived and enormous cardboard boxes were piled high in the living room. I was starting to unpack the boxes when my husband said he had something to tell me.

So, there amongst the large cardboard boxes he told me he was leaving me. He said his girlfriend was about to arrive and it was time for him to go to the airport to meet her. With ill-concealed excitement he said, "She'll be living with me in the flat. All her belongings and car will be arriving from Houston". He said no more and left.

My world tumbled about me and my heart felt as if it was going to bound out of my chest. I started to cry and couldn't stop. Alone I sat amongst the cardboard boxes and cried. Shock and despair overcame me, and I cried until I was too exhausted to cry anymore.

Once I stopped crying, I realised I had no choice but to get on with life and unpack. Every day there were times when I couldn't hold back the tears. To cope with them I put a box of tissues in every room so that I could mop up my tears as I worked.

One day I returned from shopping to find footprints in the snow leading to the front door and guessed they were my husband's. They were. He told me afterwards he'd called round to invite me to ice skate with him as his girlfriend didn't skate. He said he was disappointed I wasn't in. I never ceased to be amazed at his attitude to our marriage break up. I don't think he had the remotest idea how I felt. He'd once suggested a "ménage a trois". For him that would have been the perfect solution as then I'd have been on hand to go skating with him.

Some weeks later he phoned to ask if he could call round to see me. I made a supreme effort to look attractive and then waited with my heart in my mouth wandering what he was coming to tell me. I could hardly contain my excitement at the thought of seeing him again. When he arrived, he said "I want to come home". I couldn't believe my ears. We walked round the garden hugging and kissing. I was so happy. He'd finally had the change of heart I'd been waiting and longing for.

He sent his girlfriend, plus her car, back to Houston and moved into our house with me. He brought the bicycle he'd bought for her with him and put it in the garage. While Andrew was home on holiday from university, he needed a bicycle pump, so he took the pump from her bicycle. He told me he'd just taken "The Slag's" pump. From that day onwards my sons and I called her "The Slag". We hadn't the heart to use her name so that worked for us.

I helped my husband unpack his clothes and put them away. A piece of paper fell out of one of his pockets. It was a love note from "The Slag". After that I looked in all his pockets as I put his clothes away and found love note after love note. I found a CD with a note telling him to listen to one of the tracks. She clearly hadn't given up the fight for him. In her love notes she listed the reasons he should choose her over me.

She was a master of manipulation. He'd never really stood a chance.

My husband's mother had her say, too. She wrote to him, and I came across the letter and read it. She said how delighted she was that he had finally seen the light of day and left me. She wrote "What took you so long". There was no help coming my way from my mother-in-law from hell. I really shouldn't have expected it.

We tried to get back to leading a happy life, but my husband's mistress continued to contact him. When I found out I let him know that continual contact from her unnerved me and could threaten our happiness. He assured me that I had no reason to worry. It wasn't long afterwards when he told me she needed him, and he would have to go to her. I think she might have been threatening suicide. The bottom fell out of my world once again. How could he torment me in this way?

But that night we had a wonderful night of passion. Hope returned. He obviously still loved me and had decided to stay. However, the next morning he walked out of the front door and left me. As he went through the door, he turned back to face me and said, "Have a nice life". I felt numb and a feeling of hollow emptiness flooded through me.

What did he just say? "Have a nice life". How could he possibly think that was an appropriate thing to say as he abandoned me once again? Did he have any idea what he was doing to me? Where were his emotions? Did he feel nothing for me? Where was his loyalty? Did he have no moral compass? A cavity opened inside me, and I felt as if I was going to pass out.

He rented a house for himself and his mistress in Wassenaar, not far from where I was living. It was on my route to Wassenaar town, so I passed it frequently. One day I noticed the American number plates from the dark green Firebird I'd driven in Houston placed on an upstairs windowsill with the numbers facing outwards towards the road. My Firebird had been imported and now had Dutch number plates, but why were the U.S. plates displayed like this for all to see? The sight of them caused me pain every time I drove past their house. Were they placed on the windowsill, not for all to see, but for me to see as a sign of victory? Possibly. I can't think of another explanation.

After a few months my husband contacted me once again. He said he'd had enough of his girlfriend and wanted me back. He complained she was unpredictable and petulant. He told me she'd thrown a suitcase at him. How I went on forgiving him and wanting to welcome him home I've no idea. Love is a strong emotion, and I still loved him.

When I opened the door to him, I threw my arms around him. But he'd changed his mind. He wasn't coming back to me. He told me he couldn't as his girlfriend's need for him was too great.

I'd had enough. It was time to leave Holland and get on with my life. I booked a boat from Hoek van Holland to

Harwich and asked my elder sister, Sally, if I could stay with her in Reading. I was going house hunting.

With the entire U.K. to choose from I needed to decide where to live. I didn't want to move close to my mother or any of my sisters as I wanted to start a new life by myself. My sons had been at school at Charterhouse in Godalming, and I'd visited frequently and liked the area. Godalming, Farnham, Guildford, and surrounding villages were all possibilities. With my sister Sally's help, I started to house hunt.

I found a house in the village of Bramley, near Guildford. It was perfect, small, cosy with a big garden and within my price range. It only took one visit for me to fall in love with it and put in an offer. Then I returned to Holland. I stayed in Holland for several more months while the house purchase went through. I also wanted to give my husband one last chance to come back to me.

Having bought a house, I felt stronger. I didn't spend all my time in despair mopping up tears and waiting for him. I played badminton, swam, and played tennis with expatriate girlfriends. They were a tremendous support. Updates on my husband and his girlfriend's bizarre behaviour fascinated them. I recounted the content of the numerous emails she sent me. She wrote telling me how much she and my husband were enjoying life together and how she suited him so much better than I had. She sent photographs of the two of them on the yacht my husband and I had bought when we were planning a future together in Holland. She was no gentle soul.

One day I had a story to tell my friends which was even more bizarre than usual. *The Slag* had phoned me very early one morning while I was still in bed. She'd phoned as she had a complaint. She said, "your husband is behaving like a 2-year-old". I was dumb struck. How could she possibly think it appropriate to phone me to complain about how my husband was behaving? It was certainly nothing to do with me if while living with her he chose to behave like a 2-year-old. Was I supposed to help her out with some kind of explanation? Who knows. It was good to have friends to share her outrageous behaviour with.

I enjoyed the sports I played and the companionship of friends, but I needed to achieve something as well, so I started a photography business. This new venture proved to be my salvation. It gave me a purpose and something to get out of bed for in the morning.

I decided to become a professional photographer and make some real money. My photos were already selling through Tony Stone, the stock agency that had bought Focus, after they'd contacted me in Canada. I found a photo agency in Holland who liked my work and started to submit photos to them as well. I'd also had offers from photo agencies to represent my work as the result of being highly commended in the Wildlife Photographer of the Year competition in the U.K.

My photos had been hung in the Natural History Museum and been spotted by photo stock agencies.

Keeping myself busy helped enormously. My overwhelming feelings of rejection and worthlessness were starting to take a back seat, and my thoughts were no longer constantly dwelling on my plight. Life was becoming more bearable.

Then the police contacted me. They said, "you've got to leave Holland, as you're divorced". The Texan woman had registered with the police telling them she was living with my ex-husband, and we were divorced. I told the police we weren't divorced. But to my surprise I discovered that another woman living with my husband had more rights to stay in Holland than I did.

I pleaded with them saying I needed time in Holland as I hoped my husband would return to me. They generously gave me 6 months to sort my life out. But the summons to the police station had been upsetting and unsettling. I'd also had my wallet stolen with all my credit cards in Amsterdam and was only just managing to cope with the shock.

By then I'd waited 18 months for my husband to recover from the excitement of a new relationship and see the error of his ways. He'd always loved challenge and excitement, and his affair had given him a boost in both. But finally, I'd had enough. I'd been robbed in Amsterdam and interrogated by the police. I no longer wanted to stay in Holland.

I called in the packers and prepared to leave for good. It was the easiest house pack I've ever experienced. I chose small pieces of furniture for my cottage and happily left all the big pieces; they included the very heavy oak table and carved chairs my husband had chosen. It gave me great pleasure to walk away from anything and everything I disliked. For some reason I vacuumed the house before I left. I can't think why. I suppose I didn't want to let myself down.

On my very last day in Holland, when I put the keys to the house through the letter box and got into my car I was pleased to be going home. I had my cosy little house waiting to welcome me and a photography business to fill my time and provide me with an income. I had a future to look forward to.

CHAPTER 11
Home Alone

It was spring of 1997, and I'd arrived in England to start a new life, alone. I was still hurting from my marriage breakup but now with a new home and having left Holland for good it was time to set about reinventing myself. I had a new life to fill, and I could please myself how I did it. Now from morning until night, the day was mine. There was a good chance I would never return to my former life as a Shell wife, so I had to put that behind me where it belonged. I didn't give my husband my address as contact with him never ended well. It was finally time to make a fresh start.

My first task was to create a cosy home for myself in April Cottage. I painted the walls, ordered furniture and had a coal effect fire installed. I also had the window frames and door to the patio replaced. I'd had enough of freezing air rolling down the sloping garden and creeping in around the patio door.

My son, Andrew, and I had spent a very chilly New Year's Eve hiding from draughts. He didn't want to go back to Holland during his Christmas vacation as it held too many sad memories. Instead, we'd stayed together at April Cottage, despite it being only sparsely furnished. On New Year's Eve we sat in the sitting room, on worn borrowed chairs, close to a very smelly gas fire trying to keep warm. Icy air crept into the room through cracks in the ill-fitting patio door, but we managed to brave the conditions and stay up until midnight. At midnight we popped the cork of a bottle of cheap champagne and clinked our glasses to welcome in 1997.

I reminisced with Andrew about New Year's Eve 1996 later and he told me the worst part of the evening was the cheap champagne. That really was a big mistake. If all around, you is uncomfortable the least you can do is to drink good champagne. Anyway, I promised myself there would be no more New Year's Eves like that one. April Cottage would be a cosy home from now on and the champagne would be good.

As soon as my new home felt welcoming, I invited all the greater family to a housewarming party. There were twenty of us. We all fitted in somehow. Family members who couldn't fit into a room stood in the hall or sat on the stairs. It was wonderful to have all the greater family around me. I had shrunk from a size 14 to a size 10 so I didn't take up much space. Weight had dropped off me at half a stone a week when stress levels were at their highest in Holland.

Andrew brought a letter to the party which he'd received from his father's mother, my mother-in-law. He handed it to me to read. It was the most shocking letter I have ever read. It attacked Andrew personally with pages of unpleasant criticism and accused Andrew for not being grateful to his father. She wrote, "you enjoyed the good things your father provided, but now the gravy train has dried up". Andrew was willing for the letter to be passed around so that everyone could read it. They were all shocked and disgusted. I hope sharing the letter with his family helped Andrew to come to terms with its shocking contents. My mother-in-law from hell had struck again and she'd chosen to send the letter just before his finals.

With April Cottage welcoming and snug, my next task was to draw together the shattered pieces that were once a confident Shell wife and create a new person. My self-worth was at rock bottom and without my husband I felt only half a person.

We'd met when we were at school, had known each other for 7 years before we married and been married for 28 years. We'd always done things together and faced life as one. When my husband abandoned me, I felt the togetherness we'd once basked in was split in two; like Siamese twins being separated after a lifetime together. The loss was overwhelming. I was alone, cut adrift from the man I loved and had shared my life with. To compound the loss the only lifestyle I'd known as an adult was swept away, whipped from my grasp like a leaf being caught up by an unexpected gust of wind. All that I was left with was a cavity of nothingness. It takes courage to try to rebuild yourself after being rejected by the man you love and courage to become a whole person again. Somehow, I had to find that courage.

My photography became a life saver and the key to the new me. Each morning, I had work to do so there was no time for grieving. I loved photographing flowers, and they were an easy subject to find. I photographed flowers I grew in the garden and bought bunches of flowers from the florist. The Royal Horticultural Society gardens at Wisley were only a 45-minute drive away so I made frequent visits there. I paid £200 for a permit which permitted me to sell my photos. The gardens were great for photography and visiting made a good day out. I'd stop for coffee at 11 a.m. and for a sandwich at lunch time. It gave me a reason to leave the house, and it was good to have people to chat to.

I could at last present myself as somebody other than an abandoned wife. I'd sit surrounded by all my photographic gear and proudly tell people that I was a photographer. I was becoming a proper person with a profession.

The magazine *Amateur Gardening* used many of my photos taken at Wisley. As soon as my film was processed, I'd mount my slides and send a selection to the magazine. A month later my photographs of flowers would fill the pages of *Amateur Gardening*. My photographs were used on the front cover of *Amateur Gardening* 53 times. The money rolled in.

I began to look for social activities so that I could start to meet people. I joined a choir, a camera club and an amateur dramatics society. Some clubs are set up to welcome newcomers. Unfortunately, the choir I joined wasn't one of them. I didn't find the members welcoming and probably left before I'd given them a chance.

The camera club was welcoming at first. Then I started to win competitions, and that upset them. A committee member came to me with a question. "Are you the Rosemary Calvert who writes articles published in the *Practical Photography* magazine?". For a minute I thought I was going to be congratulated, but no, that wasn't what she'd come to say. She spoke sharply to me saying, "You shouldn't be entering photos in the new member's group if you're a professional photographer, you should be in the more experienced photo group. But", she added, "you can't be in the experienced group until you've submitted a portfolio of your photos to the committee, and they've judged them to be of the required standard". Camera clubs are known for their pettiness, and this was a prime example. I duly gave them a portfolio of photos and they were passed by the committee, but I wasn't impressed.

Shortly afterwards the chairman of the club asked if he could nominate me as chairman at the next election. I'd taken on a difficult committee as president of the Calgary Camera Club and enjoyed the challenge, but I didn't feel up to any extra challenges in life right now. I needed to be a whole person first.

I was making progress but hadn't got there quite yet. After a year of attending the camera club meetings, I felt they weren't bringing me any pleasure, so I left.

The amateur dramatics society didn't fare much better. In Borneo I'd taken part in many successful productions put on by the Miri Amateur Dramatics Society, MADS for short, but I found MADS and my local amateur dramatics society operated on different levels.

I was delighted to be given a part in the next production. But my delight rapidly waned when I discovered that the cast didn't stick to their lines; they ad-libbed all the time. This meant that a line which should have been the cue for my next line was composed of other words. In MADS productions the cast would never have got away with not learning their lines. But in my local amateur dramatics club it appeared to be acceptable. I appreciated MADS productions even more when I found I had to make my own costume and help design the scenery. I'd been used to a stage manager in charge of scenery and a team to make the costumes. But it was the lack of correct cues that really finished me. I didn't turn up to the auditions for the next performance. So, it was something of a surprise when the producer of the next production phoned to ask if I would play the lead. I refused. In my fragile state I couldn't leave myself open to more stress.

I certainly didn't get much right at first. A friend introduced me to a Shell wife who had also been dumped by her husband

and was divorced. She had lots of tips about divorce and invited me to join a group of women who were all divorced. She arranged a lunch so that I could meet them which was very kind of her. They were planning a break together in Wales and asked if I'd like to join them.

This turned out to be exactly the wrong thing for me to do. The ex-wives spent most of the time talking about how awful their ex-husbands were and how they were cheated financially in their divorces. It destroyed my optimism and made me unhappy. I didn't stay long as a member of the divorced wives group.

I then made another error. I joined a mixed walking group of singles. The same happened again, except this time it was the men complaining about their ex-wives behaviour and how they'd been cheated in their divorces. I went on two walks and decided to abandon the mixed walking group of singles as well.

In the summer of 1997 Andrew finished his 4-year master's degree in engineering at Durham University and invited me to the degree ceremony. This I attended on my own. it saddened me when I discovered Andrew's father didn't bother to go. After the ceremony I asked Andrew where he would be living when he left university and was surprised when he told me. "With you," he said. I wasn't expecting that. April Cottage wasn't very big, and I'd bought it just for me. Nevertheless, it was wonderful to have Andrew's company for the next 4 years.

Everything Andrew owned was in Durham and somehow it had to be brought down to Surrey. I thought that might be something his father could help with, but I was dreaming. I drove up to Durham in my old Volvo Estate and Andrew filled it with his belongings. The back was stacked to the roof as was the passenger seat. There was no room for Andrew, so he took the train to Guildford. I put more air in the tyres and set off.

One thing that did build my confidence when living on my own was having to do things I'd never done before. It made me realise I was more capable than I thought I was. I was pleased I knew about putting more pressure in the tyres when a car is fully loaded. At the very start of my lone existence in Holland I was impressed with myself when I went to a hardware shop and bought fireproof cement and cemented up a crack in grate behind the fire.

Having Andrew living with me was a great boon. I was no longer alone, and he also did things for me which I would have found difficult. He put up curtain rails, dug a hole in the garden for a pond and fitted a glass fibre liner. I went to Antarctica on a photo trip and when I came home, he'd totally removed a broken greenhouse as a surprise. I was a proud and very grateful mother.

Travel was a luxury I'd been used to in my previous lifestyle and now I had an opportunity to travel again but this time I could choose where I went. I was making good money selling my photographs, so I used my earnings to fund my photo trips. I could claim trips against tax which helped. One year I spent £17,000 on travel which HM Revenue and Customs questioned, but they were legitimate photographic trips backed by receipts, so all was well. They were also suspicious of me spending £12,000 on cameras the same year but I could back that up with receipts as well.

I was happiest when I was preparing to go on a trip and already had plane tickets for the next trip in a drawer. That way I always came home to the excitement of preparing for another trip.

I'd always wanted to visit Antarctica and the opportunity had arrived. I booked a three-week expedition to the Falklands, South Georgia and the Antarctic Peninsula. Next, I needed clothes for the arctic and specialized camera gear. I bought thermal underwear and packed my down jacket and thick ski socks. Camera gear had to be protected from water damage when travelling in a rubber inflatable from the ship to the shore, so I ordered a special waterproof backpack for my camera gear. A photographer friend recommended I bought a neoprene fisherman's suit with fitted integral rubber boots. That was very bulky and increased the weight of my luggage no end. I just hoped I'd find it useful.

I flew to Buenos Aires, then down to Ushuaia, where I boarded the ship. It was a Russian ice hardened ship, Akademik Ioffe, once used for polar research. We left Ushuaia and sailed down the Beagle Channel. It took a day to reach the Falkland Islands where I explored the town of Stanley. I found the inhabitants were comfortable with talking about the Falklands

War and how they had suffered during the invasion. Those living in the Falklands still had a strong connection with the U.K. and visited for holidays using RAF planes for the journey.

After we'd anchored, we climbed onto Zodiacs, rubber inflatable boats, which took us ashore. We made landings in remote parts of the Falklands Islands which couldn't be reached by road. The wildlife was awesome with different species of penguins, fur seals, elephant seals and albatross. The gentle, hilly terrain with grassy slopes and fields was pleasant but not dramatic. Some passengers said it reminded them of the Scottish islands.

After exploring just, a small part of the Falklands we set sail for South Georgia which lies 800 miles east-southeast of the Falkland Islands. When I first caught sight of South Georgia on the horizon it looked like a massive, jagged rock covered with snow emerging from the sea. As we came closer and travelled along the South Georgia coast, we saw mighty snowy peaks and a huge glacier. It was impressive; remote and inhospitable but very beautiful.

We moored off King Edward Cove and used Zodiacs to reach Grytviken. Grytviken was once a centre for the whaling industry which ceased in 1965. When we landed, we found the whaling station was now a mass of tangled rusty corrugated iron with rows of large rusty tanks used at one time to store whale oil.

Further inland was the wooden Whalers' Church, or Grytviken Church, erected by whalers in 1913 after being pre-built in Norway. It was beautifully kept and looked incongruous in a valley full of rusty tangled metal. There was also a museum and shop run by Tim and Pauline Carr. The captain of our ship invited them on board for dinner and I was lucky enough to be chosen to sit on their table.

They'd arrived in South Georgia in 1992 in their engineless 32-foot yacht, Curlew, built in 1905. For many years they lived on Curlew sailing her to other parts of South Georgia to collect artifacts for the South Georgia Museum they created. They'd arrived in South Georgia for a stay of a year and remained for 14 years. Their yacht Curlew is now an exhibit in the National Maritime Museum in Falmouth, Cornwall, after the Carrs donated it to the museum in 2003.

After visiting Grytviken, the Akademik Ioffe made its way north to South Georgia's Salisbury Plain where an unbelievable treat was in store for us. Three miles of glacial outwash backed by snow-covered peaks was packed with 60,000 breeding pairs of king penguins. This mass of penguins standing on the sand was an awe-inspiring sight and it was hard to know how to capture its splendour on camera. We landed the Zodiac and waded ashore. Wellington boots were essential for wet landings, but I'd gone one step further and was wearing my neoprene fisherman's suit with integral boots. This meant I could stay in the sea with the penguins to take photographs. I find animal behaviour fascinating and dressed in my fisherman's suit I could stand in the water with the penguins observing and photographing them.

There was another treat in store for me on Prion Island. Wandering Albatross nest on the ground and although visitors to Antarctica aren't permitted to approach wildlife on shore at a distance of less than 5 metres Wandering Albatross are so big they are easy to observe at that distance. It gave me a supreme sense of privilege at being able to be so close. The birds seemed undisturbed by my presence, and I was lucky enough to have the opportunity to see them stretching their beautiful wings. They have the largest wingspan in the bird kingdom at 11 ½ ft wing tip to wing tip. The number of nesting pairs have sadly diminished but at that time there were 170 nesting pairs on Prion Island.

From South Georgia we set off on the long passage to the Antarctica Peninsula. This should have taken two days, but it took four. A storm raged in the Southern Ocean. It's the most powerful body of water on the planet as the ocean stretches around the globe uninterrupted by land. This allows high winds and strong currents to build up. With a storm raging the ship was struggling to make progress.

The Akademik Ioffe had an open bridge policy, and I made my way to the bridge to experience the storm. The towering waves sent spray crashing onto the bridge windows and the wind screen wipers were in constant use. During the 4-day long passage I made frequent visits to the bridge to observe the ship's headway through the most dramatic seas I've ever been exposed to.

We finally reached the west coast of the Antarctic Peninsular and calmer waters. I went on deck when it was deserted. It was wonderful to stand alone surrounded by icebergs and snowy mountains and let the feeling of isolation and remoteness soak into me. It was like being on another planet, not connected to the world I live in.

At sunrise we sailed through the narrow Gerlache Strait with dramatic snowy peaks and glaciers close to the ship on both sides. Everyone was on deck and there was a great clicking of camera shutters during the passage.

There were only 96 passengers on the Akademik Ioffe. This had advantages as each ship anchoring in Antarctica was allotted a limited period of time when their passengers could be on shore at each anchorage. No more than 100 passengers were allowed to land at one time so if there were 200 passengers each passenger had half the time on shore. With only 96 passengers we had plenty of time to enjoy, observe and photograph the wildlife. I used every available minute and loved my time on shore with the wildlife.

I used to wander away from the other passengers so that I could be alone with the wildlife. I didn't think this put me at risk but while photographing fur seals I had a frightening experience. Three seals approached me from different directions and closed in on me trapping me so that I couldn't escape. My heart began to race. Fur seals have a reputation for being aggressive and giving a nasty bite when angered and I was scared. It looked to me as if they were coming in for the kill. I upended my tripod and holding it out like a weapon I lunged towards each seal in turn. A gap between them opened and I hurriedly escaped through it, but my heart didn't stop thumping for a while. I've never felt comfortable being anywhere near fur seals ever since.

The ship made its way further south and dropped anchor in a bay. The itinerary had to be flexible as the captain never knew where it would be calm enough to get ashore. This beautiful bay was close to a gentoo penguin colony. Unfortunately, the colony was at the top of a snowy cliff. I struggled up the cliff carrying my heavy camera gear and made myself at home sitting in the snow behind my tripod. I sat there and observed nesting gentoo penguins for 2 hours. They were building their nests out of small rocks and if a nest was left unguarded, an opportunistic penguin would deftly steal a rock and take it to its own nest. It was fascinating to watch.

I struggled up many a snowy cliff to reach penguin colonies carrying my heavy camera gear until I struck a deal with the ship's doctor. One day he brought his camera to me as it wasn't working. I couldn't fix it, so he was cameraless. He suggested a deal. If he carried my equipment, which included a heavy tripod and massive 500mm lens, up the snowy slopes would I send him copies of the photographs I took. It was a fantastic offer. My climbs were made easier, and he was delighted with the photos I sent him. What a perfect deal it turned out to be for both of us.

I wasn't short of challenges, but the crew offered us an extra challenge; that of sleeping for a night in the open on the peninsular. Most of us agreed to take part as we didn't want to appear weak. Couples were supplied with a tent, but single people were only given an arctic sleeping bag. A portable loo was erected but we were told not to use it unless we had to. All waste would have to be carried back to the ship in the morning, so the crew were anxious for there to be as little as possible.

The Zodiacs took us to the shore before dark and each of us chose a spot to place our sleeping bags for the night. The sleeping bags had hoods so we could cover ourselves completely, but I was concerned that I'd feel cold during the night, so I made myself snug in my North Face down jacket. A writer for the Times, who was camping next to me, said "you won't feel the benefit of your sleeping bag if you wear that jacket". I thought she was some kind of authority as she was a writer for the Times so took it off. I soon put it back on again.

I woke up in the night and needed the loo. But I had to consider if it was worth getting out of my cosy sleeping bag to use the restricted facilities. As all the sleeping bags looked the same, I worried that I might not be able to find my sleeping bag when I returned. I decided to go anyway and if I couldn't find my sleeping bag, I'd creep into one of the couple's tents.

It was pitch dark, but I had a torch and was able to memorise markers on the way to the loo. I found my way back safely, but I'd taken a risk. If I hadn't found my sleeping bag or a couple prepared to keep me warm, I could well have frozen to death.

At first light I was snug in my sleeping bag wearing my North Face down jacket when I noticed the woman who wrote for the Times pacing around trying to warm up. She wasn't alone. It had been a tough night for many of the campers. Their plight was made worse by a long wait for the Zodiacs to take us back to the warmth of the ship. The sea had frozen during the night and the Zodiacs had to laboriously cut their way through the ice using their propellers as ice breakers to reach us. I was very grateful for my North Face down jacket.

Eventually the Akademik Ioffe turned round and headed north towards Ushuaia. We called in at Deception Island, an active volcano in the South Shetland Islands, and anchored in the caldera. When I went ashore, I took my swimsuit with me. Hot springs seep out of the black sands and run into the sea. This warms the sea up a little, but not enough. I dug a hole in the sand mixing the water from the hot springs, too hot to tolerate, with the seawater which was icy cold. I wouldn't say I had a swim, but I did have a very pleasant warm dip with snow on the ground around me.

The same day we set sail to cross Drake's Passage which is well known for its rough seas. Two bodies of water meet, cold from the south and warm from the north, which results in powerful eddies. Coupled with high winds this makes Drake's Passage one of Earth's roughest waterways. I felt sick, very sick. I took to my bunk, medicated with Stugeron, and there I stayed. The 48-hour crossing seemed to take forever but we finally reached the calm waters of the Beagle Channel and were soon docking in Ushuaia.

My first trip to Antarctica on Akademik Ioffe had far exceeded my expectations. I was travelling alone, but at no time did I feel lonely. We queued for our meals, and it didn't matter who I was standing next to in the queue, people were both friendly and interesting to talk to. It seemed that anyone interested in taking a trip to Antarctica was no normal tourist.

The company that organized the trip invited me to go on another trip to the Antarctic in March, the following year. The trip would be free and all I had to do was to help passengers with their photography and give presentations. It was a surprise and a wonderful gift from the trip organizers. Canon contacted me and lent me a professional digital camera so that I'd have immediate access to my photos during the trip for presentations.

I was lucky in so many ways as not only was my trip free and I'd been lent a digital camera, but I was given an upgraded single cabin, far more luxurious than the cabin on my first trip which I'd shared.

I'd first visited Antarctica in January, when the penguins were raising their chicks in their colonies. But by March with the breeding period over most of the penguins had left for the ocean to fish. It was only the moulting penguins that remained, and they were a sad sight standing like statues only clad in a thin layer of feathers. Moulting penguins stay in a sheltered position fasting during the 2-4 weeks it takes for them to lose and replace their feathers. During this process they are no longer waterproof so unable to enter the water.

The March trip turned out to be a whale watching trip. We went out in the Zodiacs and found there were hump backed whales all around us. They swam under the Zodiacs, shot out of the water spy-hopping, and provided the classic shot of a tail flip, or fluke, with water dripping from their tail fin. The driver of my Zodiac spotted a minke whale. We stayed with it for some time and watched it swimming around the boat. We felt very privileged to have its company and be able to observe it closely. The March trip was enjoyable and turned out to be altogether different from the January trip.

Travel and my photography business took over a large part of my life. I'd settled to a happy existence with thoughts of my husband only lurking harmlessly in the background. I was alone but I wasn't lonely.

I joined a tennis club and although this wasn't a great success it meant I met an acquaintance from my time in Borneo who was living close by. She organized a small walking group of friends who hiked 5 to 6 mile in the Surrey countryside every Wednesday morning, finishing with a pub lunch. She invited me to join the group. I loved the walks and made new friends. Joining the walking group turned out to be a gift and one of the most valuable things that happened to me during my 10 years in Bramley. We walked in the pouring rain and searing heat; the weather never detracted from my enjoyment. It was good to be outdoors with friends and surrounded by the natural environment. We came across wildlife, too.

One Wednesday we were walking past Loseley Lake, near Guildford, when I saw two Canada geese badly entwined in barbed wire at the water's edge. I was able to reach them easily and as I came close, they seemed undisturbed by my presence. I gently removed the barbed wire trapping one goose, and it swam off unhurt. Then I carefully set the second one free. It was a moving experience. They were so calm as I freed them and the trust, they showed in me made me feel emotional. It's a feeling I often get when I'm close to wildlife and sense their trust in me.

Jenny, the organiser of the walking group, had only been an acquaintance in Borneo, but she soon became a close friend. She was the most talented and beautiful person. She would make herself available to help anyone. When I was struggling emotionally with my divorce, she was there for me. Tragically Jenny collapsed and died from sudden cardiac arrest during a walk 12 years later. Losing Jenny was a terrible loss then, and still is to this day. She had been such a wonderful friend and a companion for extra walks at the weekends. She was good company, and I loved to chat with her over a coffee. She left me with great sadness. But she also left me with happy memories of our special friendship. Why is it that death claims the very best people when they're giving so much to others?

Very close friends are precious and rare. I had, and still have, a close friend, Liz. who I met in Holland in the Victorian theatre with a leaking roof. We became firm friends in 1970, and both our husbands dumped us at about the same time. She was a great comfort to me, and I hope I was to her.

She was living in Cheshire when my marriage broke up, but she got on a plane and flew to Holland to cheer me up. We always had fun together, even when we felt sad inside. When I returned to England, Liz would drive down to April Cottage bringing a bottle of champagne with her. I'd have a bottle of champagne chilling in the fridge, and we'd drink both bottles the first evening we were together. We went on holiday and had some marvellous times in Devon eating smoked salmon and strawberries on cliff walks. We'd wash our picnic down with a gin and tonic then take a nap in the long grass. Being together made us both happy.

We had holidays in Africa, Iceland and Antigua. The African safari was a great success. Our first night was in Victoria Falls Hotel which we'd chosen for its elegant Colonial Style. It made a great start to the holiday. There were views of Victoria Falls from the hotel's extensive green lawns and the flowers in the grounds, which were watered every morning, were glorious.

In Botswana we slept in a tree house which we reached by ladder and each morning one of the staff would bang a drum at the foot of the tree to announce breakfast. It was so different and exciting.

We were driven in a Land Rover to Chobe Lodge and taken to our room We were told that everything in the room fridge was free, but we'd have to pay for drinks at the bar. We opened the fridge to find it filled with bottles of wine and a bottle of champagne. As we're both fond of champagne we drank the champagne immediately. Shortly afterwards the cleaner came into the room, checked the fridge, found the champagne missing and added another bottle.

We stayed at Chobe Safari Lodge for 2 nights and each evening took the free cruise on the Chobe River. My great delight was to watch the herds of elephants coming down to the river to drink. One evening a baby elephant stumbled on its way down the sandy slope to the water's edge. Its mother gently put her trunk under it and lifted it back onto its feet. I was enchanted. I fell in love with elephants and bought a very large book full of elephant pictures. I struggled to fit it into my suitcase when I packed to go home but it did make it back to April Cottage.

While holidaying in Antigua we enjoyed all the delights that a Caribbean holiday offers, except for the one night when we went into St Johns to attend a concert. We sat down in a vast arena with tiered seats. The concert began with loud, almost deafening music, and then an argument started a few seats away from us. The argument turned into a fierce fight. We were terrified and fled the arena. We scoured the streets for a taxi, with fear in our hearts, but couldn't find one. A policewoman found us and scolded us for being out alone on the streets of St Johns late at night. She called a taxi to take us back to our hotel and we didn't venture out again.

Friends played an important part in my life while I was recovering from my marriage breakup. Close friends, Anne, and Chris had moved from Holland to Perth, Australia and they showed support by inviting me to stay with them for three weeks. They gave me a brilliant holiday and took me on wonderful trips. They made me feel very welcome and I felt comfortable with them in their home. Their support was an important part of my recovery.

While I was staying with them, I flew to Uluru from Perth on my own. Clearly visible below the plane was a red sandstone desert with a dirt road running through the red rocks and across the sand. For much of our 2 ½ hour flight the plane seemed to follow the road. I was fascinated by the remoteness of the road and tried to imagine what it would be like to be driving for hours through inhospitable terrain miles from civilization. I'd rather have been driving on that road than in the aeroplane—it looked so enticing.

As the plane approached Uluru it flew low over the Olgas and then Uluru came into sight. There it was a block of red sandstone rising from the flat semi desert. I was at last seeing a feature of the globe I'd only learnt about in geography lessons. It was a glorious moment.

The next day before breakfast I took a coach trip from the hotel to see the famed spectacle of Uluru glowing red at sunrise. A group of Japanese tourists were already there sitting in a row. They'd brought folding seats with them and a small cardboard box each containing their breakfast. We all waited for the sun to rise but it didn't, or rather we didn't see it. A layer of cloud hung along the horizon blocking it from view. Eventually we all packed up and went back to our hotels disappointed.

In the heat at midday, like a fool, I decided to go for a walk. I wanted to explore. I met some camels which surprised me, but I also met a lot of flies. As I walked, they crawled into my ears, eyes, mouth and up my nose looking for moisture. It was horrible. I wished I'd been wearing the mosquito net I used in Canada. It would have been perfect. It was an interesting experience, although dangerously hot, and an unwise thing to do.

After I arrived back in Perth Anne and Chris took me on an exciting trip to Pinnacle Desert, north of Perth. It was fun driving along the beach in their 4×4 vehicle for part of the journey. We stayed in a hotel and Chris offered to get up before dawn and take me to photograph the extraordinary yellow sandstone pinnacles at sunrise. Chris and Anne also took me south to the wine growing region of St Margaret's. They were such good friends and really put themselves out for me. Trust, love and support from good friends when needed is invaluable.

Having Andrew living with me brought normality to my life which I appreciated. I cooked supper every evening instead of living on current buns, my staple diet during my time in Holland. I ironed his shirts and had someone to care for. We took trips to London to the theatre and ballet, but best of all we went on holiday together.

Andrew and I had a fascinating trip to Egypt. We went to a sound and light show at Karnak Temple in Luxor which was awe-inspiring. It was a surreal experience to watch the light playing on the ruins.

Another highlight was a hot air balloon ride. We started very early in the morning and had breakfast as we crossed the river Nile by boat. When we arrived at the launch site the balloon was already inflated and waiting for us to climb into the basket. We drifted over the Valley of the Kings and the temples below were pointed out to us as we travelled. Our landing was gentle, and we were taken to a table already laid for lunch in the shade of a group of trees. The trip was brilliantly organized. Andrew and I felt lucky to have the opportunity to take such an incredible hot air balloon flight.

We enjoyed a week's cruise down the river Nile and a flight to Abul Simbel. We explored numerous temples and visited the Tomb of Tutankhamun. The whole experience was astonishing.

Later during the trip, I photographed Tutankhamun's death mask in the Egyptian Museum in Cairo. My photo is still available for use on the Getty Images website today and sells almost every month.

Andrew and I flew to China and followed the tourist route visiting the Great Wall, Terracotta Army at Xi'an, Forbidden City in Beijing and cruised up the River Li to Guilin. It was wonderful to see all the sights I had only heard about and longed to see. How very fortunate we both were.

Our flight home was from Shanghai. We arrived at our hotel after dark. The hotel was at a high elevation and across the road there was a phenomenal view of the skyline of downtown Shanghai lit up in all its glory. It was 10p.m. when we crossed the road and with my camera on a tripod, I started to capture the scene. As it was late I suggested to Andrew he might like to go back to the hotel while I took photos. He firmly refused to leave me saying, "I'm staying right here with you". I'd experienced my eldest son, Alexander, protecting me when his father was leaving us and now Andrew, my youngest son, was doing the same. It's heartening to know that my sons have become my protectors, and our roles have been reversed.

By the start of the year 2000 I had reinvented myself and was an established professional photographer with a good income from my photography, but I was still vulnerable.

On New Year's Eve I welcomed in a new century with my greater family by letting off fireworks on Lee-on-the-Solent beach at midnight. Afterwards we all found floor space to sleep at my youngest sister's house; I slept under the dining room table.

I woke up early the next morning, surrounded by my greater family, but with a feeling of terrible emptiness. The idea of starting a new century on my own distressed me and I retreated to my car to cry. I was missed and two of my sisters came to find me. They climbed into my car and tried to comfort me, but nobody can really comfort you if you feel you have no one of your own to share your life with. All the same it was good to know my sisters were there for me and loved me. Having friends and family as I struggled to recover was invaluable and went a long way towards me being able to face the year 2000. I told myself I had to get on with the new life I'd created and discover ways myself to fill my feeling of emptiness.

In that year my father died. He was 87 so a good age but his death made me desperately sad. I didn't see him for 2 years after he left my mother but eventually my strong bond with him was renewed. He moved to Exmouth with his new wife, Janet, and we always stayed with them during our home leaves. One year Janet offered to look after our young sons Alexander and Andrew for 2 weeks while we went skiing. She had a good heart, and I was grateful to her.

In September 2001 I travelled from the U.K. to Alaska for an organized photo safari in Katmai National Park to photograph grizzly bears catching salmon. I flew from Anchorage to Katmai in a floatplane, it was a thrilling experience when the plane touched down on water instead of land.

We stayed in cabins and photographed grizzly bears fishing for salmon in the river. Our photography was done from a secure raised platform with a gate to protect us from curious bears. But to reach the platform we had to walk for some distance along a path beside the river. We were told to bang the legs of our tripods together as we walked to alert the grizzly bears of our presence as surprising a grizzly bear can provoke an attack.

One morning we were walking along the narrow path beside the river when we saw two grizzly bears charging towards us, one chasing the other. The leader of our group told us to roll down the bank out of harm's way. I thought it was an opportunity to have a closer look at grizzly bears, so stayed where I was. The bears thundered passed me and were so close I could have touched them. I could see the moisture condensed on fur around their mouths caused by their hot breath. It was wonderful.

But I didn't bask in my privileged experience for long. The leader severely reprimanded me for putting both our lives at risk. He said he had to put himself at risk by staying with me, rather than seeking safety. This surprised me as I always thought I was responsible for my own safety. I hadn't intended to put the leader at risk. I'd just thought that if the grizzly bears were chasing each other, they were unlikely to stop and attack me.

The next morning when I opened the cabin door a grizzly bear was standing on the door mat. This time I felt less curious and shut the door quickly.

We flew back to Anchorage and everyone in the group except the safari organizer and me, took planes home to the U.S. that evening. I had to wait until the next day for my plane to the U.K. The following morning as I walked down the corridor towards the dining room for breakfast, I could see everyone was standing and looking in the same direction in total silence. It gave me a feeling of unease. When I reached the dining room, I found they were all looking at the TV. It was September 11th. A plane had flown into one twin tower of the World Trade Centre in New York and as we watched another plane flew into the other tower. We were all aghast.

I had witnessed a tragedy unfolding and felt very shocked. Then I realised how this devastating terrorist attack was going to affect me as all planes in the U.S.A. were grounded. I asked the trip organizer what I should do. He told me the photo safari was over so what I did was my responsibility.

The hotel I was staying in was full, so I couldn't book for more nights there. Other hotels in Anchorage were also full, partly as passengers who had arrived on cruise liners were unable to fly home so they were filling up the hotels. There was absolutely nowhere for me to stay in Anchorage. The only option left to me was to hire a car and drive out of the city to try to find somewhere to stay. It was a situation I was totally unprepared for. I hired a car and drove towards the town of Homer on the tip of the peninsular. I was deeply unhappy and uncomfortable with the situation. I stopped each night at a hotel but when I switched on the TV all that seemed to be showing was the twin towers collapsing. This video clip was far too distressing to watch over and over again, so I stopped switching on the TV.

I came across a hotel my husband and I had stayed in 6 years earlier during our disastrous trip to Alaska when we left Houston after his affair. To help secure a room for the night I mentioned that I'd stayed in the hotel previously with my husband. They kindly looked up their records and gave me the same room we'd stayed in, the very room I really didn't want.

I reached Homer at the tip of the peninsular and stayed the night. Then I made my way back to Anchorage checking every evening with the airlines to see when I could fly home. International flights were resumed on 14th September, three days after the attack, but there were no seats available when I checked each evening. One night I stopped at a remote log cabin and booked a room. I asked reception if I could use their phone to contact the airlines. This request surprised them as they had no phone connection.

When I checked with the airline a week after I'd left Anchorage, I was told I would have to wait another week. I couldn't hold back the tears and sobbing into the phone explained I was alone in Alaska and needed to go home. They took pity on me and suggested I came to the airport and queued for a seat. Eventually I manage to get on a plane to London. It was such a relief.

Being stranded in Alaska with no accommodation was unexpected and it's at times like this that I turn to my maxim, "it's not what happens to you but what you do about it that matters". Sometimes it takes enormous courage to do anything at all but fortunately most of us manage to find courage from somewhere when it's needed.

One evening son Andrew handed me a large pink envelope he'd found under one of the windscreen wipers on my car parked outside the house. On the envelope was my name but it was written in my husband's handwriting. I was surprised and shocked. I hadn't given my husband my address, but he had somehow found me. Inside the envelope was a Valentine's card and inside the card was written, "I love you and need to see you? Please contact me"

I'd established a home, a lifestyle and had gone a long way towards reinventing myself. Now it seemed my husband had decided he wanted me back. I wasn't entirely sure how I felt about that. A lot had happened in the seven years since he'd first told me he was leaving me. I still loved him but was there a way back to living happily together after everything that had happened? Nevertheless I decided I should see him and take it from there.

He arrived at April Cottage in the dark green Firebird I'd driven while we were living in Houston. He told me he'd finished with his mistress and sent her home. He'd realised it was me he loved. We hugged, then sat on the sofa, kissed and cuddled. It felt good. I gave him back his wedding ring which I'd asked if I could keep as a keep's sake. It was precious to me and had my name written on the inside. We were going to have a life together again; it was hard to believe.

My husband wanted to take me to Devon for a camping holiday and he'd brought a tent with him. I thought a night in a hotel first might give us a chance to talk in comfort, so I booked a room in a delightful hotel in Devon where I'd once stayed with my friend Liz.

As we drove down to Devon it was like old times sitting beside my husband in the Firebird and I felt happy. We had dinner in the hotel and things continued to go well. I felt optimistic about our future together. We snuggled down in our king-sized double bed. It was wonderful. Love and contentment claimed me as I fell asleep in his arms.

To my surprise in the middle of the night my husband suddenly sat bolt upright and said, "she loves me". Rather odd behaviour but I was happy that he'd realised halfway through the night how much I loved him. So, imagine my despair when I discovered it wasn't my love for him he was talking about; it was his girlfriend's love for him. I couldn't get back to sleep after such a devastating announcement and after tossing restlessly got up and made a bed for myself in the bath. How could I lie beside my husband when he was thinking about his girlfriend? The chance of healing our relationship and moving forward in life together was rapidly evaporating.

In the morning, we left the hotel to pitch our tent in a campsite. I was expecting an apology and lots of talk about how he regretted his actions and how he had always loved me, but nothing was forthcoming. His declaration in the middle of the night that his girlfriend loved him showed me that his heart and mind were not set on repairing our marriage. I began to lose faith in there being any future for us together and in my heart the feeling grew that the revival of our love was doomed; our marriage had been damaged beyond repair. I abandoned all my hopes of a happy future with my husband and asked him to take me home.

He dropped me off at April Cottage and as he left, he said "I've ruined our marriage. I've made my bed, so I'll have to lie in it". Recalling his words now makes me feel so sad and brings tears to my eyes. I will never understand why he kept coming back to me only to leave again. I was desolate when he left this time as I knew our marriage was finally over. I'm not sure there was a way I could have saved it. Could I have acted differently? I don't know, and I never will know. I did the best I could and that was all I could do.

Fortunately, this time I had a lifestyle to return to. I resolved to get on with my life. I booked a trip to New Zealand.

I'd never visited New Zealand before and the prospect of three weeks driving around the perimeter of South Island in a bus with 12 other passengers sounded exciting.

Before I left, I had my ears pierced. My mother was against pierced ears, so I hadn't had mine done and neither had any of my four sisters. With my newly pierced ears I set off for New Zealand. This gave the New Zealand trip an extra twist of excitement as every time the coach stopped for a coffee I shot off into the nearest jewellers and bought myself some earrings. I amassed quite a collection.

I shared a room with a 35-year-old woman who was a Buddhist. She was wonderfully easy about everything, and I enjoyed sharing with her. The others on the trip were mostly young single women and I very much felt part of this young group of females, although I was 56.

One evening we were sitting on the balcony of a bar having fun when one of the young women in the group said to me "You fit in very well considering how much older you are than us". I'm sure the remark was well meant but I didn't want to just fit in, I'd thought I was one of them. Her remark made me feel old.

As we drove into Queenstown a list of activities we could do while we were there was passed to everyone in the bus. We could choose three activities. I scanned through the list but didn't see a single thing I fancied. Sky diving, bungy jumping, tandem paragliding, whitewater rafting, Shotover Jet river extreme boat ride and horse riding were on list, plus a few more challenging activities. I looked for the tamest activities and settled for an extreme jet boat ride, whitewater rafting and horse riding.

The extreme jet boat ride was scary and not really my thing. I was glad when it was over. The whitewater rafting trip was fine until the oarsman thought it would be fun to turn the boat over and tip us all in the river. I didn't appreciate his idea of fun. I just thought it was dangerous and irresponsible. Then came the horse riding. I wasn't worried about that.

When we were all astride our horses we were divided into two groups. A group of Japanese tourists were put in one group as they'd never ridden a horse before. I opted to join the more advanced group. We set off. The countryside was magnificent, and I was having a wonderful time until we were told to canter. I'd never mastered cantering, so I just hung on to my horse and prayed we'd be told to stop soon. But cantering seemed to be the fun thing to do so we were asked to canter time and time again. It was an exhausting couple of hours.

Back at the ranch when I'd dismounted my rather lively horse the organizer asked how I'd found him. I didn't want to admit to my inadequacies, so I said the horse was fine. "Good" said the organiser, "we wondered how you'd get on as your horse is new to the stables. He was a racehorse". That explained a lot.

One of the highlights of my New Zealand visit was a trip to Stewart Island on a fast catamaran. The plan was to look for kiwi birds in the woods at night, but we didn't see any. What I did find fascinating was talking to people who had chosen to live on an isolated island, with a population of 406, cut off from the mainland during much of the winter. They were larger than life characters escaping from something. The young woman who ran the cafe had been there for years and had no plan to leave. She loved the remote, solitary life she could lead on Stewart Island.

There was a paua shellfish farm with pauas kept in tanks to produce pearls. Paua is the New Zealand name for what we call ormers in the U.K., in the U.S. they are known as abalones. The pearls are large, highly coloured, and more like opals. They're exported all over the world and fetch a high price. They were stunning and I didn't have to think twice before treating myself to a pair of paua earrings.

I had a wonderful 3 weeks in New Zealand and felt that if I'd met someone, I wanted to be with, I would have been happy to spend the rest of my life there. It's a beautiful country, welcoming and with a strong flavour of Britain.

After my husband returned to Holland, from our hopeless camping trip, he'd applied to Shell for a posting to Houston, so that he could be with his girlfriend. His request was granted. As he was leaving Holland, possibly for good, he needed to sell our house in Holland, but as he'd put it in both our names he couldn't. He thought the easiest solution was to send legal papers to me to sign granting him sole ownership of the house.

He told me it hadn't increased in price, so there'd be nothing in it for me. I had heard differently. I phoned the neighbour in Holland and made enquiries. She told me house prices in Holland had rocketed, particularly those in Wassenaar.

The time to divorce him had come. I took my marriage certificate to a solicitor and passed it to him over the desk saying, "I love my husband, but I want to divorce him". There followed two of the most trying years of my life. My husband failed to declare all his assets and I spent my life trying to think like a lawyer to make sure the settlement was fair.

My husband's Shell pension formed a large part of his assets, unfortunately all except for t 5 years of his pension was held in Bermuda where Shell invested international staff pension funds. In a U.K. divorce a wife is entitled to half the pension, but in Bermuda law there is no agreement for a pension split so I couldn't be awarded any of it.

Eventually the lawyers awarded the proceeds from the house sale to me, and my husband retained his Bermuda pension. I was relieved I'd investigated the value of the house and not signed over sole ownership to my husband. In the end having my wits about me and battling for justice made an important difference to the settlement.

There was an amusing side to the divorce. While the divorce settlement was in progress, I received information from my solicitor by text. My text machine was part of my phone and produced reams of paper resembling loo roll. One day I came home to find a cloud of paper covering the text machine. I straightened it out and laid it down the length of the hall in April Cottage, it must have been 12 feet long. It reached from the loo door to the front door. It looked so bizarre I just stood there and laughed. I'm so glad I have a sense of humour and can see the funny side even when I'm feeling desperate.

Our divorce went to court. My lawyers had suggested a 60/40 split in favour of my husband but he had turned it down. Late on the evening of the day before the final hearing my lawyer contacted me. My husband had told his lawyers he was prepared to accept the 60/40 settlement they had suggested. We still had to go to court the next day anyway, but I was glad as I would be able to see my husband for one last time. I knew it could be the very last time in my life that I would see him.

The judge questioned the fairness of the split. He couldn't see why the split wasn't 50/50. However, I was happy with the settlement as I felt through hard work my husband had done well in his career, and he deserved a bigger share. I've never questioned the wisdom of my decision.

I didn't take my eyes of my husband's face throughout the hearing. I was absorbing every tiny detail to cherish for the rest of my life.

It was 2003 and I was divorced. With my divorce settlement I bought a house in Guildford which I let to provide an income. I was at last free to lead life as I pleased. I had a home, a business and an income and I intended to make the best of my freedom and independence. I'd reinvented myself as a professional photographer and finally I'd built myself back into a whole person. What I needed now was to spread my wings and take another photo trip.

I flew to Svalbard, also known as Spitzbergen. It was the second time I'd been there, and I was getting to know the town of Longyearbyen quite well. We sailed from Longyearbyen heading west towards Greenland on a ship with only 30 passengers. It was September and the Greenland Sea was partially frozen. When the sun set it turned the ice pink and with the blue water and shadows created a glorious patchwork of colour.

We visited Ittoqqortoormiit, a small settlement, one of the remotest villages on the east coast of Greenland. The wooden houses, painted in bright colours, were linked by dirt roads and the small church had a simple yet beautiful interior.

We sailed into Scoresby Sund, the world's largest fjord, passing the most stunning icebergs. Then suddenly we were plunged into thick fog, and everything disappeared, giving us time to grab a much-needed quick cup of coffee. The ship gradually emerged from the fog, and I continued to take photos. The sight of massive icebergs looming out of the fog was spectacular. It was a fantastic trip and helped to heal me after my divorce.

I loved my visits to the arctic but for me it didn't claim my affections as much as the Antarctic. Antarctica was special.

I think, because it was a natural environment and home to wildlife, not human beings, apart from those living in the research stations.

I travelled widely during the years I lived in April Cottage. Andrew was with me for the first four years and then when he was offered a job in London, he bought a flat in Putney and moved out. But I didn't go back to living on currant buns as I had in Holland. Instead, I lived on fish and broccoli. I cooked two trout in the oven, ate one and warmed the other one up in the microwave the next day. I seemed totally incapable of cooking a proper meal for myself. It just seemed a waste of time.

Some of my trips didn't fulfil my dreams and sadly my trip to Namibia with the Royal Photographic Society was one of them. I love observing and photographing wildlife, but Namibia was arid with little wildlife compared to the abundant wildlife I'd seen in Zimbabwe and Botswana. On the Namibian trip we were taken to photograph a diamond mining settlement of derelict houses full of deep drifts of sand. They looked dramatic and I photographed them, but the photography didn't satisfy me. However, despite my lack of enthusiasm for ruined houses full of sand the photographs I took continue to sell on the Getty Images website to this day.

When I signed up to go on the trip to Namibia it was partly to see the massive red sand dunes in Naukluft Park, near Sesriem and this part of the trip was everything I'd hoped for.

The giant sand dunes were spectacular. I photographed one with a leafless tree dwarfed at the foot of the dune giving it scale, and the photograph has sold well.

When we returned, I was nominated for a prestigious position with the Royal Photographic Society. I was asked to join a panel to judge the Fellowship awards in the travel section. I felt honoured. I continued to judge fellowships for the next 4 years.

I returned to Greenland for another visit. This time I left by ship from the east coast of Canada and visited Disco Bay on the west coast of Greenland. The ship moored off Ilulisatt and we visited the enchanting wooden Zion's Church, built originally in 1782. It was moved further inland and enlarged in 1929. The wooden houses in Ilulisat are painted bright colours making the town picturesque. We were taken out into the icefjord in a Zodiac and circled the most spectacular iceberg resembling an ice sculpture of a cathedral. It had arches and columns and looked breath-takingly beautiful. The iceberg had broken off the Sermeq Kujalleq glacier, also called Jakobshavn glacier, which is thought to have produced the iceberg which sunk the Titanic.

My third visit to Antarctica in late November 2004 turned out to be beyond my wildest dreams. It provided me with one treat after another. I joined a group of photographers to spend a month on a Russian icebreaker visiting emperor penguin colonies.

We needed to fly to the Falklands to board the icebreaker, but there are no flights from Argentina for political reasons, so I flew from London to Santiago in Chile and from there to the Falklands. From Santiago the plane flew south following the Andes mountains to Punta Arenus. The view of the Andes from the plane was magnificent and offered a wonderful opportunity to see the fabulous mountain range from the air.

In Punta Arenas the internal flight became an international flight to the Falklands. This meant we all had to get off the plane, with our cabin luggage, collect our hold luggage, pass through customs, have our passports stamped and then get back on the plane and sit in the same seats!

The icebreaker sailed from the Falkland Islands to South Georgia, which took 48 hours, and we dropped anchor off Grytviken. It looked very different from the first time I'd visited. All the tangled rusty metal had gone. The derelict whaling settlement had been transformed. It had become a beautifully organized and well-kept open-air museum. On the beach were two whaling boats which looked as if they had just beached after being at sea, whaling.

We sailed north to Salisbury Plain and I was impressed for a second time by the tens of thousands of king penguins on the glacial outwash. We then sailed south to the South Orkney Islands which I hadn't visited before. The only inhabitants on the South Orkney Islands were Adele penguins. I found them fascinating to watch as their attitude to each other and body language looked almost human. The islands emanated a strong feeling of remoteness. I felt as if I'd arrived on an icy planet inhabited solely by penguins.

The fun started when we entered the Weddel Sea and made our way south towards Halley Research Station, operated by the British Antarctic survey. There were two helicopters on board the ship which took us onto the ice. They landed no closer than a kilometre from an emperor penguin colony, so as not to disturb the penguins. We walked the rest of the way. This is something only the young or fit should attempt. I found it hard going as I was loaded with heavy camera equipment and from time to time my feet would break through the layer of thin ice, and I'd have to lift them out. A Dutch photographer had the perfect solution. He'd packed a collapsible sledge which he loaded with all his equipment and pulled over the ice behind him. He became the envy of all the other heavily laden photographers.

We were required to keep 5 metres away from the penguins, unless they approached us, so once I'd reached the penguin colony, and regained my breath, I set up my tripod and camera and sat in the snow behind my equipment. Penguins are curious creatures, and they'd come to have a good look at me, peck at my lens and rummage in my camera bag. Close-up photographs were easy to come by and often the penguins were too close to photograph. Once again, I felt very privileged to be accepted and trusted by wildlife.

There were many photographic opportunities. Emperor penguin colonies were usually found on flat areas of ice with an ice cliff behind them to give the penguins some protection from the weather. Penguins with their chicks, backed by a beautiful ice cliff, made a great photo. Another photo opportunity was provided by emperor penguins tobogganing down slopes on their stomachs. It was fun just to watch the way they behaved.

From time to time a queue of emperor penguins would build up at right angles to the water's edge. This penguin queueing behaviour was for a reason. Leopard seals often lurked in the water under the ice shelf waiting for a meal. If the penguins in the queue plunge into the water in rapid succession they have a better chance of survival.

I wanted to capture the moment the penguins dived into the water, so I kept my eyes glued on the queue waiting for action. I was amused when I noticed the penguin at the front of the queue decide it would rather not go first and make its way to the back.

One evening the helicopters dropped us for a night of photography. As it was light all night there was always something to see and photograph, but it became increasingly cold. We tried to keep our cameras warm by putting them inside our coats but finally the cold proved too much, and all our camera batteries died. There was no point in staying out in the freezing cold any longer, so we called for the helicopters to collect us.

When the icebreaker reached Halley V Research Station, built on the Brunt Iceshelf, we flew in the helicopters to visit the station. We took with us fresh fruit and vegetables which they were thrilled to receive. In return they served us coffee, with strange biscuits from an elderly looking tin. I felt a bit as if we were eating their precious supplies and couldn't bring myself to have any. To get some idea of what it might be like living in this remote research station for a year at a time I found an empty lounge and sat in it by myself trying to imagine it being my home in the dark winter months. I think I managed to conjure up a little of what it must feel like to be isolated in freezing conditions in almost 24 hours of darkness.

We didn't go further south than Halley but changed direction and made passage west across the Weddell Sea towards Peninsular Antarctica.

The helicopters regularly left the vessel to look for leads, fractures, or gaps, in the pack ice which the icebreaker could use to make passage. If the ship met solid ice the icebreaker would start the ramming process made possible by the ship having a specially shaped bow and an ice hardened hull. Ramming was done with the ship's engines at full speed harnessing the weight of the ship to break the ice. It was carried out a maximum of three times. If on the third attempt a path through the ice didn't open up, then the captain would seek an alternative route. All the passengers were warned when ramming was about to start and most took the opportunity to go on deck to witness the ship's progress as it carried out a rarely seen process.

Once we reached the east coast of the Antarctic Peninsula, we made our way north. We called in at Deception Island, then crossed Drakes Passage to the Beagle Channel and finally docked in Ushuaia.

My month on the icebreaker had given me experiences I couldn't even have dreamed about. We were so lucky to be able to visit 7 emperor penguin colonies. I shared a cabin with a woman who had made the trip before. On her first trip bad weather throughout the trip had prevented passengers from visiting a single emperor penguin colony. On this trip the weather had been kind and we'd seen everything we'd hoped to see.

When I returned home, I not only had endless digital photos to sort through but an internet dating project to continue.

I'd put my details on the internet dating page of the Times and before I left for Antarctica, I'd had a phone call from a man who'd seen them. When I picked the phone up, after he'd explained who he was, he said, "I'm looking for a wife and you sound nice". I admired him for his direct approach, but he didn't sound right for me. Not liking to say I didn't want to see him I used my month-long trip to Antarctica as an excuse not to arrange to meet him. I'd already had dates with 17 different men in the 9 months since I started internet dating, and I'd learnt to choose who I dated with care.

CHAPTER 12
Internet Dating

I'd dated 17 different men so far, but I hadn't felt the desire to have a long-term relationship with any of them. Was I expecting too much? Probably. I didn't have the need for a man, I was fine by myself, and I certainly wasn't looking for a pair of trousers to sit on my sofa while I ironed his shirts. If I found someone, I would have to make enormous changes to my lifestyle. That would only be worthwhile if I found a man who could bring depth to my life, someone I could share my life with and who would change it for the better.

People said I was brave to internet date, but I had few qualms about it. I felt that with a strong strategy it would be safe and could even be fun. When I told my sons I was internet dating they received the news in very different ways.

My younger son was living in Putney when I first started dating. I drove up to London from Bramley to have dinner with him, as I often did. We were walking along the pavement on the way to the restaurant when he casually remarked "you're looking very smart this evening, Mummy". So, he'd noticed the change. Friends had suggested that I needed to smarten up if I was going to find a man. A girlfriend even took me shopping and I was wearing the jacket we'd bought together.

I told my son I'd bought new clothes as I'd started internet dating. He came to an abrupt halt on the pavement. A look of utter horror spread over his face, and he said, "Is that wise?"

My eldest son's reaction was very different. All he said was "You'll get into triple figures before you find anyone". I'd like to think by that he meant I was picky and would be hard to please, not that the first 99 would turn me down.

So why was I internet dating? I was working on my computer one Saturday evening when a pop up suggested I looked at a dating website called *Tickle*. I'd been on my own for 10 years and had a full and satisfying life. But I had time on my hands, so I clicked on the website. Photographs of men started to pop up, I scrolled through what seemed like hundreds of them. I had no idea there were so many men out there looking for a special someone. So why was I sitting at my desk working on a Saturday night not out there enjoying myself? I could join the website and perhaps I'd find someone I liked or could grow to love. To cast a wider net seemed a plan, so I signed up to four dating websites and paid my dues.

First, I needed to find a photo. I chose one of me with windblown hair, in an anorak taken in the arctic with an iceberg as a backdrop. It seemed a sensible choice as it hopefully wouldn't attract anyone with sex in mind on the first date. I filled in the forms and answered numerous searching questions about myself. Then in the want boxes I put over 6 ft, with a degree, nonsmoker, no tattoos, divorced or widowed, reader of the Times and at least £50,000 a year. I didn't want someone I'd have to support financially or was only interested in me for my money. That done I was ready to meet the first applicant. Several times a day I checked the internet to see if anyone was interested.

Internet dating, for me, was not going to be simply a process of dating random strangers, but a series of serious job interviews. There's no point in starting a relationship if problems show up on the first meeting. As we women quickly learn if a dress doesn't look quite right in a shop it will look a great deal worse when you get it home.

It wasn't long before I had my first applicant. It was a man with a Russian name. In his photo he was wearing a magnificent Russian fur hat and looked rather attractive. I was intrigued by his name as he shared it with a member of a historic Russian royal family. I agreed to meet him for a drink at a nearby pub.

I parked my car and walked into the pub. A slightly built, balding man with a beard was propped up against the bar. He looked vaguely familiar. Then the realisation hit me; he was my date. Gone was the Russian hat and the royal bearing. I didn't find him at all attractive. What was I going to do? I very much wanted to leave the pub and drive home, but that would have been a cowardly and unkind thing to do. I approached him and he confirmed his name.

We sat opposite each other and sipped our wine. Conversation was a struggle. "I have a fur hat like yours I bought in Moscow," I ventured. "Oh, I got mine in Aldershot," he replied. He'd never been to Russia. and his Russian roots seemed questionable. I had hoped they'd make a good topic for conversation. I realised then that the Russian name and magnificent Russian fur hat he sported in his photograph could be just a ruse to attract interest and make him seem intriguing. I had certainly fallen for that one.

Our conversation gradually wilted and died. He offered me a second glass of wine and I refused. He started up the conversation again. "I've been dating for 2 years, and you are number 21," he said. "Most of the women I've dated have said they'd like to see me again, but the next day emailed to called it off. Would you like to see me again?" The poor man was obviously desperate. How was I going to give him the bad news that seeing him again wasn't going to happen. As gently as I could I explained that I didn't think he was looking for me and I wasn't looking for him.

The next 9 months were busy. I seldom saw the same man twice. Reasons for not having a second date varied. Number two thought that having seventeen windows in his flat was interesting. The length of leg room in the back seat of his gold Jaguar also seemed worthy of mention. He wasn't for me. We had a good meal in the Seahorse pub and there it ended.

Number 3, an architect from London, showed more promise. He was interesting to talk to and things were going well. We'd been dating for about 3 weeks when drinking tea on my patio one afternoon he asked, "how am I doing?" He'd felt it necessary to ask this question because part of my policy when dating was not to give feedback during the job interview. I wanted to know if my dates were suitable for me before I committed to sharing my feelings with them. The architect was obviously wondering how much I liked him. I assured him I was enjoying his company.

After tea I took him for a walk in the Surrey countryside. It was going well until we came to deep tracks in the path filled with muddy water. I climbed up the bank at the side of the track and down the other side avoiding the muddy water. He stayed where he was and refused to go any further. The architect from London was clearly a towny who couldn't cope with thick mud and pools of muddy water There was no way he was going to fit into my lifestyle. We walked back to April Cottage and shortly afterwards he drove back to London. I never saw him again.

I accepted a date with a would-be politician who sounded interesting. We met in a pub and we got on well. He invited me to his home for a second date and cooked a meal. He was a good host, and we enjoyed some lively conversation. Things were starting to look promising.

For our third date he took me punting on the river Wey and brought strawberries and champagne for our picnic lunch. That was the sort of luxury I enjoyed. He was fun and we enjoyed doing the same things. What could possibly go wrong?

We had 5 or 6 dates but gradually I got the feeling he was a bit weird. He supported one of the off the wall political parties and seemed to live and breathe politics. In the end offbeat politics proved too much for me. His commitment to politics would have come between us and once I realised this there was no point in continuing to see each other.

Next came the solicitor from the Isle of Wight. He asked me to meet him from the ferry in Portsmouth, which I did. He was over 6 foot, reasonably good looking and had a degree; he ticked the right boxes. He climbed into my car and sat down. But that's all he did. He just sat there. He had no plans for the day. I didn't know Portsmouth so what was I going to do?

I drove around until I found a café and stopped the car. We went into the cafe and had a cup of coffee. That went reasonably well. I enjoyed talking to him. After coffee we got back into the car. He sat down solidly beside me and that was it. He didn't offer any suggestions as to what we could do next.

I drove around until I found a restaurant and parked the car. We got out and had lunch. This date wasn't coming up to my expectations. I enjoyed his company, but he seemed to be totally devoid of any initiative. After lunch we got back in the car and as he settled himself comfortably in the seat beside me, he asked, "What's next?" There was only one answer to that. "Back to the ferry," came my exasperated reply. I nicknamed him "the lump", dropped him off at the ferry and drove home, relieved to be free of my passenger.

For me there needed to be some kind of initial attraction if I was going to enjoy a date with a man, even if they did tick the right boxes. Love can develop gradually, I know, but there needs to be some good vibes or a spark in the beginning. I don't believe in love at first sight, but it must start somewhere. So how did I feel about a man who would like to see me but only had one leg. He sounded okay and looked all right, with his clothes on. I felt I shouldn't let his truthfulness in admitting his disability prejudice me against him, but how did I feel about the possibility of eventually going to bed with a man who only had one leg.

He asked if we could meet at Westonbirt Arboretum. As I already had a visit to Westonbirt arranged with the editor of a photographic magazine, I suggested he joined us there. It was early October and the editor, and I were planning to capture the stunning autumn maple colour. The three of us met up and while we took photos my long-suffering date hung around looking bored. It wasn't a great start and probably wasn't a good idea.

We had lunch and the magazine editor took me to one side "you can do better," he said, "with the date that is, not your photography". I sort of agreed as there didn't seem to be much of a spark between us.

My date and I had supper in a restaurant in Tetbury and he explained how he had lost his leg. "I lived in Africa as a child," he said. "An exploratory procedure went wrong, and my leg had to be amputated". It was a shocking tale, and I felt sorry for him, but compassion isn't a good reason to start a relationship. It's a mistake many people make, and it usually doesn't end well. I wasn't about to make this mistake and as he simply didn't light my fire I drove home after supper without agreeing to see him again.

Blue eyed wonder boy was number 7 and he caught my interest the moment I saw him crossing the petrol station forecourt where we first met. He was tall and leggy with blue eyes and blond hair. I thought I'd pulled. His looks fulfilled my dreams. However, eight weeks into a euphoric relationship, peppered with marriage proposals, the mist cleared, daylight flooded in, and I drove away from an enlightening weekend positive I never wanted to see him again. Number seven's glossy cover concealed a darker story.

I was fast believing there wasn't anyone online I could tolerate for long, let alone have a relationship with. When you love someone, you tolerate a lot of undesirable traits but if they're obvious on your first meeting they could prove terminal to a relationship very quickly or prevent it from starting in the first place. As I'm quick to judge, one of my failings, I wondered if I'd given some of my dates much of a chance. I decided to continue internet dating and try to be more tolerant. That couldn't be too difficult, could it?

A friend knew number 8. Her husband had worked with him abroad. As she knew him, I was happy for him to collect me from April Cottage for our first date. I opened the door to a smartly dressed dapper little man in a silk shirt with well pressed trousers. He was slightly built and not very tall and my heart sank. I didn't find him attractive, not like number 7, but I tried not to be quick to judge. Personality is more important than looks I told myself. This candidate had lived the same expatriate life as I had so we must have something in common.

Over lunch he quizzed me. "What are you looking for?" He asked. It was rather an intense lunch and not much fun. To my surprise he wanted to see me again and offered to take me sailing on his 30ft yacht. I love sailing so that was a plus and I accepted his offer.

We went down to the south coast in his BMW convertible and motored out in his yacht to East Head in Chichester Harbour where we dropped anchor. No sailing so far. We had lunch, and I swam. He came down below while I was getting dressed. I'm not sure what his intention was but I was relieved when the yacht suddenly started to drag anchor, and he had to rush back on deck. He decided not to re anchor the yacht but to motor back to Hayling Island. We never did have a sail, or, fortunately, anything he may or may not have had in mind either

As we were driving home, he said, "you don't need anyone". True I didn't need anyone, but a companion to share my life would have been nice. I'm of the opinion that *needy* and *desperate* are dangerous reasons to internet date. For that reason, I hadn't sought to date anyone after my marriage broke up. I wanted to feel a whole person first, complete in myself, before I started a relationship. Feeling rejected and only half a person would have meant I could only bring weakness and need to a relationship.

I didn't see number 8 again and I had no regrets, but he did leave me with a memento. He suggested I submitted my website www.rosemarycalvert.com to the Royal Geographical Society and applied for a fellowship. My website was full of photos from my travels and number 8 thought trips to the Antarctic, Arctic and Africa would qualify me for a fellowship. My request was granted, and I can now put F.R.G.S. after my name.

Number 9, a doctor, took me to lunch at the Withies, a rather smart pub restaurant. I really enjoyed his company, and the lunch was excellent. I felt I'd found someone who I could communicate with on an intellectual level. We talked about medicine, and I asked him if he specialised. "Oh yes," he said, "I'm a psychiatrist". He had a practice in Harley Street. Wow! So, had everything I'd said so far been analysed for personality traits? Anyway, I can't have come off too badly as he wanted to see me again and offered to cook lunch for me at his home. He served me a tasty meal but then he took me on tour of his house. It was a very detailed tour, and I got the distinct feeling he was preparing for me to move in. I took fright.

As I was about to fly to Denver, Colorado to stay with my son and his wife, there was an opportunity for a cooling off period. We continued to email but I had cold feet. I felt I needed to stop contacting him. I think he must have finally got the message as emails between us dried up. I don't think it was just the tour of the house which put me off. I'd quickly developed an intellectual interest in the psychiatrist but nothing more. The assumption that I would like to move in with him had come far too early.

When I returned from Colorado, I continued receiving emails from men from different dating websites asking me for a date, but none of them interested me. My lack of progress was discouraging, and I wondered if I should give up.

One man who emailed me asking for a date ended every sentence in his email with "eh?" Not liking his style, I refused his offer. He was swift with his reply. He wrote "You're the one for me even if you don't know it, eh?". To encourage me further he said, "My parents didn't like each other at first, eh." Emails from him flooded into my inbox and I replied as politely as I could. But in the end, I had to tell him I would no longer reply to any more of his emails.

I didn't date every man who contacted me. The applicants had a to get through my filter system first. Some emails were highly suggestive and gave me more than a hint of where the first date would be going. These I didn't reply to. Emails full of grammatical errors didn't go down well either. I'm afraid I refused dates with anyone unable to write English correctly.

I can't allot a number to every man I dated, although I did keep a tally of the total number of men I met. Every date I had was different and every date left me with a story to tell. My weekly walking friends waited each week in eager anticipation for the next instalment.

I dated a promising sounding applicant. We had a drink at the Seahorse pub and talked about music. He said he played the guitar. This was exciting news as I love guitar music. I hadn't played for several years, although I had 6 guitars. I invited him back to April Cottage so that he could play one of them.

I proudly handed the newfound musician my favourite, rather special, guitar. The only problem was he didn't seem interested in it. He'd come back to April Cottage as he thought I was providing him with the opportunity to sleep with me. How could I have been so naive? Had I learnt nothing about men in my 59 years on this planet? I had absolutely no intention of going to bed with him, so I packed him off home, this time to his home. He emailed me a couple of days later to tell me he'd met a wonderful woman on the dating site who was prepared to sleep with him.

Sex seemed to be the goal of many of my dates. I met another one of my 6-foot suitors in the Sea Horse pub for a drink. After one glass of wine, he said "will you sleep with me tonight?" I said "no". So he said "Well how about tomorrow night?" I only saw him once and remained intact.

A man I'd been exchanging emails with asked if he could Skype me. He seemed okay so I agreed. We hadn't talked for long on Skype when he asked me to take my top off. My interest took a dive, and I refused. It was fortunate that I refused, as suddenly he said, "I'll have to get back to you later as my wife has just come home". Our contact ended right there.

There were partial truths and downright lies amongst the descriptions tended by some of my potential dates. A pleasant-sounding man emailed me asking for my phone number so that we could have a chat. The conversation was going well until I mentioned that he was a year younger than me. "No, I'm not," he replied, "I'm 68, (I was 59), but my daughter told me that if I put my true age on the dating site no one would want a date with me". I can't tolerate being lied to, so I told him in no uncertain terms that what he put on the internet dating website was entirely his responsibility. "So, I suppose you don't want to see me," he said. I confirmed this and the call ended.

Another potential date fell at the first hurdle in his job interview. From his emails he seemed nice, so I gave him my phone number. The phone call we had was bizarre. Most of it was taken up with stories about his failed second marriage to a woman who used up all his money before leaving him. He felt very sore about that. He'd been flattered when a much younger woman had agreed to have a date with him, so flattered that he'd proposed to her, and she'd accepted. He then went on to discuss his washing. He said, "I like my shirts to be dried on the clothesline, because if they have a good blow, they smell so much fresher." Why on earth did he think I'd be interested in his washing? I don't find washing or housework interesting or good subjects for a debate. This man was not suitable for me even if he was 6 foot tall. I ended our phone call as quickly as I could.

I met a mathematician for a drink at the Seahorse. He turned out to be a half a glass mathematician. He looked great on paper. He had a degree and was over 6 foot; he ticked the right boxes. But we struggled to make conversation and interest died quickly. We finished the rest of our wine and parted knowing we weren't right for each other.

I continued with my 6-foot applicants. A businessman of over 6 foot contacted me and we dated. On the second date he parked his sinister looking long black Jaguar with tinted windows outside my house. My neighbour, something of a voyeur, was watching. It didn't take him long to call round and tell me this chap wasn't suitable for me. I had a couple of dates with the black Jaguar man, but I was inclined to agree with my neighbour. There was "something of the night about him" as well as his car.

Number 14 drove all the way from Taunton for our lunch date. I rather liked him, but a long-distance relationship would have been difficult. It takes many meetings to get to know someone and I couldn't see me building a relationship with a man who lived in Taunton. Besides which he told me he had a female friend who lived nearby he quite liked. I sensed competition and another date wasn't mentioned by either of us.

Some men I met didn't leave much of an impression, even when they had the appropriate job qualifications. The *Amateur Photographer* didn't live far from me, which was a positive, and he was keen on photography. We had a glass of wine at the Seahorse and another date when we met for a cup of coffee in a cafe in Odiham, near where he lived. But after two dates my interest in him waned. We shared a love for photography, but you can't build a relationship on just one thing you have in common. There must be so much more. We didn't have a third date.

The man I met at the Cricketers was a lovely person and lunch was convivial. He'd been on his own for 30 years after his wife died. He fulfilled the criteria, but he was set in his ways. He'd developed a lifestyle to suit himself, as you'd expect, since he'd been on his own for a long time. I wanted to have fun, but he struck me as a bit staid. I watched him as he walked to the loo after the meal and thought "no, he's not for me". He was a perceptive man, as when he came back, he said "I know you won't want to see me again, but I wouldn't have missed this lunch for the world". How touching, but sadly he was right.

As time went by, I was adding to my tally of dates but not one had flourished into a relationship. I began to wonder if there was a single man out there that had the qualifications, I'd specified on the dating website and suited me. I was considering giving up the search when a friend suggested I put my details on the Times dating page. That seemed a good idea so in went my description, no photo.

I received a phone call. "I like the sound of you and I'm looking for a wife", said the applicant, "I've got a nice car, a Golf," he continued. He listed his attractive features, or rather things he believed I might find attractive. "Me dad died," he said, "so I've got an 'ouse,. You could come on 'oliday with me 'cos I got two free tickets." He was a BA cargo handler, and they were a freebie he'd been given. No doubt he would be ideal for someone but that someone wasn't me. I was about to leave for a month in Antarctica, so I used that as an excuse not to see him. I didn't want to tell him I wasn't interested and felt sure he'd find someone during the month I was away. However, the day after I got home from Antarctica the phone rang. "Did you have a nice time in Antarctica," he enquired. I tried to let him down gently, but I don't recall exactly how I did it. I didn't advertise in the Times again.

So, we come to number 17. He ticked all the right boxes. He was over 6 foot, had a degree and was good looking. He suggested we met at Wisley Gardens in Surrey. He clearly liked gardening, and it was one of my passions, so that was another plus.

But while we walked round the gardens, he didn't mention gardening or plants. All he was interested in talking about was his ex-wife. He was consumed by the injustice of his divorce and clearly couldn't move on. His ex-wife was living in their marital home, she'd kept the car and all he was left with was the Winchester College school fees for their son. He lived in rented accommodation and had a clapped-out car. So, I can see why he was upset. To top it all his ex-wife had held on to his family silver.

Certain in the belief that he would be able to move on during our next date I accepted to see him again. We went to the theatre. I was delighted until I found it wasn't so much the plot of the play he wanted to discuss in the interval as his broken marriage and the injustice of his divorce. He'd been in the army, so I nicknamed him the *Poor Soldier*.

I continued to look at the internet dating websites while I dated the *Poor Soldier,* but I seemed to have drawn a blank with the over 6 footers. Friends told me there actually were very nice men under 6 foot, so perhaps I should try one of those. On the *Udate* website there was a feature which made it possible to see who was online at the same time as you, so I switched to that.

A photo of a man behind the wheel of a yacht, holding a large mug popped up. He looked okay and he obviously liked sailing, so we had that in common. But would he turn out to be any different from the 17 who had gone before. They ranged from the half a glass chaps, who managed to let themselves down halfway through the first glass of wine, to blue eyed wonder boy.

I examined his photo carefully and asked myself a question; "could I fancy this man?" Well, he looked wholesome enough, so I sent him a one-line email, "I see you like sailing". Back came the reply, "Yes, and other things, too". "Oh no!" I hoped that didn't mean what I thought it might since sex was high on most dates' list of likes. I was confident, however, that I could handle any problems in that area. He'd ticked the 5ft 10in to 6-foot box and he had a degree. He was a year younger than I was. His qualifications were close to the job description I'd specified on the dating website, so I decided if he wanted to meet me, I'd accept.

We started emailing each other. I was a bit concerned as sometimes he was online, but I could see he was emailing someone else. He sent me poems and chatty emails, but he didn't suggest we met. This wasn't the usual behaviour I'd been used to from men on a dating website. I had to assume he wasn't serious about having a date with me, perhaps he just liked writing emails to women.

I continued to date the *Poor Soldier* and our relationship was improving. His conversation had become less one tracked, and we'd moved on to subjects other than his ex-wife. I'd entertained him at home, and we continued to have trips to the theatre. Things were looking promising, but I wasn't sure he was ready for a relationship so soon after his upsetting divorce.

In one of my chatty emails to the fellow I'd nick-named *"Mr Email Only"* I described the latest play I'd seen with the *Poor Soldier*. To my surprise in his return email, he asked for my phone number. As I'd enjoyed our email correspondence, and he seemed genuine I gave it to him.

All the men, so far, who'd ask if they could phone before meeting me had fallen at the first hurdle and I'd refused a date with them. I couldn't wait to find out how a phone call with *Mr Email Only* would work out. Was I about to arrange a date with number 18 or would his phone call prove as disappointing as the rest of them? I'd soon find out.

The phone rang. I picked up the phone and the rich tones of my new applicant's voice resonated from the receiver. He had a very attractive voice and spoke well. My enthusiasm mounted. Our conversation flowed effortlessly and when he asked if he could take me out to dinner I accepted. We arranged to meet at the Sea Horse.

When I first set eyes on number 18, he appeared much shorter than I'd imagined from his description. I must admit to being surprised and rather disappointed. I then discovered he didn't have a degree, and he was a year older than me, not a year younger. His internet box ticking had been creative, rather than accurate. Any hope of a relationship could have ended right there. But I felt comfortable with him. It was the first time I'd felt like that. It was almost as if we'd met before. I didn't feel a spark, more the affection you might feel for a brother. We sang from the same song sheet, as if we'd grown up together. I decided not to give up and see how things progressed

I arranged to see number 18 again and felt it was only fair to stop dating the *Poor Soldier*. It was a shame, but I think he probably needed time to get over his divorce and reclaim his family silver before starting a new relationship.

Valentine's Day was approaching, and I wondered if number 18 might invite me out for dinner. He had a more practical suggestion. He felt restaurants would already be booked up, so he suggested he came to April Cottage and cook dinner for me at home.

When I told my younger son of number 18's offer to cook a Valentine's dinner for me his words were, "most admirable but a little inadvisable". I have never asked him exactly what he meant by this. I assume he meant that I had high standards and was hard to please. His concern, clearly, was not for me but for number 18 as he believed the meal might well fall short of my expectations.

I put a white embroidered tablecloth on the dark oak dining room table, set it with the silver tableware I'd inherited from my mother and put new long pink candles in my newly polished solid silver candelabra. With my crystal wine and water glasses the table looked ready for our Valentine's dinner.

Number 18 arrived loaded with lots of kitchen equipment which included a large wok and all sorts of utensils. He put on his pinafore and got to work preparing supper. I must admit to being a little amused seeing him standing in my kitchen in his pinny.

As a starter he prepared lettuce, which he embellished with a few drops of balsamic vinegar. He surrounded the lettuce with fresh strawberries and drizzled them with honey. The main course was salmon and prawns in a carbonara sauce poured over spaghetti. I can't remember what he brought for pudding, but it was something in two small pots bought from the supermarket.

My son was right, Number 18's efforts were "admirable". Cooking a meal for me was such an endearing thing to do. "Inadvisable", well perhaps. I'm not a picky eater but I'm not keen on balsamic vinegar or strawberries drizzled with honey served with salad and I'm very much not a fan of spaghetti.

However, in every other way the meal was a success. I sat at the table opposite Number 18 and beheld the face of a good man. My feelings of brotherly affection towards him were developing into something else. I reached for his feet with my feet and gave them a little affectionate nudge. He returned the nudge. It was that nudge which became the turning point in our friendship. I'd met a warm, kind, good looking man I felt comfortable with and what was more I was starting to fancy him.

CHAPTER 13
Dating Angus

So, I'd finally found a potential boyfriend who I felt comfortable with, and I was even starting to fancy him. I'd no idea what the future held for either of us. Would he want to go on seeing me? Would I find him interesting enough to satisfy me? I was hopeful. I stopped looking at internet dating websites and moved dates 1-17 to my bin of dating experience. Number 18 already showed more promise than any of his forerunners. It was going to be worth trying to get to know him. There might yet be a number 19, or perhaps number 18 was going to prove the man for me.

I knew he was good looking, not very tall, a year older than me and his name was Angus. On the internet questionnaire he'd filled in that he had a degree, but that wasn't true. He'd spent 2 years at RAF Cranwell, a prestigious college, which educates RAF officers. It now offers a 3-year degree course so perhaps that's why he counted his training as a degree. Getting to know Angus would be a long process, like making a jigsaw with a lifetime of pieces.

Angus seemed to like walking, and we went for some lovely country walks. I noticed he used a stick. He'd had a knee replacement a couple of years before, so I guessed that was why. At least he didn't shy away from mud like the architect from London did. He played Scrabble so at last I had a Scrabble partner. We seemed to be getting to know each other as friends, and there was a strong element of attraction between us as well. But would our friendship blossom into a relationship?

The phone rang one morning. It was Angus. I remember sitting on the stairs at April Cottage to receive the call. "Are you free at the weekend?" he asked. When I confirmed that I was he said, "Would you like to go to Venice with me?" I was amazed. To go away for the weekend with one of my dates would be a step further than I'd been with any of them. It was an unexpected and exciting offer which I accepted.

Going on holiday with someone other than family, or female friends, was a novel experience. For the first time for 10 years, I had a manfriend sitting beside me on the plane, I snuggled up to him. Angus put his arm round me, and I felt protected. The feeling of having a man friend to take care of me had been missing from my life for a long time.

We had some lovely meals in Venice and one evening while eating in a fancy restaurant Angus said, "I need some feedback". An interesting remark, and legitimate, as I don't give feedback at job interviews. That's a bit harsh, but I had a policy of telling my dates as little as possible about myself until I'd started to get to know them. I was enjoying Angus' company which is what I told him. The weekend went well. When we joined a long queue to check in for our flight home standing with Angus in the queue was so enjoyable I didn't mind how long we took to reach the desk. I felt that must mean something.

We didn't see each other often but Angus sent me poetry and lovely emails. One email asked me if I fancied the wind in my hair on his yacht or navigating for him rallying his classic car. I fancied the yacht more than the car, but it occurred to me that if he asked me to navigate for him first, I wouldn't be likely to see the yacht. I knew nothing about navigating and I wouldn't have been my first choice if I'd been looking for a navigator.

Unfortunately, the invitation to navigate in a classic car rally came first. Angus invited me to join him on a competitive rally in Spain. I do like a challenge, but I didn't want to let him down. I accepted in the hopes I would learn how to navigate quickly.

We took the ferry to Santander and during the passage, Angus handed me a sheet of numbers saying, "That's for you". I had no idea what the lists of numbers were. Were they distances, or perhaps times? I would need more than a sheet of paper with numbers on it if I was going to learn how to navigate. I was also given two stop watches and a "road book" full of diagrams called "tulips". I had a steep learning curve ahead of me.

Angus' Jaguar 150 drophead, manufactured in 1959, broke down on the ramp as we disembarked the ferry in Santander. I thought that might put an end to me having to learn to navigate, but it didn't. The accompanying maintenance car had a petrol pump that would fit. It was Spanish siesta time, so we had to hang around for a while waiting for the garage to wake up, but eventually we left the car to be repaired.

The rally started the next morning, and we missed the start, but we joined the rally in the afternoon. Now we had the additional job of trying to catch up time which compounded my task of learning to navigate.

The sheet of numbers turned out to be average speed tables. There were three columns of numbers; distances, times and the speeds needed to achieve the distances in the times listed. I hadn't reached the first rung of my learning ladder. There was a Branz machine attached to the dashboard which showed the miles covered. So, I had the miles in front of me on the Branz machine and I could set the time we started each leg of the rally on both stop watches. It was fortunate my arithmetic was reasonable as there were lots of numbers to play with. Now I just needed to work out how to decipher the "tulips" and we'd be on our way.

There were check points at intervals on the route, but we had no idea where they were. We just had to arrive at them at exactly the right time, to the second. Fortunately, Angus was very patient as I progressed slowly up my learning curve. I worked out a system which I was quite proud of, and it worked well. At one check point we checked in within 3 seconds of the time we were supposed to be there.

Unfortunately, one day I misread the "tulips" and we got badly lost. As we zoomed down a motorway, I knew something was wrong as rallies tend to keep to winding side roads. Then we noticed a check point on a hill to the right, but some distance behind us. A check point can only be entered in one direction, so we doubled back and took a lane which appeared to go in the direction we wanted. The lane got narrower and more uneven until it became a track. We came to a narrow rickety wooden bridge and without slowing down Angus shot over it, I was surprised it took our weight. We ended up in a rural settlement that looked like something out of the Middle Ages. Chickens scattered and women in head scarves stood open mouthed as we sped passed their shack-like wooden houses.

We saw cars ahead and joined a metalled road which soon brought us to the check point. But when we checked in, we found we weren't late, as we'd imagined, but a minute early, which was just as bad.

Angus was a superb driver, and, in the end, I didn't do too badly as a navigator. Our group of cars came first in the rally, and we came third in our group. With this success under my belt, I thought I might now stand a chance of seeing Angus' yacht. I'd quite enjoyed the Spanish competitive rally, and it had been a challenging experience. It had been memorable, too. The luxurious hotels, fabulous classic cars, Angus' patience, daily stress and large gin and tonics every evening left an impression on me for life.

In early summer 2005 Angus invited me to join him on his yacht, "Palawan". He kept it in Croatia and the plan was for me to fly out to join him for a 2-week holiday. I welcomed the idea of spending two weeks with him as it would give me an opportunity to get to know him.

"Palawan" was a 42-foot yacht, which had spacious and comfortable accommodation. I immediately felt at home. She was much bigger than "Snowflake", the 32-foot yacht I'd spent so much time sailing with my family when we lived in England and Holland. Angus kept "Palawan" in Kremik Marina, just north of Split on the Croatian coast which was ideal for visiting the numerous islands close-by. As I packed for the holiday, I had feelings of excitement but also of nervous anticipation.

We sailed from Kremik Marina to the Island of Trogir and moored alongside a pontoon. A grey Marine Police launch pulled in behind us. I was on deck when they called to me and asked where my husband was. I was more taken with the assumption that I had a husband than I was worried about why the Marine Police were asking for him. I didn't disillusion them but went down below to find Angus. The Marine Police wanted the ship's papers as we hadn't registered the boat and crew for the present year. The boat had to be registered each year, and the crew registered whenever it changed. We sailed straight to Primosten where we could get our papers signed to make "Palawan" legal. While I waited, I reflected on what it would be like if one day I did have a husband.

We started to explore the islands, and it was lovely to be on the water again. We anchored in a bay in Solta but heard that a strong northerly Bora wind was forecast which made it unsafe to stay. It was already dark when we left the bay and sailed to Milna on the island of Brac. It looked as if my sailing holiday was going to be just as exciting as the classic car rally.

We visited Hvar which I liked very much. It had an attractive waterfront with palm trees and lots of welcoming restaurants. Sitting in a restaurant having a beer was a perfect way to end the day. Our holiday was progressing well.

The weather forecast for the next few days was poor with high winds, so we headed north and sailed inland to Krka National Park to visit Krka Waterfalls. We motored up a narrow waterway with sheer cliffs on either side and moored at Skradin Marina. A footpath beside the Krka River led to the beautiful Krka Waterfalls. The falls were breath-taking and well worth the 3km hike beside the river.

At the end of two weeks, it was time to fly home. I'd got to know Angus a little better and we'd had fun, but I had no idea if our relationship had a future. At Split airport, I met Angus' crew for the following 2 weeks, a group of male friends. Life on *Palawan* would be different for him with them, and I wondered if he would miss me or just slip back into old habits.

Once back in England I continued with my photographic business. In June I flew to Svalbard, Spitzbergen, to join a photographic expedition looking for polar bears. Every day the ship sailed backwards and forwards searching for bears on the ice floes, but they were harder to find than we'd hoped. One day there was great excitement as two cubs had been spotted following their mother across the ice and swimming between islands of floating sea ice. They were such a joy to watch, and I managed to get some pleasing photographs. We also found a rather dejected polar bear standing on a muddy island which should have been covered with snow and ice. It was a sad sight. I took a photograph which I thought might be useful to illustrate global warming. When the two weeks came to an end, we'd covered great distances in the ship but to my disappointment we'd seen very few polar bears.

Angus was house hunting when I first met him, and he'd had his offer accepted on a house in Fareham. When he returned from Croatia, he took me to see his prospective new home. It was close to the water, and I noticed the house was lower than the water level in Portsmouth Harbour. How do you tell someone you don't know very well that the house they're about to buy looks as if it might be prone to flooding? I remember standing beside the water and wondering what to say. I had to tell him somehow. I pointed out the level of the water and the level of the house and he saw my point. When he checked records for the area, he found the house had been flooded twice. He withdrew his offer.

Eventually, Angus found a pleasant house in Havant with a double garage, which was important as he needed to garage his precious convertible classic car. He moved in and I started to visit him at weekends. I remember how excited I felt as I drove down the A3 to Havant from Bramley early on a Saturday morning to arrive in time for breakfast. I'd ring the doorbell and wait in anticipation. One morning I looked through the frosted glass in the door to see the shape of Angus coming downstairs. A thrill of excitement ran through me. I had a boyfriend, and I was developing strong feelings for him, maybe I was in love. Whatever it was it made me feel happy and young again. Coffee and toast in the kitchen tasted better than I ever remembering it tasting.

On Saturday we'd shop at a convenience store and sit at the kitchen table eating the quiche we'd bought for our lunch, accompanied by a glass of chilled white wine. It was heaven. What did puzzle me, however, was Angus' Saturday evening arrangements. Every Saturday evening, he invited a relative or friend to join us for dinner. I couldn't understand why he needed company in addition to me. I still don't know. Did he not find being alone with a new girlfriend enough? I wondered if I should be worried.

After a few months Angus started to introduce me to his family. I met his eldest daughter for the first time in a pub in London. A beautiful tall, blond girl slipped into the seat beside to me. To my surprise she seemed quite relaxed, although she probably wasn't, as meeting her father's girlfriend couldn't have been easy. I hoped I didn't disappoint her.

Angus' second daughter met me later at his house in Havant. She was petite, dark and clearly not relaxed. My heart went out to her. When she left to go home her elder sister buttoned up her coat for her. I think she was in shock. Poor girls, it must have been so tough meeting me. Having their parents go their separate ways and then having a strange woman coming on the scene must have been hard for them.

On a different occasion Angus' only brother came to the house in Havant to meet me. He seemed in shock, too. I think at one point he was close to tears. I could only hope time would help them to get used to me and the situation. I was beginning to build a relationship with Angus but my relationships with his daughters and brother were like a collection of jigsaw pieces I hadn't even shaken out of the bag, let alone started to put together. If Angus and I continued seeing each other his family would be part of my life, too, and I would need to get to know them. They would need to get to know me, too.

In the autumn of 2005, I joined Angus again on *Palawan*, this time for a 3-week holiday. We sailed south to Dubrovnik which was exciting as it was the first time I'd visited it. We took a memorable walk along the top of the wall which encircles the old city almost completely. The wall is 82 feet high in places and is continuous for over a mile. Afterwards we found a perfect restaurant and had an excellent meal sitting outside in a street in the old town. It was so good we decided to go back the following evening. But it must have been the chef's night off as the following evening the meal wasn't very good at all.

After Dubrovnik we retraced our passage northwards towards Split and called in at Korcula. It was a beautiful island but what I remember most was breakfast outdoors on tables placed alongside a wall at the water's edge with the open sea just the other side. Breakfast in such a scenic place was quite thrilling

I enjoyed swimming from *Palawan* and swam at every opportunity. We dropped anchor in a cove off the coast of the island of Sveti Klement and again I swam. I could see a sign on the beach, so I went ashore to see what it said. It was a signpost to Restaurant Paradiso. We both like exploring so in the evening we went ashore in the dingy and set off to find the restaurant. The sign directed us along a narrow path through bushes of wild rosemary. As we walked, we brushed against the wild rosemary and its fragrance filled the air.

Finally, we came to the restaurant which was in a remote spot and seemed abandoned. Eventually someone appeared, as if from nowhere, greeted us and showed us to one of the many empty tables outside. It looked as if we might be the only customers that evening. We chose pork spareribs from the rather restricted menu.

The waiter brought a large tray to our table and a bowl of salad. The tray appeared to be covered with bones. There was little meat in evidence. It was either a very slim pig or someone had already eaten the meat and we'd been given the spareribs. We ate the salad and paid. As we made our way back to the boat along the narrow path through the fragrant rosemary in the pitch dark we couldn't hold back the laughter. Our meal had been a strange experience.

Looking at the restaurant's website today it seems to be an up-market establishment serving good meals but in 2005 it was very different. At least it made us laugh and added to our history together. A new relationship has no history, no past to mull over and recall. It was something I missed. It made me happy to be building history with Angus, but we seemed to spend most of our time in Croatia either sailing to an island or eating in a restaurant.

With bad weather forecast we sailed north and motored inland to Skradin Marina, once again. We walked to the Krka falls to enjoy the splendid sight for a second time. Afterwards we were walking in the streets of Skradin when we came across a pig being roasted on a spit in a pop-up restaurant. We were intrigued.

That evening we went back into Skradin to sample the roast pig. Angus loves crackling and once the chef realised this, he provided him with a continuous supply. Angus ate plate after plate of it.

The next morning, he was feeling sick. He stayed in bed for 2 days moaning and only getting up from time to time to be sick. Overindulging in crackling had made him quite ill. Poor Angus! There wasn't much I could do but wait until he recovered. He now has a healthy respect for pork crackling although when it's available he finds it difficult to resist.

Once back in England Angus continued to invite friends and relatives to supper every Saturday evening. One Saturday he invited my sister Marilyn to join us. She lived near Southampton, so not far away, and he wanted to start to meet my family. Angus made an excellent fish pie for supper. He really was rather a good cook. Perhaps that was why he liked entertaining every Saturday evening.

Marilyn is a lovely person and Angus got on well with her. She told me afterwards that if Angus treated me well, she would be there for us. It was clear that if my relationship with Angus continued it would have a ripple effect which would affect both our families, our greater families, and our friends.

Angus had Christmas with his family, and I flew to Denver with Andrew to spend Christmas with Alexander and his family. Angus and I were still very much doing our own thing and although we'd enjoyed several holidays together, we hadn't talked about sharing a future.

In April I flew to the Galapagos Islands for 3 weeks to join a group of wildlife photographers. Twelve of us stayed on a small luxury yacht and visited many of the islands. The wildlife was fearless, and it was a real treat to be able to be close to so many birds, reptiles and other animals. Blue-footed boobies stood on the path as I passed, and I could take close-up photographs of the magnificent frigatebird on its nest; "condor of the oceans" as Charles Darwin called them. I saw the dragon-like marine iguana on every island we visited, and I was impressed by the magnificent Galapagos giant tortoises. After much searching, we found Galapagos penguins. We swam with sea lions several times, but they paid us more attention than we'd bargained for by tugging on our flippers all the time.

The Galapagos Islands offered a feast of wildlife, but three weeks away from Angus seemed a long time and when he met me at the airport, I decided I had taken my last long photographic trip. I wanted to spend more time with Angus.

At the end of May, son Alexander and family flew from Denver to stay with me at April Cottage. I organized a greater family get together so that everyone would have the chance to see Alexander and his family during their visit. There were 23 of us in total, my 4 sisters, their husbands, and their children, as well as Alexander's family and Andrew. Angus had only met my sister ,Marilyn, and Andrew before the gathering so for him it was a baptism by fire. He coped well but he did say he noticed everyone having a good look at him when they thought he wasn't looking. It must have felt like judgement day.

We all lined up for a family photo in the garden and Angus was included. Now everyone would have a record of Angus as part of our family. But was he?

Afterwards my elder son had some questions for me. He wanted to know why my relationship with Angus hadn't progressed beyond friendship. We'd been dating for over a year, but nothing was being said about a future together. He wanted to know which of us was holding things up. I didn't want to say Angus wasn't ready for commitment. Instead, I said we both had to be sure we were right for each other before we could commit to a future together. Alexander seemed to accept that as an explanation.

Angus spent the rest of the summer of 2006 on his boat in Croatia with friends and family. I was a little surprised that he chose to spend weeks away from me, but old habits die hard. He'd spent much of the latter years of his marriage pursuing his own hobbies when he and his wife started to follow different interests. Angus enjoyed his independence, and I enjoyed mine, but I missed him when we were apart. I had to remind myself that Angus was a boyfriend. We were not a couple or, in modern language, an item. I was aware that there could still be a number 19.

When Angus returned from Croatia, we started seeing each other again at weekends. We stayed alternate weekends in Havant and Bramley. Angus was due to be with me at April Cottage the next weekend when son Andrew phoned with a question. "Will Angus be with you this weekend?" I had no idea why he wanted to know. He just said he wanted to visit me while Angus was there.

When Andrew arrived, he said he had something he needed to tell me. "It's about my father," he said. I'd been divorced from his father for 3 years so I couldn't imagine what news about him could possibly concern me. When he told me I was shocked. "Daddy has been diagnosed with terminal bowel cancer and has been told he has a maximum of a year to live," he said. I couldn't hold back my tears. I'd loved the man who'd been my husband for so many years and now I was going to lose him in the most final way possible.

Angus comforted me. Here I was weeping for my ex-husband and being comforted by my boyfriend. It was an odd situation, but it did demonstrate to me Angus' compassionate and loving nature. Andrew must have had faith that Angus would support me when he gave me the distressing news.

Once I recovered from the shock, I started to think about my life long emotional tie to my ex-husband and how his death might affect me. When I'd married him, I'd taken my marriage vows seriously. I'd married him for better or for worse and for the rest of our lives. I felt now I was going to lose him forever

I'd no longer be tied by my marriage vows and free to love someone else. I wondered if it was my feelings of commitment that had made me welcome him back every time he chose to return to me. Or was it simply that I loved him?

In September Angus' dog, Tiggy, fell ill and died. Tiggy, a giant schnauzer, had been so much part of our relationship. Angus maintains it was Tiggy who I fell for first, not him. Tiggy had big brown eyes and was always so excited to see me, perhaps he was right, I did fall in love with Tiggy. Angus was very upset at losing her and we both missed her enormously. How sad life can be. The most joyous things in life can be lost and the more we love them the greater the loss.

In November 2006, to my surprise, in the kitchen at April Cottage, Angus asked me to marry him. I was sitting on a high kitchen stool, and it came out of the blue. I didn't need to think twice before giving him my answer. It was a very firm "yes". I knew by then I had fallen in love him. He gave me one of his mother's rings which fitted perfectly. It had a central diamond with small marquise diamonds each side. I was delighted to be given one of his mother's rings. Now we were engaged I could look forward to a future with Angus. It was an exciting prospect.

We decided to take a holiday together and chose western Canada which is magical in winter. It was a perfect choice as it gave me an opportunity to show Angus all my favourite haunts from the time I lived in Calgary. We flew to Calgary on 15th

December 2006 to spend Christmas in the Rocky Mountains together. I couldn't wait to share my love of snow, ice and winter mountain scenery with Angus.

We stayed a few nights with Fran and Chris who were our neighbours when I lived in Calgary. Fran and I had exercised together every morning and chatted over coffee afterwards. It was good to see her again. I'd missed her so much when we moved to Houston. My Canadian friends had proved to be irreplaceable when we left Calgary. I didn't meet anyone I could call a close friend in Houston, except Joanne who I met on the dive drip in Australia right at the end of our time in Houston.

After visiting Fran and Chris in Calgary we drove on Highway 1 towards the Rocky Mountains and stopped in Canmore to stay with Mavis and Andrew. I'd first met Mavis and Andrew in the Europa Hotel in Scheveningen in 1969 when we moved to Holland the first time. They'd been given a Shell posting to Calgary and loved it so much they'd decided to emigrate there. When my marriage to Rodney broke up, they had been very upset and angry. They were thrilled I was engaged and delighted I'd brought Angus to meet them. However, Mavis had a few words of warning for Angus. She found a moment to speak to him in private. Angus told me of their conversation afterwards. She said, "I hope your affection for Rosemary is genuine as she has a lot of friends". Neither of us are quite sure what she meant by this, but she was clearly concerned about me and wanted to make sure Angus wasn't just playing with my affections. I was very touched by how much she cared.

Next, we drove to Banff to start exploring. There were so many places I wanted to show Angus. We travelled up Sulphur Mountain in a gondola and admired the stunning views of snow-covered mountains. We swam in Banff hot springs in an outdoor pool in freezing temperatures. I was having a wonderful time, and I hoped Angus was enjoying it as much as I was.

Lake Louise was another scenic place I wanted Angus to see. We stayed in Deer Lodge and had a champagne afternoon tea at Chateau Lake Louise. I'd reserved a table with a picture postcard view of Lake Louise and Victoria Glacier through a cathedral style window. A horse drawn sleigh stood outside in the snow waiting for passengers with blankets piled high to keep them warm. The view was like a pop-up picture from a fairy tale story book.

From Lake Louise we took highway 93, Icefield Parkway, to Jasper. It was quite an experience for Angus. He drove our hired 4×4 Jeep along a slippery snow-covered road, through a blizzard and passed a sign saying, "no petrol for 230 km", nearly 140 miles. It must have been a first for him.

After visiting Jasper, Medicine Lake and Mount Robson we drove back on Icefield Parkway to Highway 1. I'd booked a cabin in Emerald Lake Lodge in British Columbia for

Christmas. It was my favourite lodge in the Rocky Mountains and wanted Angus to experience a few nights there.

It was just as I'd remembered it. Our first glimpse was of frozen Emerald Lake stretching out beyond the lodge and the outdoor hot tub steaming invitingly. Ice sculptures of deer stood each side of the path which linked our cabin to the main lodge and with the snow-covered fir trees decorated with bright Christmas lights it looked like fairyland. There was a log fire in our bedroom and each morning a man wearing a pixy-like hat brought us logs in a fabric sling. It was perfect and very romantic.

We skied round the lake falling frequently and collapsing in youthful laughter. We were having fun together. We built a snowman and decorated it with a Christmas hat and scarf. I felt younger and more light-hearted than I had done for years. Christmas 2006 turned out to be magical.

Back in the U.K. we looked forward to 2007 as an engaged couple with an exciting future to plan. We both had a house and Angus said he'd be happy for me to move in with him after we married. There were two reasons why I couldn't do that. Angus' house was opposite a tennis club and the sound of tennis balls going plop as they landed, then continuing to go plop, plop, plop until the game ended, irritated me. If I'd moved there the constant plopping sound would have driven me mad. The other reason was a long-held belief that it's better if a newly married couple start anew, living in a house they've both chosen rather than living in one already owned by one of them. Fortunately, Angus agreed with me. We put both our houses on the market and started to house hunt.

We had a plan. We'd have coffees in cafes in different towns and villages and see if we could imagine living there. This resulted in us falling for the most expensive place, Haslemere. We tried to feel comfortable in other towns and villages but for some reason we couldn't. We hunted for houses on the internet hoping we'd fall in love with a house in a cheaper area but each time we returned to Haslemere for a coffee we felt we wouldn't be happy anywhere else.

We sorted through descriptions of house after house. It's amazing how misleading estate agent's descriptions can be and how much information they somehow omit. Motorways, railway lines, factories and flood plains were always omitted however close they were to the house. Wide angle lenses were put to good use to make the drives look misleadingly wide. You couldn't turn a mini round in most of them. We weren't keen on north facing patios either and we saw a few with those.

Visiting a house in Haslemere one morning we were aware of a continuous bleeping sound. The house was on a hill and at the bottom of the hill was a builders merchant's yard. It was some distance away but bleeps from a backing forklift truck filled the air. The sound was even more irritating than tennis balls. The thought of relaxing in the garden on a warm summer's day listening to bleeps from the forklift truck, instead of bird song, made living there out of the question. We looked round the house but had no intention of buying it.

We found a house with a double garage in Haslemere within our price range and went to see it. A house can feel promising from the start, and this was the feeling we both had as soon as parked on the tarmac drive in front of it. It was a Scandia-hus of simple design with big windows and it had an open plan, welcoming feeling. The price had just been lowered, after it had been on the market for 6 months, and it was now in our price range. The 17 electric wall heaters, instead of central heating, may have been why it hadn't sold, but we could easily have central heating fitted. There was a big garden, and the orchard was bright with yellow daffodils when we viewed the house.

Afterwards, sitting on the stairs at home, I realised it was the only house I'd seen that I could possibly swap for my beloved April Cottage.

As neither of our houses had sold, we recklessly arranged to take out mortgages on both. It was an expensive and risky move but a necessary one. It was the only way Amberwood House could be ours. Sometimes immediate action is essential when you find something which is just what you're looking for. Living with "we should have" and regrets just adds to life's disappointments. There are plenty of disappointments in life without adding to them if you don't have to. So, with the decision made and the mortgages arranged we bought Amberwood House.

Regarding disappointments, how do you tell your fiancé that the gold on his mother's ring he'd given you as an engagement ring is wearing off? I pondered on the best way to break it gently to him. There really wasn't an easy way so I just said, "the gold on my engagement ring is rubbing off". Angus had told me his mother had had some lovely jewellery, but it seemed that this ring was a paste imposter.

Angus took the upsetting news well and quickly bought a replacement ring of a similar design on the internet and gave it to me. But when I looked at the central diamond in my replacement ring my heart sank. It was a low-grade diamond. I'm sure many women wouldn't have noticed, or been concerned about the quality of the diamond, but collecting gems was one of my hobbies. I'd bought gems and jewellery all over the world for years. I also had a brilliant cut, top quality, grade D, one carat diamond ring my ex-husband had given me for my 40th birthday. As I had a love for beautiful gems, I found it difficult to wear a diamond of poor quality. In my head I heard my father's words of warning, "I'm worried about you Rosemary as you expect too much out of life and you're going to be disappointed". He was right. I've always expected too much and I've frequently been disappointed. So, what was I going to do about this recent disappointment?

I did the only thing I could do. I had the central diamond of my engagement ring replaced with an oval, 1.2 carat, grade D diamond. The oval diamond looked better with the marquise diamonds, so I used this as my reason for changing it. I enjoy wearing my engagement ring, it's beautiful, and I don't regret finding the courage to change the diamond. Fortunately, Angus is very tolerant of my quirks and accepted the change without questioning my motive.

We married on June 7th, 2007, at The Georgian House Hotel in Haslemere and had a reception for 100 friends and relatives. Our wedding was wonderful in every possible way. Angus looked handsome in his kilt, and I wore a dusty pink dress and coat with a matching wide brimmed hat. I'd had a Premium Bond win of £1,000 which paid for my outfit. As I walked down the aisle the hotel had created between the chairs, Angus turned round and looked back at me. I felt a thrill of love run through me. I was marrying for the second time and once again for love.

My eldest son, Alexander, gave me away and a friend took a photo of Alexander with me on his arm walking down the aisle. His expression was one of sheer joy and pride. Monica, Alexander's wife, was matron of honour, their daughter a bridesmaid and son a page. Monica had cleverly put the wedding outfits in their hand luggage, when they flew from Denver, in case the hold luggage was lost. It paid off as their hold luggage only caught up with them after the wedding.

Both Alexander and Andrew were witnesses, and I felt proud to have such adorable sons. Everything went like clockwork, the sun shone, the guests looked fabulous, some in big hats, and they all looked very happy to be witnessing Angus and me getting married. My friends and relatives had been greatly saddened by my marriage break up and were so very happy I'd found love again.

CHAPTER 14
Life with Angus

We didn't have a honeymoon, instead we looked after my grandchildren. We'd chosen June 7th for our Wedding Day as son, Alexander, and his wife, Monica, were coming to England from the U.S. to attend a conference in London. We hadn't fixed a date for our wedding and were just taking things slowly but when they told us they would be visiting England we seized the opportunity to get married so that they could be with us on our wedding day.

The day after we married, they went up to London to the conference and we took charge of 2-year-old Liam and 4-year-old Sasha. We needed to find of ways of amusing them so the next day we took them to the zoo. It was not a success. The trip was punctuated by temper tantrums from 2-year-old Liam, and we struggled to cope, but to be fair it was tough on the children; they hardly knew me, and Angus was a total stranger.

They were also having to adjust to jetlag and being in a foreign country. I was proud of my new husband as he showed his true colours and got on with the job. I admired him for that.

When my son and his wife returned from their conference in London the family left for Denver and we drove to a spa in Dorset for a break. We needed one! There was a bottle of champagne waiting for us and we had two days of total luxury. While waiting for a massage we sat in our bath robes and sipped orange juice. I reflected on my good fortune. I had a new husband who I loved and a future I hadn't expected. Angus had changed the plans I had for my future. I was going to add a conservatory to April Cottage so that I could read in the sunshine and peacefully grow old. Now I was a married woman with a precious man of my very own and a future for not one, but for two, to plan.

Angus and I had been on holiday to Spain, Croatia, Canada and Finland before we married but we'd never lived together full time. The newness of being together 24/7 was so exciting we didn't need a honeymoon. We made April Cottage our base and drove to Haslemere each day to re decorate Amberwood House.

In November 2007 Angus sold his house in Havant so we were able to furnish our new home with his furniture and move in. Before marrying we'd, both been living on our own for some time. I'd been on my own for 10 years pleasing myself from dawn 'til dusk; it was a big adjustment being with Angus 24/7.

We both needed our own space so we chose a study each so that we could be alone from time to time and pursue our own interests. It was the perfect solution.

In late November 2007, 5 months after we'd married Angus answered his mobile. It was my son Andrew. He'd phoned with the news that his father had died, and he wanted Angus to break the news gently to me. He knew I'd be very upset and need Angus to support me.

I'd been aware that Rodney hadn't long to live, but it didn't lessen the shock when I heard he'd died. His death did affect my relationship with Angus. After I heard the sad news, I could only think about Rodney and the happy life we'd had together. I had been devastated when he left me. I just hope he found happiness in the last years of his shortened life. After he left me, I could never bring myself to say his name as it meant too much to me. But when he died, I started to call him my late-ex. It made things easier, although some people did ask me why I called him latex!

Rodney's new wife didn't tell the family when he died, neither did she invite them to his funeral. She flew his body out of Houston to Dallas where he was interred in a graveyard with her family. She was the only family member to be present at his burial. It was hard for our sons, and his sister and mother to have their last chance to say farewell taken from them.

When Rodney left me, I'd consciously preserved our precious life together in an imaginary glass box, so that it couldn't be changed or sullied. It was this treasured past life with Rodney that occupied my mind and caused me to distance myself emotionally from Angus. Angus patiently waited for the tidal wave of my ex-husband's death to pass. He said he knew I needed time.

Friends who heard Rodney had died phoned to say how sorry they were. This must have been difficult for Angus. Tony, who we knew in Borneo, phoned and talked to me for a long time about how much he admired the work Rodney had done for Shell. He said Rodney had innovative ideas and had moved oil exploration forward in some important fields. I admired him for that, too.

Andrew summed up his father succinctly when he said, "he was a one off". His father had certainly had a unique approach to life. It had presented me with challenges and sometimes I'd struggled to cope, but he was a brilliant man. He also knew how to have fun, and I've always loved having fun. Andrew said he didn't think his father knew what love was. Quite an observation for a son to make. Considering what happened to our marriage perhaps Andrew was right.

It's hard to define love; perhaps to each of us it means something different. I loved Rodney unconditionally; it was an all-encompassing deep feeling. He wasn't a good communicator, but he was full of ideas, and I enjoyed the challenges living with him brought, most of the time. We had a very active life together full of excitement. It was a wonderful life.

But when he left me, he accused me of being more like a mother than a wife. In some ways perhaps I did behave like his mother as I loved him unconditionally and protected him from himself whenever he had dangerous ideas. Perhaps I filled the only vacancy which was available to me. On the other hand, his accusations may have had no foundation but simply have been a way to justify his leaving me.

I knew I was in love with Angus when there was a feeling of electricity when we touched, when I wanted to be close to him all the time and when I cared for every hair on his head. We spend hours each day talking to each other whereas Rodney and I didn't communicate verbally very much. The love I feel for Angus is not the same as the love I felt for Rodney. There is more passion, but there are so many types of love.

Angus told me he didn't feel the power of true love until after we married, and we'd spent time together. He said it was a strong feeling he suddenly became aware of. When he described how being in love felt to him, it made me realise that men's love can be different from women's. Angus knew he was in love with me when he wanted to defend and protect me and when he felt able to share everything with me, his success, his weaknesses, and his failures. The film "Love Actually" is an entire movie made about the complexities of the emotion we know as love.

I feel privileged to have married two very different men. I have learnt so much from each of them. There's a theory that we look for a different type of person for marriage when we're young, than we do for a second marriage when we're mature; that the young subconsciously look for a partner with opposite genes and the production of pheromones is nature's way of helping with mate selection and ensuring the survival of a strong species. Marrying for a second time, when breeding is not the intention, a partner more like yourself is more likely to be chosen. I had certainly adhered to this theory in my choices.

Once the house was organized and I'd sorted myself out emotionally we got on with life. I continued to submit photos to stock agencies which provided me with a good income and Angus' great interest in cars, boats, and aeroplanes kept him busy. He was in the Royal Airforce for 8 years and flew the iconic Vulcan bomber. He'd also owned his own plane. He had a sailing boat when he was 7 years old and owned several yachts over the years. His classic car, an XK 150 Jaguar drophead built in 1959 was his pride and joy. He lived and breathed cars, boats and aeroplanes.

When we weren't on holiday or doing things together, we followed our own interests in our studies. Angus watched videos and read articles related to his interests in cars, boats and planes and I processed and perfected my photographs using photoshop while listening to my favourite music. Life was harmonious and good.

In the 17 years we've been married nothing, and yet everything, has changed. Our love and commitment to each other hasn't faltered. We've grown in understanding as the pieces of jigsaw, which make up who each of us is, have fallen into place. We've found we're both sensitive and words sometimes must be chosen with care. Angus was overly defensive and quick to defend his corner when we first married, which I struggled with. Once he knew he could trust me he became less defensive, and life became easier for us both.

Many things did change in the first years of our marriage. Our boats and cars changed, not infrequently. We clubbed together and bought *Dino Volante*, a Sigma 32 yacht, and called her *Volly*. She was fast and I enjoyed sailing her. She had a tiller and handled like the dinghies I'd be used to sailing. We rallied Angus' Jaguar XK150 classic car and acquired a delightful group of friends. We were enjoying life so much I didn't want it to change. I said to Angus, "life is so good I'd like to put it on hold".

But nothing ever stays the same, that's life. Angus fancied a yacht with a wheel, not a tiller, and a self-taking jib, so we sold 'Volly' and bought 'Volly 2', a Maxi 1000. Angus sold his Jaguar XK150, as the price was right, although he did shed a tear when he said goodbye to the car he'd loved for 40 years. He bought a Honda MX which I disliked as it made me feel sick and unsafe. Angus sold the Honda MX and bought a Jaguar F type. He disliked that so much he sold it after 9 months and bought a Jaguar XKR. We both liked the XKR, but Angus hankered after a classic car. Life was a journey of discovery as we searched for a lifestyle and a sports car that would suit us both.

Angus' hobbies were, and still are, vital to his happiness and he really wanted a classic car. I made him an offer. If he bought an E-type Jaguar I would pay half, but only if he bought an E-type. In the 1960s I had hoped to find a boyfriend who owned one, but no E-type owning boyfriend had come my way. I watched E-types drive by and thought they were the height of elegance. Now I had a chance to own one, or half of one, it would be a dream come true.

E-types were first built in 1961. The design changed three times between 1961 and 1975 when the last one was built. There were Series 1 E-types, then Series 2 and Series 3. Angus found Series 1 and 2 E-types cramped when he drove them, but Series 3 are bigger, and he found them more comfortable.

He showed me pictures of three Series 3 E-types for sale in our area. There was only one I fancied, and it wasn't the lemon or pale blue E-type that Angus thought we should look at first as they were nearby. I don't believe in wasting time looking at what I know I don't want; I had the same policy when I was internet dating.

We drove 85 miles to Bicester to see a Series 3 E-type in opalescent grey metallic with dark red seats. The moment I saw it I knew it was the one I wanted.

We've been on many noncompetitive rallies with our E-type, to Holland, Spain, Southern Ireland and all over the

U.K. Only three times has it needed a ride home on a low-loader after breaking down.

The second time it broke down we were on the A27 driving down to our boat in Chichester Marina. It suddenly stopped. The AA came but they couldn't fix it; they flagged down a passing AA van, but they couldn't fix it either. Unfortunately, roadside help is not manned by mechanics who know much about classic cars. We sat on a piece of concrete beside the road for 4 hours waiting for a low-loader to collect our car.

A car pulled up and the driver wound down his window. "Would you like a cup of coffee?" he said. What a wonderful offer, it was the one thing I really needed, apart from the arrival of a low-loader. We accepted without thinking twice.

He drove off and soon returned with two large take away coffees. He handed them to us and refused payment. A modern day "Good Samaritan" had brought us just what we needed. Never in our wildest dreams could we have imagined that would happen. We marvelled at his kindness and generosity. That large cup of coffee was a life saver and heaven sent.

Our sailing days ended when Angus was diagnosed with atrial fibrillation, often referred to as AF. He feared that he might become dizzy on deck, fall overboard, and I would be unable to rescue him.

We sold *Volly 2* and went on the search for a motorboat. A Nimbus 320, 32-foot motorboat is popular with ex-sailors, maybe as the interior resembles a sailing yacht. We found one in Brighton named *Call Girl*. It had been on the market for a while and the agent blamed its name for the lack of interest. We bought it and changed its name to *Seabird*.

For 2 years we apologised to everyone for having a motorboat, not a yacht, but during the third year we realised we enjoyed the advantages a motorboat brought and stopped apologising. We didn't have to freeze in the cockpit being soaked with icy spray and we could motor to Guernsey from the Isle of Wight in 5½ hours instead of the 15 hours it would have taken us under sail.

We hadn't managed to put our life on hold and continue to spend holidays on yacht *Volly* and rally the classic Jaguar XK150, but we now had good replacements. *Seabird* became our mobile country cottage, and rallying the E-type gave our life an injection of glamour.

We found we both liked travelling, sightseeing and exploring. Most of our holidays were successful but not all of them. In December 2007 we booked a delayed honeymoon to the Maldives. We didn't do any research, which was a mistake. January and February are the best months to go to the Maldives, not December which we'd chosen. When we landed, we found high winds were whipping up the sea and the float planes were bouncing around and unable to take off. The October monsoon had arrived in December.

We eventually reached the holiday resort island and started to explore our water villa. We'd booked a water villa as it sounded romantic; perfect for our delayed honeymoon, or so we thought.

It was raining hard and there was a strong wind blowing. We went out onto the balcony and as we did so the door slammed shut behind us locking us out. It was 9 o'clock at night and dark. Angus bravely volunteered to go for help and fully clothed climbed down the wave battered steps and into the water. My new husband gained a lot of brownie points for his courage and dedication, in this noble gesture.

We laughed our way through our honeymoon. There was no other way to enjoy it. The rain and high winds persisted for 7 days and with my motto "it's not what happens to you but what you do about it that matters" ringing in my ears we chose 2 bikes from a heap of rusty old bikes and rode to the end of the island. Here we found a circular bar with a thatched roof no bigger than a large parasol. If we pulled our stools in close to the bar, we could avoid water pouring off the roof and running down the back of our necks. We were happy we'd found something we enjoyed doing.

Early in our marriage we went to the Far East. I certainly wouldn't want to do it now. In a two-week holiday we flew to Japan via Hong Kong, back to Hong Kong, then to China, Thailand, Cambodia, back to Thailand and home. It was an exhausting trip. Angkor Wat in Cambodia and the bullet train in Japan were the highlights. A glass of water in Bangkok which left me ill for days and the ironing board bed we spent a restless night on while staying in Japan were the low points. Visiting Stanley in Hong Kong was undiluted fun. We'd both been to Hong Kong before and wanted to try something other than the tourist trail. I noticed a number 6 bus passing our hotel window, so I suggested we caught it the next day and explored wherever it took us.

It was a 1970s red London double decker bus which went to the coastal village of Stanley. The seats were tiny. We balanced on our seat and hung on. The bus swayed down the narrow road taking the corners at speed. I found myself ducking as the bus swept under over hanging branches. After 40 minutes we reached Stanley where there was a wide stretch of sandy beach and a large, partly covered, market. The market was crammed with the most exotic, colourful and dazzling goods. We were enthralled. Our lucky dip approach to how to fill our free day had led to a fun day out in Stanley

In 2009, 2 years after we married, we went to the U.S. for a month. I wanted to share my love of my favourite American states, Colorado, Arizona, and Utah with Angus. We visited son Alexander and his family in Colorado, then drove southwest to Arizona. Angus was very impressed with the Grand Canyon, but less so with the endless red rock landscapes afterwards. Straight, undulating roads stretched endlessly to the horizon through barren red rocks and Angus was not happy. I was in my element and thought the scenery wonderful. Unfortunately, it didn't look as if Angus was going to share my love for my three favourite states.

We drove to Monument Valley Navajo Tribal Park, more red rocks, and stayed in the View Hotel, my treat, or so I thought. The hotel had opened in December 2008, after I'd left Houston, and staying there had become one of my ambitions. All the rooms have a view of *The Mittens*, red rock formations in the shape of giant mittens. We stood on our balcony and watched as the sun rose behind them. To me it was sheer magic.

In the evening we ate in the View Hotel restaurant and asked for a beer. We were out of luck. No alcohol was served as it was a Navajo Tribal run hotel. We'd worked up a thirst from being out in the heat all day and from looking at all those red rocks and we both felt we badly needed a beer. So, we set off to drive to the edge of the tribal park where we thought we'd be more likely to find one.

After 45 minutes we drove out of the park and there we found a *gas station* with crates of beer stacked to the ceiling. It must have been catering for a multitude of people living in a dry area and desperate for a beer. We loaded a crate into the back of the car and drove back to the hotel. Never has a cool beer tasted so good.

The next morning, we continued our travels. The scenic route I'd planned took us to the Grand Canyon Skywalk, overlooking a side canyon of the Grand Canyon. It opened in

March 2007, again after I'd left Houston in 2005, and was on my list to visit. Unfortunately, neither of us was particularly impressed. Standing on the glass floor looking down at the bottom of the canyon turned our stomachs but that was the only effect it had on us. At least I could tick it off my go to list.

I was beginning to think our trip was turning out to be more about me having a wonderful time than Angus appreciating and sharing my much-loved scenery. So, I was pleased when he said he really wanted to go to the north rim of the Grand Canyon. He'd heard the panorama from there was the most dramatic view of the canyon. At last, there was something he wanted to do. As the viewpoint from the north rim is a long drive from anywhere, we booked a night in a cabin at the edge of the canyon.

It was a very long drive but eventually we arrived full of excitement and anticipation. We checked in and went to our cabin which was at the very edge of the canyon. But looking across the Grand Canyon we saw nothing. It was shrouded in thick fog and there was no view at all. The fog persisted for our entire visit, although we did get one fleeting glimpse of the dramatic view for a couple of seconds. The long drive to the north rim had been a waste of time and it wasn't the kind of place we could pop back to. Angus was deprived of the only view he wanted to see. It was a big disappointment to both of us.

The trip didn't get any better for Angus. We drove to Zion National Park in Utah and went pony trekking. I love riding and thought it was great fun, but Angus got heat stroke, and I discovered he didn't like riding anyway. By the time we arrived at Bryce Canyon National Park Angus had had enough. He declared he'd already seen too many red rocks and refused to leave the hotel room to look at Bryce Canyon. On previous trips I'd been down into the canyon and loved walking amongst the massive hoodoos which are the largest concentration of hoodoos in the world. I did persuade him to look at them from the rim but that was all. Angus and I have many things in common, but a love of red rocks clearly isn't one of them.

But when discussing with Angus what I'd written about his dislike for red rocks he corrected me saying, "it isn't true that I hated all red rocks, I loved Antelope Canyon". Thinking back to our visit there I can see why he thought it more interesting than barren red rocks. Antelope Canyon is phenomenal, a feast for the eyes and a delight for the senses.

As it made such an impression on Angus let me tell you something about it. Antelope Canyon is in Lake Powell Navajo Tribal Park, near Page in Arizona. It's a slot canyon created by torrents of water rushing through underground tunnels after heavy rainfall. For this reason, it can only be viewed at certain times when safe from flooding.

We entered upper Antelope Canyon at midday, the best time to visit, as when the sun is high rays of sunshine filter through the narrow cracks lighting up the interior of the canyon. The intense rays of sun illuminated the banded waves of sandstone in shades of yellow, orange and red and made them glow. In addition, focused rays of light shimmered through the cracks creating circles of bright light on the floor of the cave. It was a glorious sight.

I was pleased to hear Angus loved at least part of our trip to the U.S. But it had taught me enough about his likes and dislikes to be concerned when I booked a surprise trip to Antarctica as a 70th birthday present. I was worried that he'd be as interested in endless snow and ice as he had been in endless red rocks. I love Antarctica but I'd learnt the hard way that we didn't always like the same things.

It was January when we flew to Buenos Aires and then down to Ushuaia to start our 3-week Antarctic cruise. We called in at the Falklands, then sailed on to the sub-Antarctic Island of South Georgia. When we landed at Grytviken all my worries about Angus not liking Antarctica evaporated. He was fascinated by the outdoor museum displaying remnants of the former whaling station, and particularly taken with the whaling ships pulled up on the shore looking as if they'd just arrived. When we stepped out of a Zodiac onto the shores of Salisbury Plain, he found the sight of 60,000 pairs of king penguins standing on the flat glacial outwash looking like a very difficult jigsaw puzzle simply unbelievable. For him experiencing such a phenomenon of nature was a thrill he could never have imagined in his wildest dreams. The

Antarctic cruise had started well, and I was hopeful that my birthday present to him was going to be a great success.

After visiting South Georgia, we sailed west to the Antarctic Peninsula. We stood alone on the ship's deck and Angus' feelings mirrored mine during my first trip to Antarctica. He said, "knowing there are only a few thousand people on the entire continent of Antarctica gives me a sensation of being out of this world". We shared the same feelings about Antarctica even if he didn't share my love of red rocks. Angus was very definitely enjoying the trip.

Much of the trip was memorable but one day stands out from the rest for both of us. To reach an Argentinian research station the captain had to force the ship through thick sea ice. He managed to do this by using the ship as an icebreaker. Other ships had turned back but our captain seemed determined to bring fresh supplies to the station. We all stood on deck as we ploughed our way through the sea ice. The reaction of wildlife was captivating to watch. Seals and penguins looked up in amazement as our ship bore down on them. Penguins jumped into the water one after the other and seals sat like statues gazing at the ship in total disbelief. Only at the last minute did they abandoned their icy islands and slither into the sea. It was a great opportunity for photography.

The Argentinians were overjoyed to see us, even though Argentinians don't usually like the British. They'd been cut off by icy waters and isolated with no visitors for 9 months so the arrival of visitors bearing fresh produce was a momentous event. I should imagine visitors from any country bearing fresh food would have been made to feel welcome.

I tried to use my smattering of Spanish to communicate with them and in return they took photos of me. There were no women on the station, so the sight of a woman was clearly worth recording.

For Angus his 70th birthday trip to Antarctica had been a trip of a lifetime. For me it was valuable time spent on my favourite continent. I love Antarctica as it's a natural habitat, largely unspoilt by man's intervention. I came home with over 10,000 digital images to sort through and looked forward to enjoying revisiting Antarctica as I looked at them one by one.

Our travels continued the next year, 2015, when we went to Peru on a car rally. Each couple was given a Toyota RAV4, a 4×4 vehicle. We set off from Lima on what turned out to be an epic road journey. It was a perfect way of seeing Peru, but the roads were dangerous. Lorries had the habit of taking sharp corners on the wrong side of the road. On many a corner we'd see shrines and flowers left in memory of those lost on a bend in the road. It was a hazardous way to travel, but exciting.

Driving instead of flying from place to place gave us a better opportunity to absorb the flavour of Peru. We saw shepherds caring for sheep in the fields and cattle being herded along country roads. We came across lone women in remote places walking along deserted roads dressed in their colourful peasant costumes with a woven blanket thrown over one shoulder bulging with produce. It was all new and exciting.

At lunch time one day we stopped in a small town and gingerly went into a local cafe. We asked for sandwiches, and they brought us some good-looking sandwiches accompanied by some very strange tasting coffee. Other members in our rally group, also hunting for somewhere to eat, saw us in the local cafe and joined us. The owner couldn't believe his luck. Using the loo was a bizarre process involving a bucket, but it provided us all with an experience as well as a satisfying lunch break.

We worked our way through the tourist sights. We reached Machu Picchu on a mountain train with skylights in the roof. I pointed my camera up at the skylights and photographed the mountains as they flashed by. The sight of Manchu Picchu was stunning as we'd imagined it would be. While I stood and took in the view, I noticed a beautiful and graceful alpaca-like creature grazing nearby which I discovered was a wild vicuña.

We visited the Nazca Lines, a group of geoglyphs made in the soils of the Nazca Desert in southern Peru. We boarded a light aircraft, a twelve-seater Cessna Caravan, and flew over them. Viewing them from the air is really the only way to be able to appreciate them. We were surprised when the pilot started to perform dramatic manoeuvres with the plane. In rapid succession he tilted the wings from side to side and as he manoeuvred, he pointed out the zoomorphic designs on the ground. After noting that I could grab the sick bag if I needed it, I photographed the spider, hummingbird and monkey. While capturing shots through the window I noticed the man sitting in the seat behind me had turned green and looked soaking wet. His shirt had darkened in colour and clung to his sweat soaked body.

After we landed an American passenger exclaimed, "that sure was just the biggest waste of 200 dollars". Indeed, few of the passengers had felt well enough to even look out of the window. I'd been lucky as my stomach had coped. For me the flight was an incredible experience and the pilot's manoeuvres had enabled me to take some very special photographs.

We visited Cusco but spent rather longer there than was scheduled. Angus was rushed to hospital with cellulitis.

The next morning the other rally drivers left without us. The leader visited Angus before he left and came to tell me his condition had worsened adding, "if the worst happens. I'll come back". That was a scary thought. I knew cellulitis can develop into septicaemia, with fatal consequences. That must have been what he meant. I felt frightened and very alone. I couldn't help crying into my breakfast. One of the rally driver's wives took pity on me and brought me a bag of sweets.

I spent most of each day with Angus in the clinic using the internet to look up the medication he was being given. It comforted me when I discovered that all the drugs were imported from the U.S.

Cusco is at about 3,400 metres (11,200 ft) above sea-level, so the air pressure is very low. The clinic was equipped with a hyperbaric oxygen chamber to treat altitude sickness which tourists can suffer from when visiting. It also speeds up recovery from infection, so when I was offered the treatment for Angus, at an extra cost, I didn't hesitate in accepting it.

Each day Angus was rolled into the oxygen chamber for an hour. To me the chamber looked like a glass coffin, with Angus lying in it. It was an alarming sight. I was allowed to sit beside the chamber with the nurse during the hour-long treatments. Gradually the pressure was increased to match air pressure at sea-level and then brought back to the level of air pressure in Cusco.

I took a 2 hour break each day and explored the streets of Cusco which I got to know well. I found a cafe full of single people working on their laptops and made that my regular refreshment stop. I felt less alone surrounded by people who were also on their own.

After 4 days Angus had recovered enough to leave hospital. We'd missed visiting Lake Titicaca, which I very much wanted to see, but Angus was making good progress which was far more important.

The trip leader had assured me he would book flights for us to join them when Angus left hospital. I contacted him but was told he couldn't book our flights, I'd have to. So, it was left to me to book flights to Arequipa in southern Peru from

Cusco. A phone call to the airport drew a blank so I switched on my iPad. For a nerve racking 30 minutes I entered our names and passport numbers multiple times, at the same time praying the flaky internet connection wouldn't go down. The entire episode was a nail-biting ordeal, but I did finally manage to secure seats for the next day. We were met at the airport and arrived at the hotel in Arequipa to cheers from the rest of the party.

In 2016 I was offered an Honorary B. Ed degree by Roehampton University. It came as a surprise. I went through the ceremony in mortar board and gown. So now I finally have the degree my father so badly wanted for me and a photograph to prove it.

We've been to the Maldives ten times since our first wet and windy honeymoon, and have booked to go again next year, 2025. As our first holiday was something of a wash out Angus spent time on research before booking for a second time. He came across Komandoo, a small island just 100 metres wide and 500 metres long with a beautiful and accessible house reef. We booked for the end of January, not December.

In the 12 years since Angus discovered Komandoo we've only missed our regular Komandoo January holiday 3 times. One year we went to Antarctica instead, another year to Madagascar and in January 2020 during the height of the Covid pandemic everything was cancelled, and no one went anywhere.

Two weeks in Komandoo makes the perfect holiday for both of us, but for different reasons. I love marine life and enjoy snorkelling and exploring the reef. I find it peaceful just to hang out with the fish and observe their behaviour. From time to time a shoal of black and yellow convict surgeon fish will pass by. They're fascinating to watch and I always I follow them as they rapidly swirled across the reef and with seemingly manic behaviour strip it of algae.

One of my great joys is to swim with turtles. One year I accompanied a Hawksbill turtle on its hunt for tasty morsels. I swam beside it for about 20 minutes as together we explored a large area of the reef. The turtle glanced at me from time to time but seemed undisturbed by me tagging along on its tour of the reef.

Over the years I've come to know the reef well. Each year I find something has changed but many of the fish are to be found in the same location year after year. In January 2017 when I swam out to the reef, I was shocked to find the coral looked as if someone had poured concrete over it. Sea warming had killed much of the coral. In the summer of 2016, the water temperature had risen to 30 degrees centigrade for 3 months. The once beautiful coral gardens inhabited by brightly coloured fish were dead. I was heartbroken. The only way I could deal with it mentally was to ignore the dead coral and concentrate on trying to find any coral which was still alive.

I came across an island of blue tipped finger coral full of life and teaming with bright turquoise chromis fish. It was a joyous discovery. I'd read that coral reproduces asexually by colonies of polyps breaking off and floating away to grow somewhere else. There were pieces of coral lying on the sand, so I gave nature a helping hand. I collected fragments of coral and secured them in crevices in an area where there was no living coral.

Over the years I've added to my coral garden and when I returned in 2024 there was a beautiful patch of healthy blue tipped finger coral, inhabited by butterflyfish and angelfish. It was a thrilling discovery. I've now started to create another coral garden in an area devoid of living coral.

Angus isn't a keen swimmer so his reasons for wanting to holiday in Komandoo are different from mine. He loves the heat, reading, picking up shells, relaxing and choosing from the wonderful spread of food which appears three times a day. Our 2-week holiday in the Maldives each year is a trip to paradise for both of us.

January 2020, we visited Madagascar on a Noble Caledonia Cruise. Unfortunately, both Angus and I felt we were a decade too old for the trip. The crew got us up at 6.30 a.m. to miss the heat of the day, but every day was exhausting. Clambering through the jungle on the hunt for lemurs and other wildlife was a struggle. I realised I wasn't as young as I thought I was when I had to balance on boulders walking down a stream flowing steeply down a slope. I looked forward to a day at sea so that we could get some rest but that wasn't the crew's plan. Lectures were organized throughout each day at sea, and we felt compelled to attend them to increase our knowledge of the island. It certainly wasn't what most of us would call a holiday.

One day we started early to drive for 4 hours to Kirindy Reserve. We all climbed into ancient 4-wheel drive vehicles and followed a track full of deep potholes filled with water. There was no way of avoiding the potholes, so our driver drove straight through them one after the other. It made for a bumpy ride.

Our first stop was at the 'Avenue des Baobabs' which I'd seen pictures of and longed to photograph myself. I captured a few iconic photos of the towering; majestic baobabs each side of the road and I'm pleased to say they sell well. In the Kirindy Reserve we saw ring tailed lemurs and a young Verreaux's Sifaka, a species of lemur, sitting in a tree with its mother was an exciting find.

But it wasn't only the lemurs which I enjoyed seeing. We drove past Madagascan rural settlements which fascinated me. There were clusters of small wood and grass huts with no windows. The people lived outside during the day and the huts were only used to sleep in at night. We saw multi-generational families with the women preparing food outside while the children played on the hard mud ground. Zebu cattle grazed in fields dotted with baobab trees and along the road we met zebu pulling carts loaded with hay. It was very simple living, but the people seemed happy and waved as we drove by.

One evening the ship dropped anchor off the town of Morondava, in the southwest of Madagascar. At first light traditional dhow sailing boats started to leave Morondava to fish at sea. It was an amazing sight as the dhows, with their long thin hulls, outriggers and sails of patched canvas, glided past us one after the other. We watched as a stream of them passed our ship for over an hour.

Our trip to Madagascar was challenging but despite our constant feeling of exhaustion and becoming overheated daily we felt lucky to have had the opportunity to experience a taste of this vast fascinating island, of its people, its scenery and of its wildlife.

In March 2020 we went to the Ice Hotel in Sweden to celebrate my 75th birthday. There were already cases of Covid in the U.K., but nobody seemed particularly worried about them. We flew to Stockholm and took a coach to the Ice Hotel. We'd stayed there before to celebrate my 65th birthday and enjoyed ourselves so much we wanted to visit again.

On our previous trip we'd been struck by the beauty of the Ice Hotel made from blocks of ice cut the previous spring from the nearby Torne River and stored in freezing conditions throughout the summer. Columns of carved ice supported its solid ice roof and elaborate ice chandeliers hung from the ceilings. Each bedroom had an ice bed, but a proper mattress covered in reindeer skins: the bedroom was filled with fabulous ice carvings. There were 100 rooms each designed by a different sculptor. The ice hotel was kept at -5 degrees centigrade, but we had a comfortable night in thick sleeping bags. In the morning, we were woken by a man carrying a backpack of warm lingenberry juice. Using the attached hose pipe, he filled mugs with the juice to provide us with a warming wake up drink. It was an enchanting experience, but as often happens the pleasure of visiting somewhere for the first time cannot be repeated. The second time was fun but without the magic.

After 3 nights we returned to Stockholm airport for our flight. The airport seemed deserted. Assistants stood alone in shops, only one food outlet was open, and all the airport lounges were closed. It was 14th March 2020 and Covid-19 had swept across the world. There was no service at all on the plane. The flight attendants cowered behind a curtain throughout the flight and didn't even come to check our seat belts before take-off and landing. The life we'd been used to had evaporated.

On March 23rd, 2020, Prime minister Boris Johnson announced lockdown. I had the feeling we were about to experience a historic event and started to put pen to paper to record the development of the Covid-19 pandemic. Each week I listened closely to every Radio 4 news programme and used the internet to back up what I heard and provide more detail.

Using this information, I recorded news about the Covid-19 pandemic in rhyming couplets. In January 2022 I published my records, illustrated with seasonal photos of our garden taken each month. I called my book *Covid Chronicles in Rhyme*.

I'd like to share two extracts from *Covid Chronicles in Rhyme* with you. *The Silence of Lockdown* was one of the extra pieces I wrote to express the strangeness of lockdown.

The Silence of Lockdown.
So quiet you can hear a tulip petal fall.
A bee buzzes by on its way to somewhere.
A faint breeze rustles the leaves in tall trees.
A blackbird delights with a medley of songs.
A sparrow brightly trills.
Silence falls.
The gentle warble of a pigeon breaks the silence.
No sound of voices, no dogs barking.
Not a plane in the sky or a car passing by.
No loud drumming from a car with the window wound down.
No lawnmower droning, or water flowering.
A rare moment of silence in a fresh and fragrant garden.
How can it be so quiet?
You can almost hear the silence.

I was delighted when the BBC asked me to sign a release so that *The Silence of Lockdown* could be stored in their archives.

Extract from weekly reports: -

Week 6 May 1st, 2020
Boris is back, it's week six and our leader is back in control.
Standing outside number 10 he maps out his ultimate goal.

"The tide has begun to turn," he said "we're passing through the peak,
Lockdown is her to stay for now," but then came a surprise midweek.

Congratulations to Boris and Carrie for the birth of their baby son.
Another resident for number 10 and broken nights for everyone.

A minute's silence on Tuesday for NHS staff, carers, key workers, too,
85 NHS staff have died and 19 social carers. Far more than just a few.

Captain Tom's 100th birthday on Thursday, a handwritten card from the Queen.
Spitfire and Hurricane flypast, message from Boris Johnson on screen.

Now Tom's an honorary Colonel, raising over 32 million was great.
Number one in the charts with Michael Ball, now that's what he's achieved to date.

Goal of 100,000 tests reached, 25,000 home testing kits sent out.
48 drive-through centres, 70 mobile units, success is no longer in doubt.

Testing is up, R rate is coming down, but it must stay below one before
Lockdown is reconsidered, a second spike prevented, virus infection not allowed to soar.

Remdesivir is back in the news once more and the U.S. results are encouraging.
It speeds up recovery of that, they're sure. Their trials haven't come to nothing.

AstraZeneca will produce the vaccine if Oxford University trials are a success.
End of year it could be ready and then the spread of Covid-19 will be less.

Now the death rate is shocking. A third of those admitted to hospital have died.
Ethnic minorities, obese and aged worst affected, data has now been supplied.

Death in deprived areas is greater, men more than women likely to die.
Covid-19 is a deadly virus and among the underprivileged, casualties high.

We started the week at 20,000, now it's 27,000 and rising.
We're going to be worst hit in Europe which somehow isn't surprising.

No checks at the airports, we were slow to react, PPE in short supply,
Tests not available, herd immunity considered. So why do we wonder why?

Indecision, indecisive behaviour, so much fumbling in the dark.
Should masks be worn? No, they shouldn't. Yes, they should.
What a ridiculous lark.

Weather's been mixed this week, showers with bursts of sunshine.
Gardening replaced by jigsaws and manure by a glass of crisp wine.

Angus and I weathered the Covid-19 pandemic well. We enjoy each other's company, so we didn't miss the companionship of friends too much. When it was permitted to entertain outside if we kept two metres apart, we did have a few visitors. With the gazebo erected on the patio we could place another table and two chairs diagonally opposite, and exactly two metres from our table and chairs. I delivered refreshments to our guests' table before they arrived, carefully washing my hands before touching anything, and they came to the back garden, using a path at the side of the house as it was forbidden for guests to go through the house. We bought an electric overhead heater and continued entertaining throughout the winter.

We heard that on 1st July 2021 Guernsey would open its borders to tourists, so we set sail in Seabird at 4.30 a.m. bound for St Peter Port. We were the second boat from outside the Channel Islands to arrive in Guernsey after 18 months with no visiting boats.

We were surprised by our reception. We were met by a woman dressed in a plastic pinafore, plastic gloves, a mask, and plastic visor. She was a daunting sight standing at the end of the pier. Wearing mandatory masks, we were led to a large tent and asked to provide proof that we'd been vaccinated twice. We filled in endless forms and were then released. We felt like recovered leapers being released from a leaper colony. We were given a sticker to put on our boat and once it was in place we were allowed to enter Victoria Visitors Marina.

In Guernsey no one wore a mask, unlike in the U.K. at that time. We were allowed to travel on buses and could eat in cosy restaurants. There were only 14 cases of Covid-19 in Guernsey at the time, and Sark and Herm had no cases of Covid at all throughout the pandemic. We felt free and released from captivity. That feeling of freedom was the highlight of our holiday.

On 19th July 2021 all restrictions in England were lifted but then in October cases and deaths from Covid-19 started to rise again. In November the Omicron variant was identified in South Africa and by December the highly infectious Omicron variant of Covid-19 had been detected worldwide.

We went on a cruise in December 2021 just as the threat of Omicron was spreading. Not a great idea, but precautions were put in place by the cruise ship company. Before we were allowed to board the ship, we were all given *lateral flow* tests. Any positive cases were led off by apparitions sheathed in white, looking like murder scene detectives. During the cruise it was compulsory to wear masks whenever we left our cabins. Before going ashore, we were all given PCR tests. Anyone found to be positive was immediately confined to their cabin.

In Spain it was mandatory for a ship to leave infected passengers in a *Red Hotel*. We all felt under threat and when we sailed from Barcelona we left passengers behind in one of these isolation hotels.

The Omicron variant was a threat well into 2022, but the population started to rely on multiple vaccinations for Covid-19 to keep them safe. A PCR tests was required if we wanted to travel.

We went to the Maldives in January 2022 first having had a PCR test and obtained a certificate. We filled in endless forms not only to travel to the Maldives but also to leave. We spent the last 24 hours of our holiday just filling in forms. We had to generate a different QR code for each form and it was essential that we completed the forms in the right order for the QR codes to link. Only after we'd jumped through all the hoops could we go to the airport to board the plane.

We had our annual holiday in our motorboat, *Seabird*, in June 2022 and in December went on a 2-week cruise to the Canary Islands. All restrictions had been lifted by then and few passengers wore masks on the ship. Towards the end of the 2 weeks, we both began to feel unwell. So, when we returned home, we each did a lateral flow test. We had Covid-19.

Since then, we've continued to holiday on *Seabird*, rally the E-type, give our annual Christmas party and visit the Maldives. Life has almost returned to normal, although I don't think we entertain as much. The Covid-19 pandemic changed our lives dramatically for 2 ½ years and, although we were lucky, and came out the other side unscathed, Covid stole several years of the precious years which remain for us to enjoy together. For some people Covid-19 changed their lives forever, so we were fortunate.

I've now been married to Angus for 17 years and feel blessed. I didn't expect to marry again. I had plans to stay in April Cottage into my old age, adding a conservatory, so that I could sit and read the newspaper in the sunshine. Life follows an uncertain path with luck and serendipity playing a large part. Finding Angus was unexpected. I not only have the great fortune of having Angus in my life, but I've also gained his family. He has a son and two daughters who welcomed me to the Laird clan. I get on very well with his lovely ex-wife, too.

In addition, I've got to know his brother and wife, a niece and several cousins. They all welcomed me, and I now feel very much part of Angus' extended family. Likewise, Angus has become part of my family. He gets on well with my two sons, their wives and children, my four sisters, their husbands and their children. We feel blessed to have had the opportunity to play a successful game of *Happy Families*.

Life is, indeed, a game of chance and some of us are luckier than others. I've been one of the lucky ones. I was fortunate to be born positive and with a stable and loving upbringing developed into an adult well equipped to attempt to make the best of life.

But whatever the circumstances of our birth, during our journey through life most of us slide down a snake into a pit at least once, a pit often not of our own making. When my first husband left me, he threw me into a seemingly bottomless pit of despair. Climbing up a ladder back to the surface was a struggle. Sometimes giving up seems the easiest option, but I've learnt that when we have the gift of life, climbing out of the pit and fitting the broken jigsaw of life back together again, although not always the easiest option, is the best.

I've had some wonderful years married to internet date number 18 and it amazes me to think that only chance led me to find him. If I hadn't looked to see who else was online while I was scanning the dating website, I would never have met him. Our courtship wasn't altogether trouble free, but I knew I had met someone special, and I felt it was worth persevering, not giving up and looking for date number 19. I made the right decision.

In Angus I found someone I could love and who in return loves me, unconditionally. He's a good cook and even varnishes my toenails, which is an extra perk. We have different strengths and talents, but they have fused together to create a beautiful and peaceful life. Angus celebrates things I can do well and rejoices for me when I succeed. Sadly, in my first marriage I very quickly realised my husband saw me as competition. He had to win and did his best to beat me in every way. With Angus I have the freedom to excel in things and he shares the delight with me when I do.

I had a very happy first marriage but recently I've realised I had to adapt in many ways, so that it could be happy. Throughout our marriage my first husband came up with challenging ideas which I usually enjoyed but not always. However, I always went along with them, sometimes just to keep him happy. My ideas took second place. But in my marriage with Angus my suggestions are welcomed, and he loves the fact that I'm full of ideas.

We know the animal kingdom is clever at adapting to the environment and human beings are no different. We do what we can to survive and throughout life we endeavour to find ways of achieving happiness and contentment. I'm pleased to say that I now manage to achieve happiness on most days. I've lived into my late 70s, which is a fortuitous achievement so, I've been one of the lucky ones. For me being born on 13th turned out to be lucky, not unlucky. I've had an extraordinary, blessed and long life for which I'm grateful.

Lessons the Author Learns from Life

Life has taught me many lessons throughout the years of my long life. Below are quotations or adapted quotations lifted from my life story to summarise the lessons life has taught me.

Love

- It's impossible to force, or even persuade, someone to love you.
- In life men have an ability to make a quick change when it comes to love.
- The more you love the greater the loss.
- Compassion is neither a good reason to date someone nor a good reason to marry.
- When you love someone, you tolerate a lot of undesirable traits.
- Being needy and desperate is the wrong reason to internet date.

- A new relationship has no history so there's no shared past to mull over and recall.
- You can't build a relationship on one thing you have in common.
- It's impossible to find all the qualities you desire in one person.

Friendship

- You don't need everyone you meet to like you; you only need a few good friends. If some people don't like you, it is of no consequence.
- There are no short cuts to finding friends.
- Old friends who go through life with you and share your experiences become part of the framework of life and can never be replaced.
- Trust, love and support from good friends when needed is invaluable.
- It's when things are really going badly that empathy from others is at its most valuable.
- Getting to know someone is like making a jigsaw with a lifetime of pieces.
- A stay with friends or relatives should be no more than three days.

Decision making

- Every choice we make can have a ripple effect.
- When parents make a decision, they think is the right one at the time that has to be good enough.
- You should always be two steps from danger.
- If a dress doesn't look quite right in the shop it will look a good deal worse when you get it home. (A warning applicable to choices we make in life.)
- Don't waste time looking at what you know you don't want. (It can be applied to anything).
- When things go wrong don't just worry about it, do something.
- The principle "I've started so I'll finish." should be followed with caution and forethought.
- Magic can occur by chance. Recognise opportunities when they come your way.
- Sometimes immediate action is needed when you see something you know to be just what you are looking for.
- Living with "we should have" and regrets just adds to life's disappointments.
- There's no point in doing what you don't enjoy if you don't have to do it.

Living Life

- A happy secure childhood gives you a firm base on which to build the rest of your life.
- The way your parents rear you determines your standards for the rest of your life.
- Self-doubt can creep in through thoughtless remarks from others, particularly when you're a teenager.
- There is no training for motherhood.
- Freedom returns when your children fly the nest, but youthful energy never does.
- Children take a while to learn how to hide their true feelings so as not to offend.
- How careless the young can be with their lives in the belief they are immortal.
- If you expect too much out of life, you'll be disappointed.
- Reaching for something which may be beyond your grasp is often the exciting part of achievement.
- There's a positive side to most disappointments.
- We do what we can to survive and throughout life we endeavour to find ways of achieving happiness and contentment.
- Gratitude is something we all welcome and are disappointed when it's missing.
- A computer each makes for a more peaceful marriage, and if they're in separate rooms so much the better.

- Sometimes it takes enormous courage to do anything at all but most of us manage to find courage from somewhere when it's needed.
- Why is it that death claims the very best people when they're giving so much to others?
- Those who live to a ripe old age are the lucky ones as they haven't succumbed to one of life's unexpected fatal accidents or illnesses.
- Sometimes disasters are only the starting point; things can work out for the best in the end.
- Life is full of surprises.
- It's not so much what happens to you in life as what you do about it that matters.
- It's heartening to know that my sons are now my protectors, and our roles have been reversed.
- If all around you is uncomfortable the least you can do is to drink good champagne.

Travel

- Make sure when you're travelling you buy an up-to-date travel guide.
- If you don't know a city, you don't know where the best place is to live, so do some research before you choose.
- Always be straight forward with customs officers and never think for a moment that they share your sense of humour.

Rosemary Calvert
FRPS FRGS Photographer

Author Rosemary Laird is also known as photographer Rosemary Calvert. She has a collection of 12,000 photographs on www.gettyimages.com and a website www.rosemarycalvert.com

Avenue des Baobabs, Madagascar

QR code for www.rosemarycalvert.com

Other books by Rosemary Laird.

Covid Chronicles in Rhyme published April 2022

'Covid Chronicles in Rhyme' is a weekly accurate and detailed record of the progress of the pandemic in the UK with additional reference to its spread across the world. Each weekly record is written in rhyming couplets. Details include the spread of Covid-19, variants of the virus, vaccine development and treatments trialled and used

Weekly records start from the announcement of lockdown in the UK on 23rd March 2020 and continue until January 2022 when the more transmissible but milder Omicron variant was causing widespread infections.

'Covid Chronicles in Rhyme' is packed with facts and statistics which sometimes paint a dark and depressing picture, but the last verse each week lightens the mood with a little optimism, comment or humour.

The seasonal effect on gardens throughout the year is part of the story. Photos of the author's garden through the seasons are used to introduce each month. Posters and signs which appeared during the pandemic are also used as illustrations.

www.covid-chronicles-in-rhyme.com

Printed in Great Britain
by Amazon